THEOLOGICAL INVESTIGATIONS

Volume VII

Also in this series

THEOLOGICAL INVESTIGATIONS

Vol. I
God, Christ, Mary and Grace

Vol. II
Man in the Church

Vol. III
Theology of the Spiritual Life

Vol. IV
More Recent Writings

Vol. V
Later Writings

Vol. VI
Concerning Vatican Council II

Vol. VIII
Further Theology of the Spiritual Life 2

Still to be published

Vol. IX
Writings of 1965–67

Vol. X
Confrontations

THEOLOGICAL INVESTIGATIONS

VOLUME VII

FURTHER THEOLOGY OF THE SPIRITUAL LIFE 1

by
KARL RAHNER

Translated by
DAVID BOURKE

LONDON
DARTON, LONGMAN & TODD

NEW YORK
HERDER AND HERDER

DARTON, LONGMAN & TODD LTD
85 Gloucester Road, London, S.W.7

HERDER AND HERDER INC
232 Madison Avenue, New York, N.Y. 10016

A Translation of the first part of
SCHRIFTEN ZUR THEOLOGIE, VII
published by Verlagsanstalt Benziger & Co. A. G., Einsiedeln

This Translation
© Darton, Longman & Todd Ltd. 1971
First published 1971

ISBN 0 232 51156 X

Printed in Great Britain by Cox & Wyman Ltd., London, Fakenham and Reading. Nihil Obstat: John M. T. Barton, S.T.D.L.S.S., *Censor*. Imprimatur: ✠ Victor Guazzelli, V.G. Westminster, 18th June, 1971.

CONTENTS

ABBREVIATIONS	vii
FOREWORD	ix

PART ONE *Fundamental Questions*

1	CHRISTIAN LIVING FORMERLY AND TODAY	3
2	BEING OPEN TO GOD AS EVER GREATER	25
3	INTELLECTUAL HONESTY AND CHRISTIAN FAITH	47
4	DO NOT STIFLE THE SPIRIT!	72
5	THE CHRISTIAN IN HIS WORLD	88
6	'I BELIEVE IN THE CHURCH'	100

PART TWO *Mysteries of the life of Jesus*

7	CHRISTMAS, THE FESTIVAL OF ETERNAL YOUTH	121
8	HOLY NIGHT	127
9	PEACE ON EARTH	132
10	SEE, WHAT A MAN!	136
11	THE SCANDAL OF DEATH	140
12	'HE DESCENDED INTO HELL'	145
13	HIDDEN VICTORY	151
14	EXPERIENCING EASTER	159
15	ENCOUNTERS WITH THE RISEN CHRIST	169
16	HE WILL COME AGAIN	177
17	THE FESTIVAL OF THE FUTURE OF THE WORLD	181

18	THE CHURCH AS THE SUBJECT OF THE SENDING OF THE SPIRIT	186
19	THE SPIRIT THAT IS OVER ALL LIFE	193

PART THREE *The Sacrament of the Lord*

20	SUNDAY, THE DAY OF THE LORD	205
21	THE EUCHARIST AND OUR DAILY LIVES	211

PART FOUR *Christian Virtues*

22	ON TRUTHFULNESS	229
23	PARRESIA (BOLDNESS)	260
24	THE WORKS OF MERCY AND THEIR REWARD	268
25	PROVING ONESELF IN TIME OF SICKNESS	275
26	ON CHRISTIAN DYING	285

ABBREVIATIONS

GuL Geist und Leben
LTK Lexikon für Theologie und Kirche (2nd ed.)
TWNT Theologisches Wörterbuch zum Neuen Testament (Kittel)

FOREWORD

The author has produced this further volume of studies in theology in response to the wishes and suggestions of readers, friends and collaborators. It is designed to assemble individual pieces scattered fairly widely over the field of spirituality, so as to provide a contribution to the theology of the spiritual life. In addition this volume represents a continuation of the studies which have been published in the third volume of *Theological Investigations* under the same subtitle. Of all the numerous studies produced over a long period which might be considered relevant for this purpose only those have been included which can be called *'theological'* meditations in the narrower sense. Simultaneously several meditations serving as exercises in the spiritual life in the more direct sense are appearing under the title *Glaube, der die Erde liebt*: *Christliche Besinnung im Alltag der Welt* (Freiburg, 1966). Admittedly it is not so simple to draw an absolute line of demarcation between these writings and the more theoretical type of meditations. The collection assembled here is the outcome of careful consideration, and no further justification for it can be offered beyond its actual content. The author has not hesitated to include in this volume several smaller studies as well. There is no need for a meditation always to be lengthy, and even when it is not so it can still remain a genuine and serious work of theology (at least in the author's intention). It may indeed be the case that in this approach certain essential factors can be pointed to which can hardly be expressed in the specialist parlance of the schools of theology, so that they would otherwise be forgotten, or at least it would not be possible to formulate them explicitly and clearly enough. But the inclusion of essays of this type in the present collection may serve to testify to the author's conviction that work and effort in this field is no less theological in character than the research and investigation carried on in other disciplines.

These studies are spread over a wide period. The earliest go back as far as fifteen years, while the most recent are the outcome of the work of the past few months. For the purpose of collecting the studies included in this volume, and also in the book mentioned above, a general survey has been undertaken of all the author's works, whether published or unpublished. For the unenviable toil which this has entailed in the processes both of compilation and of independent revision of the studies presented here my heartfelt thanks are due to Dr Karl Lehmann. I am also indebted to Dr Jörg Splett for his collaboration in checking and criticising the work at the manuscript stage and for making himself responsible for correcting the proofs and seeing this volume through the press. Finally I must express my gratitude to Fr B. Kriegbaum S.J, Fr P. K. H. Weger S.J., and Fr P. F. Herrler S.J. for their collaboration in reading the proofs.

Munich, September 1966   Karl Rahner S.J.

PART ONE

Fundamental Questions

I

CHRISTIAN LIVING FORMERLY AND TODAY

THERE can be no doubt that at the present time a great unrest prevails in the Church, pervading all 'classes' and groups. While it may perhaps be true that many are troubled simply on the grounds that others 'give them no rest', still there are others also who go so far as to wish that this unrest may be still greater than it in fact is. Finally we ourselves must point out calmly that the world of humanity taken as a whole, together with its life, its basic concern (*angst*) and its hopes, does not take these 'movements' within the Church and among the few Christians involved over-seriously. The true origins of this unrest are not to be found in the Council. The Council is hardly more than the occasion which throws more plainly and more openly into relief in the Church these differing attitudes and positions within it, which would have been present in any case even without the Council. Admittedly the Council has given rise to a sort of 'backlash'. The Council sought to overcome the forces that threaten the Church in the present time, but in doing so inevitably seemed, at any rate to the eye of the beholder, to impart a certain increase of strength to these forces. For he who decides, as indeed he must, to embark upon an 'aggiornamento', notices straight away – there is absolutely no way of avoiding this – that the Church is relatively out of gear with the historical situation and with the needs of the hour, which he has hitherto refused to take into consideration. He becomes uncertain, and that in itself straight away makes his position inevitably more difficult. Now anyone who feels inclined to lay this as a reproach at the door of the Council must ask himself in all earnestness whether he can find it in his heart to wish that the Church might have postponed this process of taking cognisance of her own true situation for a few decades longer – for certainly this is the utmost to which it could have been deferred – and that she should only then have been brought into the state of 'crisis' in which she now in fact finds herself, only in a far more radical state of crisis than is the case at present.

This contemporary unrest is hard to analyse at any rate in its entirety. It consists of a mixture of anxiety in the face of what is new, and an almost unbridled craving for the new merely because it is new and therefore 'more interesting'; in other words one of the elements in this unrest is truly creative in that it rightly looks to and seeks for renewal in the sense of a better way of life for Christians and for the Church. Another is anxiety over the present instability of the situation in which the Church and the believer lives. Yet another is a falling-off of the true spirit of faith, which breaks down before the onslaughts of the present world. Our task must be to consider the situation in which this unrest has arisen, to be patient with it and gradually to understand it and to endure it so that the Church may become that which she must be. Even the Church cannot choose the situation in which she lives. It is given to her, and therefore it is good.

1. *The Problem of Christian Living Today*

One of the aspects of the Church's life in which this unrest manifests itself is that of Christian living, of the religious life properly so-called. In speaking of this area of the Church's life we mean from the outset to exclude the liturgy. This is not because no unrest of the kind of which we have been speaking exists in this limited sphere of religious activity; nor is it because we imagine that the liturgy would still be the liturgy even if it was celebrated in a mere 'objective' sense, without the personal participation of the individual. Our reason for excluding the liturgy is simply that it demands a separate and prolonged consideration in its own right, and in fact by a specialist in the field.

Even with this restriction the problem of Christian living in the post-conciliar age, the 'spirituality' of tomorrow, remains a question of the highest importance. Indeed, rightly understood, it is *the* decisive question *tout court*. For if the Council had achieved or inaugurated nothing more than an improvement in the communal 'image' of the Church, an increase in its social prestige, a more attractive formulation of the liturgy or one more in tune with the popular mind, an increase in freedom and democracy in the authoritative structure of the Church and of tolerance towards outsiders, a more harmonious position in the totality of philanthropic movements of the world – if that were all that the Council had achieved, then it would have failed to attain to that which must properly be achieved in the Church *as such*: namely that man, that is 'I', may love God more, may become more believing, more hoping, more loving to God and man, may worship God better 'in spirit and in truth', may more willingly accept the darkness of human existence and death, may carry and use his freedom more freely and more responsibly. And this is, in fact, what 'Christian living' means if the word is taken as connoting first and foremost that which is explicitly religious. And by comparison with this, which is uniquely necessary, all else is secondary, important indeed as means, but in the last analysis only as means.

The question which we are putting, therefore, is: *How does post-conciliar Christian living, the Christian living of the future, appear?* In this question it is not ultimately important whether this Christian living is accorded a very large place or a relatively minor one in the decisions of the Council. In any case in the troubled question of this Christian living and the form which it takes the Council has played and continues to play to this day, the role of a catalyst. The question is extremely difficult, therefore, if only because in the Church, the Father's house which has many mansions, 'Christian living' is an extremely complex factor. It differs according to age and sex, according to nationalities and cultural milieux, according to the various ideas and traditions which have been handed down, according to worldly avocations, according to the general spiritual level prevailing at any given point, according to the categories into which the community is divided in terms of clergy, religious and laity. In the course of our present considerations, therefore, we can treat of the problems arising in relation only to one kind of Christian living, that which applies more or less to the state of the Christian layman who is an uncompromising and whole-hearted member of the Church, and whose standard of education represents that of an average cross-section of the community in our central European cultural sphere, and is not too rudimentary.

2. *Christian Living in the Church Today as Heritage and as Commitment.* It may be taken as axiomatic that *the new mode of Christian living will be Christian and ecclesiastical as it has always been practised hitherto in the life of the Church.* A little further on we shall have occasion to speak of the new form which Christian living will assume. But a factor that must be mentioned first (though this is not the same as saying that it is the most important) is that element in Christian living which endures unchanged

yesterday, today and tomorrow. This must be considered under two aspects: first *that which is true and authentic* in ancient tradition; this must be allowed to prevail against any false understanding of the Council. Second the instinct which prompts us to crystallise the spiritual life in terms of institutions and 'practices' this must be allowed to prevail against any tendency to a false existentialist subjectivism, which remains formless, arbitrary and unrealistic, and, moreover, in constant danger of being ungenuine.

First it would simply be foolish to suppose that everything *not* mentioned by the Council in the devotion of Christians as practised hitherto should be tacitly consigned to the past, and should be regarded as having no place in the future. The Council has had much to say (even though often using other terms for it) about the modes of Christian living appropriate to the layman, the priest, the religious, and even though its pronouncements may strike one as somewhat traditional and *cliché*-ridden, they are not the less important for that, or less significant as guiding lines for the future. It would be erroneous, however, to suppose that whatever subjects were not explicitly covered by the statements of the Council were *ipso facto* less important, less central and less pertaining to the essence and structure of living devotion, and the Christian living and devotion of the future at that. Even a Council operates only with a little pail as it draws upon the ocean of the spirit and the heritage of Christian living in defining what Christian life is to be in the future with all its possibilities, which are bestowed upon the Church by the Spirit. Here and there the Council does underline certain elements which must be observed in the Christian living of the future: thus that the life of the Christian must grow from a lively participation in the celebration of the Eucharist and in the genuinely communal worship of the altar; that Christians must take the scriptures as the basis for their thinking and acting; that they must exercise a spirit of fraternal freedom, and must not withdraw into a sort of pseudo-ecclesiastical ghetto, but must rather learn to regard the world with its needs and its future destiny as their Christian task. But the documents of the Council do not offer any kind of systematic programme for the form Christian living is to take in the future, nor even a truly clear, concrete and productive plan or model for such a mode of life. The references to Christian living at the Council were too random, and at the same time too much in the abstract to provide for this.

To assert that there is an underlying element in Christian living which remains the same in spite of all the differences between the new and the old in it, and in spite of all historical vicissitudes, necessarily implies that this element has survived unchanged because it has been preserved as an historical heritage in the form in which it has *de facto* developed. Perhaps we could actually go so far as to say that today the real nonconformists are to be found in the group of those who have a genuine, calm and loving respect for the religious heritage of the past and the experience of past generations – such at least is one's impression when one observes the feverish excitement of many over-zealous individuals. Certainly it would be far from true to say that some current fashion is the swallow that heralds the true spring that is to come. If anyone believes that he can practise a new type of Christian living in the Church and can make out a convincing case for it, let him submit it, this devotion of his, to the 'discernment of spirits'. He will then find that one criterion of the genuineness of his Christian living which is far from unimportant is to test whether in practising it he can preserve the heritage of Christian wisdom and experience in the spirituality of past centuries.

To take a few random examples: meditation on the scriptures as practised today presupposes a modern and down-to-earth exegetical approach, ensuring that it is the scriptures themselves that are being read, and that it is not one's own pious fantasies that are being read into them. But meditation on the scriptures is far from being merely the waging of an unrelenting and destructive struggle against supposed dogmatic taboos until finally nothing more remains than the exegete's individual outlook and interpretation. Must this tendency continue until the love of reading the classics of spirituality and even the Christian mystics withers away or simply ceases, and the religiously inclined individual of the future becomes, in his own field, like some present-day student for whom German literature begins at earliest with Benn and Brecht? Certainly the Imitation of Christ will no longer be *the* formative work for the devout Christian of tomorrow; but must it on that account vanish altogether from the spiritual library of the future? And are there not many other classics of spiritual writing with which the devout Christian must be familiar unless there is to be a glaring gap in his spiritual and intellectual formation? Again the confessional is certainly not the outmoded shell within which modern psychotherapy is practised, and must not be misunderstood in this sense from either side of the confessional grill. It may indeed be difficult to foresee, in terms that are altogether concrete, what place frequent confession will have in the life of a wholehearted Christian of tomorrow. Here too many modifications may be introduced quite legitimately on various grounds. But the more frequent 'confession of devotion'[1] is far from being on that account simply a practice which belongs to the Church's museum of antiquities. He who wreaks destruction here without at the same time building up has failed to understand the spirit of true and sincere morality, and of self-criticism in the life of the Christian.

Theologically speaking the tabernacle is certainly first and foremost the place in which the Bread of Life destined for consumption by the faithful is contained. But to reject on that account everything which has grown up in the Church and is still alive in the way of Eucharistic devotion as mere outmoded practices is still, for all that, a sacrilege.[2] Why should the Christian of the future too not kneel in prayer before the body of the Lord which was delivered up for him, before the sacramental sign of the death of the Lord and of his own death in the Lord which is made present to him? Or in the future is there to be no supplication, no forgiveness and no death? Are there only to be men who, when confronted with this abyss of existence, give themselves up to craven flight? If not, then in the future too there will be men who kneel in prayer and supplication before the shrine of the Eucharist, look upon him whom they have pierced; men who are ready to accept their fate, to which they commit themselves in the paschal mystery of Jesus[3]. In the future are there to be no more convents or monasteries of the contemplative life, in which men called by God bear witness on behalf of their brothers and sisters to the fact that all Christians, each one in his own way, must preserve that spirit of detachment from the happiness which this world offers in which alone this world acquires the beauty of its redemption? Is silent meditation no longer to be practised today as a part of our spiritual exercises? Must the clamour of the yearly fair intrude upon such times as these also? Or must we be silent here in order to learn how to endure that silence which will

---

[1] For a deeper understanding of this cf. 'The Meaning of Frequent Confession of Devotion', *Theological Investigations* III (London & Baltimore, E.T. 1967), pp. 177–189.

[2] For the relevant theological principles cf. 'The Presence of Christ in the Sacrament of the Lord's Supper', *Theological Investigations* IV (London & Baltimore Md, E.T. 1966), pp. 287-311.

[3] An attempt is made to indicate the power of Eucharistic devotion in everyday life in 'The Eucharist and Our Daily Lives' in this volume, pp. 211-226.

be broken for each one when the crisis point of his life and the loneliness of his death come upon him?

These are mere random examples, all of them intended to illustrate a single point: the Christian living of tomorrow too has a great heritage to preserve. It is genuine only when it too regains its living relationship with its own past.

Again the Christian living of tomorrow is faithful and obedient to the spirit of true Christian religion when it has a taste for that which is solidly established, practised and has already taken shape, for that which is 'the practice' – in short for forms of devotion which are established institutions in the Church. It will cease to be faithful and obedient in this sense if it allows itself to be swayed by undisciplined impulses. There is no soul without a body, there is no genuine and serious religious life without man subjecting himself to discipline and rule, exercise and duty.[4] This institutional factor in Christian living is something which the devout Christian of the future, if he is to practise it genuinely, must decide for himself to a far greater extent than formerly, and which, far less than formerly, he will be able to take over simply as the generally accepted and practised way of living as a Christian. But precisely what form this institutional factor will take is in many respects a difficult question. Anyone, however, who supposes that the institutionalised practices in Christian living are already outmoded simply on the grounds that they are uncomfortable and involve strict discipline is deceiving himself and will never attain to a genuine mode of Christian living unless the grace of God rescues him by means of some catastrophe, whether interior or exterior, from his impoverished and diminished form of existence, which has only a colouring of Christianity. Certainly there is no commandment of God or the Church directing us to say our prayers precisely when we get up or go to bed, or before meals. He who really is a man of prayer without these praiseworthy Christian customs may in all Christian freedom regard himself as dispensed from them. But will he be a man of prayer? Will he be able to lay the supremely decisive moments of his life before God in prayer if in his everyday life prayer is simply the outcome of a momentary prompting or merely the 'liturgical' prayer of the Church's public services, or if he has not previously fixed his own times of prayer which he voluntarily engages himself to observe. It is strange. The most complex techniques of Yoga are

[4] On the necessity of this 'categorical' element and its relationship to the transcendental cf. *Handbuch der Pastoraltheologie* II/1 (Freiburg, 1966), pp. 64–70.

considered reasonable, yet the old Christian methods of prayer and meditation, as for example the rosary, are regarded as unmodern. But why precisely? Is this the result of experience or is it merely that the practitioners are all too eager to know better? Many instances of such institutional practices of devotion, even such as were or are common to the entire Church – one is thinking of the prescriptions of fasting, abstinnence, fasting before receiving communion, holy water in the home etc. – may be susceptible of change, and may actually need it. Such changes in fact the official Church has already undertaken in many cases. But must the life of the Christian of the future be on that account actually devoid of any such formation by the Christian institutions? Is it already outmoded to keep a crucifix in one's own home? Why should there not be continuity between past and future in that the custom of having established usages which are Christian and human could be discovered and practised afresh? Are the students who make pilgrimages from Paris to Chartres simply engaged in a piece of sentimental folklore? Or can there not still be some meaning in such practices in the future too, even though – or perhaps because – such pilgrimages are very different in form and manner from the pilgrimage of a Polish peasant woman to Tschenstochau?

Where the power of Christian living to embody itself in concrete practices of devotion is plainly flagging then Christian living itself is beginning to die. And under these circumstances it will die however anxious its practitioners may be to express it in forms which are more tactful, reasonable and tasteful; however reluctant they may be to have a crucifix hanging in every factory workshop; however ready they may be to agree with their irreligious contemporaries that there is no need for church bells to call Christians to early Mass at six o'clock on Sunday morning. After all they have watches and alarm-clocks of their own!

All these institutional practices in Christian living are subject to manifold kinds of change. Thank God such changes are actually made.[5] But change is something quite different from demolition and atrophy. The secular institutes could make a major contribution here in testing out the merits of new, assured and practicable institutions, embodying genuine devotion, in developing these and setting an example in practising them.

[5] For a right understanding of change as conceived of in this context cf. 'Kirche im Wandel', *Schriften zur Theologie* VI (Einsiedeln, 1965), pp. 455–478; *Das Konzil – ein neuer Beginn* (Freiburg, 1966).

III. Perspectives of Christian Living in the Future

For forms of Christian living in the future the preservation of our spiritual heritage is important. But it is not the ultimate and definitive factor. For it is possible to preserve an heritage only if one keeps abreast of what is new and what belongs to the future. Mere conservatism is sterile and cannot of itself attain its legitimate goals. It is evident that as applied to Christianity the term 'new' always implies the creative discovery and adaptation to the needs of particular epochs of that which in essence has been present right from the origins. Perhaps we may draw special attention to three factors bearing upon the Christian living of the future, of which we shall shortly be speaking. Admittedly it must be plainly stated by way of preliminary that abstract and theoretical postulates for this Christian living of the future are, and continue to be, something quite different from examples in the concrete, which are living and productive. These latter in their concreteness and precisely because of it are effective by the power of the inalienable gift of the Spirit to the Church, and are not begotten in the experiments and researches of speculative theology. But Christians can pave the way for this gift of grace in the Church in that they can be patient and hold firm throughout the present situation without indulging in self will either by becoming reactionaries on the one hand, or by embarking upon any destructive quests for novelty on the other, and in that they can seek to achieve further progress in this situation wherever possibilities arise for them to do so.

1. THE EXPERIENCE OF GOD AS INCOMPREHENSIBLE

The primary and essential factor, and one which must play a decisive role in the Christian living of the future also, is *one's direct personal relationship with God*. This is a truism, for it merely points out that which constitutes the immutable essence of Christian living.[6] And yet today this point is far from being self-evident. We live in an age which speaks of God as remote and silent, which – and this applies even to the theological ideas put forward by Christians – speaks of the 'death of God'; in an age of atheism, and an atheism which, so far from being confined to the ideas to which evil and godless dispositions and rebellious attitudes might be expected to give rise, can also be the outcome of a wrong interpretation of

---

[6] cf. in greater detail the studies referred to in this chapter, Note 4 (with further bibliography).

a human experience which is at once extremely genuine and extremely difficult.[7] We live in an age in which man actively manipulates the world and himself, in which the world, from being thought of in concrete terms as subject to the control of heavenly powers, becomes the object of rational research and a quarry of arid facts from which man draws his materials for the construction of *that* world which he plans according to his own image and likeness, and where there seems to be room for wonder only where man himself is absent from the scene.[8] We live in a world in which man has made even his own interior life the subject of technical scientific investigation; a world in which he analyses himself, and in which it is by no means a foregone conclusion that among the factors arising from this analysis he will discover anything approximating to 'God'; a world, on the contrary, in which the suspicion is never absent from his mind that his religious experience may be unmasked as an outmoded and erroneous interpretation of psychological drives, needs and processes which can and must be explained and brought under control by quite different means than through a mythical and indefinable entity called 'God'.[9] We live in fact in an age in which, so it appears, 'God' (or what is understood by this term) can no longer be used in order to 'stop the gaps' which we discover in the inadequacies of our existence. We receive the impression, rather, that either we ourselves must stop these gaps or that they must remain unstopped. At any rate they cannot be stopped with the idea of God. It follows that intercessory prayer has become an extremely questionable procedure. We live in an age in which the question is not so much how as sinners we may gain access to a gracious God who will justify us; on the contrary the impression is that it is God – if there is a God – who must justify himself to his creatures in their distress, while they for their part have no need of justification. We live in an age which becomes suspicious when in answer to its questions an 'other-worldly' dimension is pointed to, in which everything is reduced to clarity and order. In such a world it is certainly far from immediately obvious that

---

[7] For a precise understanding of this experience cf. 'Science as a "Confession"?' *Theological Investigations* III, pp. 385–400; H. U. von Balthasar, *Die Gottesfrage des heutigen Menschen* (Vienna. 1956).

[8] For a clearer analysis of this situation, and for a theological interpretation which is in conformity with this cf. *Handbuch der Pastoraltheologie* II/1, pp. 178–276, esp. pp. 214 ff., 242 ff.

[9] A full discussion of the ideological attitude of suspicion towards Christian living is to be found in *Handbuch der Pastoraltheologie* II/2, pp. 109–202.

one should be devout in the Christian sense – the more so since the idea formerly accepted as axiomatic by the *community as a whole*, namely that one can and must be this, no longer exists even though ninety per cent of the children in our society still receive religious instruction.

What is obvious is that in the face of a practical, or even a theoretically worked-out or positively militant atheism the real and basic question at issue, namely the question of God, cannot be treated of here and now. This would be to go altogether beyond the limits and possibilities of so brief a consideration as this.[10] All that can be attempted is to make some few observations on the actual problem of living a Christian life in this situation. First it is obvious that in this situation Christian living must of necessity be on a modest and inconspicuous scale, and indeed that this is as it should be. For us Christians this situation is not of our own seeking. But it simply rules out for us the luxury of any elaborate systems of devotion such as were possible in the old days. Today anyone who manages to live with this incomprehensible and silent God is already practising devout Christian living. One who finds courage to call upon him ever anew, to speak to him in a spirit of faith, trust and patience in his darkness, even though to all appearances no answer is returned except the hollow echo of his own voice – such a one as this is already a devout Christian. If a man, repeatedly empties himself of all else so as to open himself to the depths of his being to the incomprehensibility of God, then, even though he seems again and again to become blocked up with direct experiences of the world in its palpable reality, the tasks with which it presents him and the needs which it demands that he supplies by his own efforts, as well as the beauty and glory of the world still unfolding before him – if he still manages to live with God and commune with him in spite of this and without the support of 'public opinion' and custom, then he is already a devout Christian. Finally if he accepts this task as the responsibility of his life, and fulfils it constantly and unremittingly in his acts, and not merely in response to sporadic religious impulses, then he is a Christian, and a devout one *today*. Obviously he will participate to a reasonable extent in the liturgical and sacramental practices of the Church (and also have a real understanding of their significance), especially today, when it is once more being realised that man is no isolated individual; but

---

[10] More in detail on this in the author's article (published in the periodical *Concilium* III (1967), Vol 3, March. cf. also the other contributions to this volume).

he will have quietly to define for himself where the real and supreme task of his religious life lies, a task which more than ever today is quite inalienable. If he is to achieve this then, in this wintry season, the tree of his devotion cannot be expected to bear such an abundance of leaves and blooms in the form of the various devotions and pious practices of the past. He will apply himself to the fundamental realities and truths of the Christian faith, and can count upon his *fides implicita* to cover many other secondary truths, derived from these, which he does not call in question. Corresponding to this *fides implicita* he also has a certain *pietas implicita* to fall back upon, without actually filling his mind and heart with the luxuriant growth of Christian devotions of earlier ages. Then the centre of live religious interest was not the incomprehensibility of God and his effective presence in the crucified one, the one abandoned by God, but rather devotion to the Blessed Sacrament – this was particularly developed – veneration of the precious Blood, the Immaculate Conception, the gaining of indulgences etc.

Now it must be admitted that if we are to have the courage to enter upon a direct relationship with God in his ineffability, to accept that our devotion must, in this sense, be cut down to the bare essentials and to accept, furthermore, the silent self-bestowal of God as the true mystery of our own existence, then we do need to do something more than merely to take up a given rational attitude to the speculative problems of the divine, and to respond in merely doctrinal terms to the teaching of Christianity. We do need to work out a certain theology of mysticism, a mysticism that leads to a religious experience which indeed many suppose that they could never discover in themselves, a theology of mysticism which can be imparted in such a way that each one can become his own teacher of mysticism. So long as we fail to realise the manifest fact of how inescapably our existence, in all its self-consciousness and self-responsibility, is orientated towards the absolute mystery which we call 'God' and which bestows itself upon us, we have not even begun to understand so much as the rudiments of this mystical theology. This approach to mysticism must rid man of his anxiety (*angst*) in the face of attack, so that the only thing that makes him tremble is the designs engendered in him by his own longing to launch himself upon the immensity of empty nothingness when he begins to call upon God and to give him, the ineffable, a name.[11]

[11] On the mystical approach to religious experience cf. the article referred to in this chapter, note 10; *Handbuch der Pastoraltheologie* II/1, pp. 269 ff. (Bibliog.).

Simply in order to make it clear what is meant here, and in the consciousness that the concept of 'mysticism' is a loaded one (rightly understood it is not the opposite of belief in the Holy Pneuma but rather identical with it) it could be said: the devout Christian of the future will either be a 'mystic', one who has 'experienced' something, or he will cease to be anything at all. For devout Christian living as practised in the future will no longer be sustained and helped by the unanimous, manifest and public convictions and religious customs of all, summoning each one from the outset to a personal experience and a personal decision. For this reason, therefore, the usual religious education as practised hitherto can only provide a very secondary kind of formation or preparation for the institutional element in the religion of the future. The mystical approach of which we are speaking must impart the correct 'image of God', based upon the accepted experience of man's basic orientation to God, the experience that the basis of man's existence is the abyss: that God is essentially the inconceivable; that his inconceivability grows, and yet does not derogate from the fact that the more rightly God is understood the more nearly does his self-bestowing love touch us; the experience that in mapping the course of one's life one can never confine God to specific points in it without being brought up against the fact that when one does so the sum fails to come out right; the experience that he only becomes our 'happiness' when we pray to him and love him unconditionally; but also the fact that he cannot be defined as a dialectical negation of the affirmative 'thrown up' by our *experiences*, for instance that he is not simply the one who is remote as opposed to one who is near, not to be thought of as the diametrical antithesis to the world, but rather that he transcends such oppositions. Our basic orientation to him is more primary, then, and prior to all such dialectical opposites, and this has the effect that he wills to be and is 'our' God in an act of absolute self-bestowal and grace as he who is 'so and not otherwise', without becoming involved in the complexities of our dialectic.

The mystical approach of which we have been speaking must teach us in the concrete to maintain a constant closeness to *this* God; to say 'thou' to him, to commit ourselves to his silence and darkness, not to be anxious lest we may lose him by the very fact of calling him by a name, as though he cannot, if he wills (as in fact he has willed) also enter into our eternal duality precisely because he does not constitute one element among others in our scheme of things. It must teach us that he does not belong to any specific place in our scheme of things (e.g. only 'outside'). Such an essentially *Christian* approach to mysticism must, of course, also take cognisance of the place which Jesus of Nazareth, the crucified and risen one, must occupy in it.[12]

For such a relationship to God theology must work out a fresh understanding and a practice of intercessory prayer corresponding to it, and so far it has not done enough in this direction. Perhaps it might be said that the particular task which man himself has to perform, or the particular fate which he has courageously to accept as inescapable does not as such need to be the direct subject of petition on his part, whereas on the other hand it is only in prayer that man can accept himself as a whole, and thereby all the particular aspects of his life. It follows from this that petitionary prayer in the concrete can only avoid being a 'troubling of the gods', and be really *prayer* to God when it consists in that opening of the heart so as to respond to the inconceivability of God as love in which alone one is *always* heard. Only that petition which is truly sure of being heard is petitionary *prayer* at all.[13]

2. LIFE IN THE WORLD AND SERVICE OF THE WORLD CONSIDERED AS PERTAINING TO RELIGION

The practitioner of active Christian living in the future will have to recognise as an integral element in his Christian living the factor of the fully free and the fully human. This is, of course, an obvious and axiomatic element in the Christian understanding of life, yet it is one which is still very far from being sufficiently brought out: namely that there is an intrinsic plurality in man's nature, a plurality such that he must not for one moment attempt to impose unity upon it, or produce an integral synthesis

[12] It is only if we include this dimension, which is missing here, that we can arrive at the depths of the Christian message in the true sense. Inasmuch as this aspect cannot be worked out here a whole series of points which are important and indispensable for establishing the Christian devotion of the future are missing from this attempted outline. For the more *speculative* aspects the author may refer to his article 'Theologie und Anthropologie' (which appeared in the *Festschrift für M. Schmaus*, (Verlag Schöningh, 1967). Indications of a more *practical* kind are to be found chiefly in *Betrachtungen zum ignatianischen Exerzitienbuch*, (Munich, 1965). Further aspects of the christological basis for Christian devotion are to be found in this volume pp. 152 ff.

[13] For a more detailed treatment of this cf. *Von der Not und dem Segen des Gebetes* (Freiburg, 6th ed., 1965), pp. 76-92.

in it by his own powers; that he has to accept this plurality of his own being patiently, whole-heartedly and without struggling against it, recognising that God penetrates with his grace even into those regions where no altar has been raised to him.[14] If we accept the teaching of Vatican II to the effect that God himself can still be the salvation of one who, in all honesty, and therefore in all innocence, believes that he must be an atheist,[15] then it is also true that in the life of the Christian *too* he can still be present wherever life in the world is lived joyfully, eagerly, earnestly and bravely even without any explicit reference to religion. Here lies the true meaning of that term which is so often misunderstood, 'the religion of the world'. The underlying conception is that this world is presented as an opportunity and a task because God wills it precisely in its worldliness and as a world made by man himself, and because he has let it grow immeasurably in breadth compared with the worlds of earlier ages and, in spite of all its ills, has also let it become more glorious. It is no longer true that the world as human begins only (or almost only) at the point at which man makes it explicitly human in forms of communal worship, and religious poetry, or in ascribing an explicitly religious meaning to it and using it in explicitly religious ways. Wherever *secular* life is lived with *unreserved honesty* there *ipso facto* an essential element in religious life is already present because God loves the world in itself, endows it with grace in itself and in no sense regards it as a rival to himself as though he were envious of it.[16] He who responds to the world with genuine *love ipso facto* encounters in it the Cross of Christ and the inconceivability of God. He has no need whatever to conjure them up first in order for them to be present there. If he practises the virtues of the world, suffers himself to be educated by it in joyfulness, courage, devotion to duty and love, then *ipso facto* he is actively practising a vital element in genuine religion in his life and such worldly virtues will one day open to him the innermost mystery which they contain, namely God himself.[17] That in man which is really of value and fundamentally alive is already summoned to receive the grace of Christ even before it is explicitly

[14] On the anthropological basis for this cf. *Handbuch der Pastoraltheologie* II/1, pp. 22 ff.

[15] The study referred to, this chapter note 10, provides an analysis of the relevant texts of the Council.

[16] The author describes certain concrete manifestations of the 'religion of the world' as understood here in *Alltägliche Dinge* (Einsiedeln, 6th ed. 1966).

[17] Examples of such virtues are to be found in this volume, pp. 229–293.

'baptised'. Indeed, provided the Christian does not close his heart to God there is actually no need for it to be so explicitly 'baptised' always and in every case. Because this is by no means always possible, and because the Christian is not the achiever of his own integrity, one who at basis is willing only to play the part of God himself. God alone remains the one true unity in the plurality which is in man.

A further aspect of 'the religion of the world' in the true sense follows as a direct consequence from this. Responsible action in the world is itself an element in active Christian living. What significance could the endeavours of the so-called 'secular institutes' have if they were only auxiliaries dressed up in more or less modern uniform to assist the clergy in their task? If secular activity as a task and as a deed did not already have a place in their lives even before it achieved an explicitly religious inspiration and was integrated into their religion? Nowadays man does not simply find himself living in a world that is *already given*; rather he himself *makes* his world. Thereby he incurs opportunities, tasks, responsibilities and dangers which formerly simply were not there[18] The active Christian living of the future, therefore, will be practised *on this plane also* – and not simply in the quiet corners of those who, because they are rich, can manage to live far from this world of work and of the humanisation of the world, practising the piety of Philothea, or else who, as the proletarian poor, have not yet been admitted as responsible contributors to the formation of the world as it evolves. Certainly making some new discovery in physics or flying in space like Gagarin does not *ipso facto* make one a man who loves God. But neither will the genuine religion of the future begin only where all that leaves off. Vatican II exhorts Christians to consider their task in the world of today, to co-operate with all in the construction of a greater freer world, one more worthy of mankind, to take the responsibility and to have the spirit not merely to depend upon the moral directives of the official Church, not merely to ask how man should act in a given case in order to avoid offending God, but to ask what man can do in order to make life more worth living.[19] Now in directing

---

[18] On this new situation cf. 'Experiment Mensch', *Die Frage nach dem Menschen. Festschrift für Max Müller*, (Freiburg, 1966), pp. 45–69.

[19] The fact that the Council too makes demands of this sort upon Christians in their lives is shown in particular by the pastoral constitution 'On the Church in the Modern World'. On this cf. the author's article, 'Zur theologischen Problematik einer "Pastoralkonstitution"' (which appeared in the *Festschrift für J. Höfer*, R. Bäumer and H. Dolch edd., (Freiburg, 1967)).

these exhortations to Christians the Church is not betraying her message of the Cross, of humility and desire for the eternal in order to adapt it to a world which has become emancipated from religion. Rather she enjoins upon believers to bring their *Christianity* to bear upon their task, a task which did not exist in this form in earlier times,[20] but which does present itself now and, moreover, for the Christian as such, and therefore as a true part of his religion, though admittedly in this, as in all other spheres each one must act according to his own gifts and calling, and perform his own task and not that of another. The Christian cannot simply dismiss politics as a 'dirty business', and expect God to give this 'dirty business' to others to carry out and not to him, so that he himself can pursue his own quiet devotions in the comfort of the petit-bourgeois. The world as developing and unfolding, as a 'worldly world' operated by man lays claims upon the Christian today, and the fulfilment of these claims in what might be called a 'political' form of religion is today or tomorrow an integral element in genuine Christian living.[21]

3. THE NEW ASCETICISM: IMPOSING ONE'S OWN LIMITS

Among many other aspects of the Christian living of tomorrow which we might also take into consideration, and which are certainly also necessary, a third one has still to be mentioned: the fact that there must be a radical change in the forms of asceticism that are practised. In earlier times certain limits were imposed upon man in his activities to a large extent by the sheer force of external circumstances, by the situation in which he lived. His faults swiftly brought their own retribution and exacted their own revenge. The majority of men at least led lives that were brief and hedged about with dangers, and in which there was little or no opportunity for luxury, caprice, free time, travel, enjoyment etc. Christian asceticism, therefore, consisted in the patient acceptance of the poverty and toil in one's life which this implied, or in additional ascetical practices which were to some extent imposed from without as e.g. in monasticism, but far less in a positive summons to a form of asceticism

[20] On the concrete tasks which the Christian has to perform in the world cf. *in extenso, Handbuch der Pastoraltheologie* II/2, pp. 40 ff.; 42 ff.; 148–175 (with numerous further references); 208–228; 236 ff.; 243 f.; 248 ff.; 258 ff.; 262 ff.

[21] For the justification in theory of the basic ideas put forward here cf. K. Rahner, 'Christlicher Humanismus', *Orientierung*, 31.5.1966; J. B. Metz, *Verantwortung und Hoffnung* (Mainz, 1966).

which was the outcome of life itself and of the actual daily circumstances in which it was lived. Under these circumstances asceticism – if it was undertaken over and above such hardships as have been mentioned – acquired the 'image' of something extraordinary and heroic. In this way Christian asceticism consisted in passive endurance[22] or else supplementary, extraordinary measures. Today man, who to a large extent has gained control over nature by his technical achievements in the sphere of medicine and all other fields of technical mastery, has to an ever-increasing extent the ability to play the part which perhaps, in virtue of his true nature, he should play.[23] He can live without restraint and still avoid incurring thereby any of those disadvantages which used to ensue as a natural consequence upon such a course. Sexual excesses are no longer 'punished' by children or by disease. The misuse of power no longer brings about its own downfall so swiftly as formerly, when a king who was immoderate in the exercise of his authority quickly incurred a tyrant's death at the hands of some assassin. The idle are no longer brought to heel under the stimulus of hunger. Medicine today rather helps than restrains the quest for enjoyment. Moderation is no longer imposed from without. Man must practise it of his own free will. And thus a new way of practising Christian asceticism is opened up, one which, precisely because it proceeds 'prudently' is not so manifestly heroic or spectacular as the asceticism of former times, which took more active forms. The ascetical practices of those former days had the character of that which is extra and out of the ordinary. But today ascetical practices have rather the character of freely fulfilling one's responsibilities in the performance of one's duty. Yet this is almost more difficult than the former kind precisely because it must necessarily appear in the guise of that which is manifestly the 'prudent' course.[24]

This 'asceticism in the consumer society' (which, however, applies to

[22] On the true significance, theologically speaking, of such traditional asceticism cf. 'The Passion and Asceticism', *Theological Investigations* III, pp. 58–85.

[23] On the difficulty of this question cf. the study referred to in Note 22, especially pp. 56 ff. and, on the ascetical aspects, pp. 65–68.

[24] Such prudence or reasonableness must not be understood to be 'obvious' in the sense that it is dictated by a prior rule of 'nature' which applies always and in all circumstances (theologically speaking in the sense of 'natura pura'). For this applies in any case to all exercises of the human reason throughout the world in virtue of the constant vulnerability of human nature. It applies even to the baptized ('Concupiscence'). Hence the *theological* concepts of prudence and freedom must be thought out afresh.

all areas of life) is difficult.[25] At basis, and as applied to the generality of men (we are not thinking here of those individuals in whom a certain weakness of the acquisitive instincts goes some way towards lightening the burden of taking their own decisions and renders them immune to the claims of an acquisitive society with its suggestions of new needs) it will be achieved only by one who is *open to God*, and therefore can undertake in all sincerity a renunciation.[26] which seems to be unattainable to the man who is weighed down by anxiety in the face of death. Certainly God and the state of being open to God are far from rendering one psychologically immune to pain, ideas which can be exploited in order to facilitate the asceticism so necessary in a consumer society. To think of them and to attempt to apply them in this sense would be *ipso facto* to negate them. Only where *God* is *loved* for his own sake does he also become a source of blessing. Only where an individual is *open* to the absolute future of God[27] will he also overcome the tendency to immoderate greed, to fill his life with the greatest possible enjoyment (taking this to include power also), and so ultimately to destroy himself by sheer excess.[28] And conversely: when man observes that moderation which is appropriate to his nature *genuinely without any thought of reward* then he is already in a mysterious sense giving his assent to God and to his absolute future even when he does not realise this.

Such is the new asceticism appropriate to the practice of Christian living in the future. It can be the new way of putting into practice that more fundamental mystery of Christian asceticism which consists in sharing in the death of Christ on the Cross, and which is offered to us because today too life still continues mysteriously to be the Passion. Today, in contrast to earlier times, this self-imposed moderation is to a large extent no longer capable of being crystallised into a general

---

[25] A comprehensive analysis of the 'consumer society' and its background is to be found, with bibliography, in the *Handbuch der Pastoraltheologie* II/2, pp. 130 ff.; 175 ff.

[26] On this cf. 'Reflections on the Theology of Renunciation', *Theological Investigations* III, pp. 47–57, and also, in greater detail, 'The Theology of Poverty' in this volume, Part B, pp. 168–214.

[27] On this concept, and on the manner in which it gives the lie to all ideologies which promise a future utopia in this world cf. *Theological Investigations* VI, pp. 59–60, and also this volume, pp. 49 ff. and the article referred to in Note 22, especially pp. 62 ff.

[28] On the anthropological basis for this cf. *Handbuch der Pastoraltheologie* II/1, pp. 34 ff.

institution. But for all that it must not remain at the level of theory and abstract commandment. It must assume a form in which it can be *effective in the concrete and can provide a practical pattern of living* and, from being morality in the abstract, must precisely become 'morals' in the concrete, 'ethics' and good habit.[29] This again is a major task for those secular institutes whose members genuinely do continue to live in the world: to provide examples which show how even in the contemporary setting it is possible to live a life that is moderate, self-disciplined and pure, in which one rises above that state of doubt and anxiety about death at the bottom of one's heart which makes one acquisitive and so, in the last analysis, unready also to take selflessly upon one's self genuine responsibility for the good of others in a practical and down-to-earth way, and in doing this silently and cheerfully to endure renunciations. In so acting the members of such secular institutes must be genuine, uncompromising, gentle and at the same time strict with themselves.

A few concluding observations still remain to be added. The impression may, perhaps, have been given, that it has not been made altogether clear precisely *how* all these factors and rules for the new kind of Christian living can be assembled into a unity. A further point also requires clarification. We might have entered still more deeply into the question of how the old and the new could be fitted together in the concrete into the unity of the devout Christian living of tomorrow; how in this Christian living the heritage of former times could be preserved and harmonised with the new forms of devotion; how mystical experience of God could be harmonised with humanist activities in the world. We could have given a still better idea of the ultimate and underlying unity of these factors.[30] But even then the full synthesis of all these factors in the concrete would still remain a prime problem and a task which is to be achieved only *in living practice*, and not by means of theological theorising.

---

[29] A task which still remains to be accomplished by the philosophy and theology of the future is to define the new form which such habits must assume in existential and ontological terms (cf. e.g. the works of G. Funke), so that this category, so important, yet, precisely in contemporary thought, so misunderstood, of the 'habitus' of classic theology, may be made available to the theology of Christian living.

[30] Special reference must be made at this point to the works of W. Dirks: 'Wandlungen der Frömmigkeit', *Weltverständnis und Glauben*, J. B. Metz, J. Splett edd. (Mainz, 1965), pp. 254–264; 'Vernunft und Heiligkeit', *Integritas*, B. Stolte, R. Wisser edd. (Tübingen, 1966), pp. 294–305. Many suggestive points are also raised by H. J. Schultz, *Frömmigkeit in einer weltlichen Welt* (Stuttgart, 1959).

Living practice itself, when undertaken in patience, in a quest which is constantly renewed, in self-critical 'discernment of spirits' always remains the gift of the Spirit to the individual and to the Church. Above all patience is necessary because it must always sustain us in times of transition from that which was formerly accepted and approved but has now become out of date to that which is new and still has to gain approval. Patience will preserve us from any premature reactions in this situation. For these represent a danger to conservatives and progressives alike, each in their own way. As an irreducible amalgam of many factors life in the truest sense and rightly understood always entails compromise.[31] But this takes place on the historical plane and is not capable of being worked out in theory beforehand in any adequate way. For this it is necessary to have patience, courage and trust in the incalculable wisdom of life, and above all in God.

In the future there will be *many* forms of Christian living. The fact that in spite of the development of mass societies man can develop many more and more varied ways of living than formerly even in the worldly sphere – this fact alone is of itself sufficient to make this true.[32] In former times, in spite of all differences the mode of Christian living adopted by those Christians of central Europe who sought earnestly to practise their faith was relatively homogenous. This appears, for instance, in the styles adopted in the orders of tertiaries, Marian confraternities etc. It is also clearly illustrated by the fact that the prescriptions of canon law for the spiritual life of the secular clergy are uniform almost down to the smallest detail. The range of variations in the modes of Christian living of the future will be greater than these, and this is as it should be. It is important to have a full and clear realisation of this situation. Otherwise, as so often happened in the past, it will be falsely suggested that the many Christians who deviate from the normal and average way of practising this Christian living are in bad conscience, and that all is not well with their way of life as Christians and members of the Church. The young Christians of today must quietly develop a new way of Christian living and demand the right to practise it in the Church. If it leads to charity, joy, peace, patience, kindness, self-discipline and other manifestations of the presence of the

---

[31] This word must not be understood here in a bad sense. The very fact that the manifold factors in man's own nature cannot adequately be harmonised is in itself enough to demonstrate this point.

[32] cf. *Handbuch der Pastoraltheologie* II/1, pp. 206 ff.

Spirit one can only say with Paul (Gal 5:23): 'Against such there is no law'. Not even the law of the Church.[33]

Finally one cannot divide the old and new elements in Christian living into different compartments because the new is genuine only when it preserves the old, and because the old only remains living when it is lived anew. In the old and in the new, however, one element must be the same, which survives yesterday, today and for ever, and of which we have not been able to speak nearly enough: God the incomprehensible source of life's blessing, the mystery of the crucified and risen Christ, the blessing which extends its holiness in and through all the monotony of everyday life, the hope for that eternal life which consists in the unveiling of God in his incomprehensibility. Where this is present and living there is a Christian, and that Christian is living his faith. This is true of the future also.

---

[33] As a further small example of such new attempts cf. the songs of Père Duval, and on these the author's article, 'Ein kleines Lied', *Glaube der die Erde liebt* (Freiburg, 1966), pp. 157 ff.

2

BEING OPEN TO GOD AS EVER GREATER

On the Significance of the Aphorism 'Ad Majorem Dei Gloriam'

It is well known that the saying 'Ad Majorem Dei Gloriam', 'To the Greater Glory of God' is the motto of St Ignatius, of the Society of Jesus and of its constitutions.[1] It is also well known that it is roughly the equivalent of that 'more' or 'greater service and praise' (of God or of Christ) etc. referred to both in the Constitutions and in the Exercises.[2] Again and again it is taken as the maxim which gives expression to the very nature of the Jesuits, their Order and their spirituality.[3] In truth this maxim constitutes a very obscure saying. It is reasonable, therefore, to offer certain observations concerning it. They touch upon a question which is basic to Christian life as a whole.

No attempt can be made here to present an historical background to our question. Instead something must *first* be said concerning the deficiencies of this saying, and this by way of an introduction to our considerations. This will lead on *secondly* to certain preliminary observations. Thirdly we must indicate the context in terms of the history of spirituality against which this saying must be viewed. *Fourthly* we shall have to treat of the

[1] The expression occurs in this or a similar form 376 times in the regulations of the order written by Ignatius.

[2] On the meaning of this 'magis' in the Exercises cf. K. Rahner, *Betrachtungen zum Ignatianischen Exerzitienbuch*, (Munich, 1965), pp. 27 ff.

[3] In fact, however, the motto of the Benedictines, 'Ut in omnibus glorificetur Deus' (cf. 1 Pet 4:16) has materially the same meaning, unless it be objected that in this case no special value is attached to the *major* gloria, the *greater* honour. The motto of the Friars Minor runs: 'Ad Majorem Dei Resurgentis Gloriam' ('To the Greater Honour of God [Christ] in the Resurrection, in memory of the birthday of this order on the first Sunday after Easter 1589). It is known that for Calvin too, a contemporary of Ignatius, God's 'fame' and 'honour' is the prime motive for God's actions, and therefore must be so for the actions of all Christians too (cf. *Corpus Reformatorum*, Braunschweig, 1863-1900, XXXVI, 294). Hence the motto 'Soli Deo Gloria' appears over many reformed churches. cf. also A. Favre-Dorsatz, *Calvin et Loyola* (Paris-Brussels, 1951), pp. 20 f.

meaning expressed in this saying, and *fifthly* of certain dangers entailed in an attitude such as that expressed in this saying.

I

Let us as Christians examine this saying more closely. The moment we do so it seems wholly unsuitable to express what is distinctive and characteristic of one particular order. First, as might be said by way of objection, it is quite clear that a maxim such as this is binding upon every saint and every Christian. There is no such thing as a saint who neither practises nor intends to practise heroic virtue. But included in the very notion of heroic virtue is the idea that the individual concerned wills to do what is better, and what is better in an heroic degree. In other words the decision to do all for the greater honour of God seems capable of expressing only something which must apply to everyone who strives for sanctity. Furthermore every Christian is actually bound to strive for sanctity in this sense, a fact which has only recently been reiterated by the Second Vatican Council (*Constitution on the Church*, c.5). For according to the teaching of the gospel every man must love God with his whole heart and his whole strength. Perhaps he does not do this yet; perhaps he has not yet succeeded in the concrete in drawing his whole being, his whole resources, his whole life and his whole effort together in one total act of love for God, but in the last analysis he would be sinning mortally if he deliberately decided to refuse to give God a greater love than he has so far managed to achieve. Perhaps in some particular case or other he can refrain from taking the better course without sinning, or at least without sinning gravely, perhaps only thereby committing an imperfection or a sin of omission, even though he sees what is the better course and is capable of taking it. But he can only act in this way because this neglect in the here and now does not constitute any absolute decision concerning his basic attitude.[5] For the total integration of one's whole life, with all its powers, in perfect love of God is far from demanding, as a matter of absolute necessity, that precisely here and now we must always take the better course, and for this reason, precisely here and now, we can take the course that is less good. But if anyone were to decide to adopt this attitude, which he has taken up in some concrete individual case and at a particular

[5] On this conception cf. recently H. Reiners, *Grundintention und sittliches Tun*, Quaestiones Disputatae 30, (Freiburg, 1966).

point in space and time in his life for the fundamental attitude that governs his whole life he would be sinning gravely. In other words, according to the gospel the spirit of the Sermon on the Mount demands as a matter of absolute duty and under pain of grave sin that every Christian shall strive after a greater perfection than that which he has already attained in the concrete circumstances of his life. Man is *par excellence* the being which is *in fieri*, the being which, in virtue of its very nature (in virtue of nature and grace alike), is bound to keep itself in openness to an ever-greater future. And from this point of view the maxim of St Ignatius and his order seems to be totally incapable of providing any meaning which precisely for the spirit of his own foundation and for himself can be regarded as a distinguishing characteristic.

One can regard the inadequacy of this saying from another viewpoint also. If one is honest and makes no claim to asceticism, if for instance one rids one's self of the habit of speaking so facilely in 'devout' circles of sanctity, striving for perfection and willing to take the better course, then one can only be profoundly shocked at a saying such as this one, concerning the 'major Dei gloria'! For is man not the lowest of creatures and the sinner among them? But if he is both of these can he then exist for the greater honour of God in any true sense?

But there is still more. In the theological treatise 'De Deo Uno', 'On God the One', we are taught that man cannot say that God has created the best of all possible worlds. Therefore he is far from willing his own greater glory at all times and in all cases. If one may so express it he is one who is thoroughly 'realistic and down-to-earth', one who wills sometimes one thing and sometimes another, who views it in all its finite limitations and accepts it for what it is – so finite as it actually is, so easy as it would be to improve upon.

A further point which must be made is that from the biblical aspect the honour of God for which we must work is first and foremost the revelation of the 'glory' ('doxa') of God to us. As creatures we are essentially those who have to receive the deed of God upon us, the deed of his compassion, his self-bestowal. Now if we are indeed those who must receive the deed of God upon us, and if God is he who creates that which is finite and limited, that which falls short of his divine omnipotence, what then can it really mean to say that we must do all for the greater honour of God? What does this saying mean if in the last analysis we have always to recognise that we are sinners, those therefore who essentially fall short of the possibility of honouring God which God himself offers us? What, in that case, can this saying concerning the greater honour of God really be intended to signify?

It might even be said that this saying is typical of the new age, inspired by the spirit of the renaissance. It seems to be the saying of a man who feels himself to be the perfector of the world, and in this awareness purposes to usher in the kingdom of God and *thereby* give God honour. In Calvin too we meet this fervour to set up the kingdom of God upon earth, the fervour which aims at a spiritual conquest of the world. Have not many great Christians of this age felt themselves called to bring about the greater glory of God in the world – that, in other words, which was not there before, that which is unprecedently great, that which is audacious that which puts all previous possibilities in the shade? Now when Ignatius adds to this that he intends that all that he does shall be done to God's glory this does not of itself entail any fundamental difference in this basic attitude. But does he not feel himself to be the one who has it in his power to bring about in person this greater glory of God? If against this view the objection is raised that as Christians we are obviously aware that this ability to achieve the greater is still itself a gift of God, then the question immediately arises: If this consciousness of having received the power to achieve the glory of God is really alive in us can we then really speak so facilely, so boldly, with such conviction of our own powers to do something for the greater glory of God, or should we not rather say with the psalmist that God himself must take steps to ensure at least that his name is not dishonoured in the world through us?

The ardent conviction that one is as it were, the representative of God, who defends, maintains and increases the glory of God in the world is in fact to a certain extent an attitude of mind that belongs to the new age, and is therefore conditioned by it. But if one reflects upon the 'end of the new age', as it has been called, then one is compelled to say that this world into which the man of the new age has entered as creator and perfector has in the meantime grown cruelly profane. It is a worldly world, one which, however much it may throw man into relief, does not so clearly reveal God and his *doxa*; a world which has been made by man for his own greater glory. But to speak truly one experiences all that man is capable of doing in the world either as profane or at least as ambiguous. We no longer find it so easy as the men of former centuries to recognise precisely *what* is in fact 'more' to the glory of God. For this God whom we have to honour in this world is still he who is inconceivably transcendent over all that exists, all that we experience and can do. The result is that to us of the present day all that we can offer God by way of his external glory in the world seems to be so immeasurably beneath God himself, so ambiguous, so insignificant that it does not (or would not) come in the least easy to us to say: 'What I now undertake is for the greater glory of God'. Left to ourselves we would be inclined to say, rather: 'We hope that at any rate it has something to do with God!'

From various aspects, therefore, this aphorism 'Ad Majorem Dei Gloriam' is far from being as self-evident as perhaps it may seem to the devout man with his traditional stock of phrases.

Now before proceeding any further and coming to consider the meaning of this saying certain further preliminary observations remain to be made.

II

Every attitude, every idea, every distinctive form of spirituality in the Church emerges from a particular situation and is conditioned by the circumstances of a particular epoch. The situation itself does not remain, but this idea or attitude can survive and continue. The situation in which it emerged is historically conditioned, but what emerges in this situation, so far as the Church of God is concerned, and the life of the Church of God in the true sense, is not something which simply vanishes with this situation. It would be foolish to refuse to recognise those elements which are appropriate only to the particular epoch, the historical context in which this saying, 'Ad *Majorem* Dei Gloriam' emerged precisely in its existing form so as to become, as it were, the beacon or the motto which sums up the spirit of the Society of Jesus. But this should by no means be taken to imply that this spirit must once more disappear. The birth of the Franciscan movement was conditioned by the cultural, and indeed by the economic circumstances prevailing at a particular point in history, those namely in which the city first emerged as a distinctive cultural environment. Monasticism as such arose from certain cultural and, in fact, economic circumstances prevailing in Egypt at the time, which are quite distinctive and well defined. Again, if we consider the institution of the papacy, the definition of its infallibility is rooted in a particular situation in the cultural history of the 19th century, that namely in which the idea of monarchy was emphasised in reaction against the liberal and pseudo-democratic ideas which were threatening to destroy it at the time. Without this atmosphere, without this basis in a specific situation no movement would have emerged even in the Church. Jesus himself in his teaching, directly from heaven though this came, spoke precisely in and from the particular situation with which he found himself confronted. So true is this, indeed, that we have, as it were, to look closely in order to realise that ultimately something which is in fact radically new has emerged at all from the situation. In view of these considerations it can be said that we must look into and evaluate impartially the particular historical context of such circumstances, in which movements have emerged within the Church, and must yet be convinced that something has been born here which is not subject to the conditions of time in the same sense as our other movements and fashions belonging to particular epochs, which do arise only to disappear once more. Much that arises in the Church has come to stay. It is taken up and destined never more to be relinquished. It becomes more developed, more explicit and finally arrives at a stage of development and explicitation at which it can never more be forgotten. What is taking place here is exactly what takes place when, for instance, a definition is produced of infallible teaching authority, whether by the pope or by a Council. Such a definition has its own particular 'kairos', its appropriate point in time, that point at which alone it could have emerged, a situation which once more disappears, whereas that which has arisen as a result of it still remains as a vital factor in the life of the Church. This does not, of course, mean that what has once arisen in this manner remains always and in all circumstances the 'last word' on the subject, the ultimate point of development which must necessarily stand as far as possible in the forefront of the Church's conscious faith and life. The definition of the Assumption is only a few years old. Of course it is a dogma and continues to be such, and, moreover, will always be taught as such. Yet already at this stage how little lasting or effective impact it has! This is a real factor. There will always be such withdrawals into the background of factors which were once more 'actual' in the life of the Church.

To this first preliminary observation a second must be added, necessary if we are correctly to evaluate the maxim concerning the greater glory of God precisely as the watchword of a particular order. If we take a cross-section of the members of any organised society we shall find that only in a very restricted sense do they realise the distinctive aims and spirit of that society. Quite in the abstract and in general it can be said that it is not in the least necessary for any one individual member of a great community always and in all circumstances to be representative of the distinctive spirit of that community. To demand this would be mere childish pseudo-idealism, which, in its ultimate implications, would be ridiculous. This in turn implies that we are not contesting the interpretation of a maxim which expresses that which is typical in the spirit of the Society of Jesus by saying: 'If this interpretation were correct, then Fr so-and-so or brother so-and-so would have to be quite different. But since he is a good Jesuit, and since the life he leads and the work he does in the order is wholly correct, and since his spiritual life is such that he "dies in the Lord", it follows that this interpretation cannot be correct.' Such a line of argument would be false. For there is no need whatever for every member of an order to express in his manner of life what is distinctive and typical of his order in a particularly outstanding degree. It is necessary to emphasise this point so strongly (although strictly speaking it is obvious) because if we do not have a clear realisation of this principle we might, for instance, be able to object to a particular interpretation of the words and maxims of St Ignatius by saying: 'This has never yet been entertained by such-and-such or such-and-such a particular devout and praiseworthy Jesuit; therefore this interpretation cannot be correct'. This line of argument is false. There are a thousand matters in the Exercises which might be worked out theologically, which are authentic ideas of St Ignatius himself, yet which have passed quite unnoticed by individual Jesuits, who have never realised their significance. Moreover, this is far from being a bad thing. The individual as an individual has no need whatever to bring to fruition in his own life and in an especially representative manner what is basic and distinctive in the ideal of his order. In this sense there are among the Jesuits not only Franciscans, but also Capuchins, Benedictines and secular priests etc., who are, nevertheless, completely authentic members of the order, and the converse too is equally true.

There is yet a third preliminary observation to be made, one which it is likewise important to recognise clearly in this context. That which is highest is always the most dangerous too, the most easy to misinterpret and also that which is always and inevitably only half understood. The great inspiration, the comprehensive idea, the most exalted spirit in an individual is necessarily that which at basis is least of all talked about in order that it can be most of all lived. For this latter is harmed and threatened by too much ingenious or pious talk – for both are dangerous. By these means it is very easy for some principle to degenerate into a mere catchword which everyone has on his lips, and which everyone invokes; and then it loses its true value, and from being most often referred to becomes most often misunderstood.

III

Now let us turn to that situation in the history of human thought in which Ignatius was placed, and which initially made it possible for this aphorism to be formulated. Taking account of the Spanish tradition to which Ignatius belonged we can undoubtedly regard him as in many respects a man of the late Middle Ages and of the 'devotio moderna' which, in the last analysis, does in fact belong to the 'autumn of the Middle Ages'. But ultimately speaking he is still, in a true sense, a man of the New Age. In saying this we do, of course, once more have to distinguish: there is a new age which is now gradually drawing to its close – as Guardini has pointed out – and also one which was initiated in those centuries to which Ignatius belonged, never more to cease: the age of the rational, the planned, the scientific and technical. It is at this turning-point that Ignatius stands, a turning-point at which interest begins to be directed towards the subjective, towards the question of salvation as it bears upon the subjective life of the individual, of the sense in which God is a 'gracious God' precisely to *me*. This is the point at which attention begins to be turned from the cosmo-centric to the anthropocentric (as J. B. Metz would say), to man who controls and directs himself and his world by means of rational planning, and directs himself and it towards a future that is open. It is a time when attention is turned to the subjective viewed as a task and as the object of a conscious mission in the Church and for the Church. There have, of course, always been apostolic men. But in the case of Ignatius something peculiar and special emerges in the relationship of the apostle to the Church, something which precisely has not appeared in earlier ages.

Our scholastic background and our sense of the Church always make us prone to think of things as though everything in the Church of God were always the same. Often we suppose that there has always been an awareness, so far as man and his problems are concerned, of his relationship to God, the Church, the sacraments, the word of God, his fellow men etc. In a certain sense this is, of course, thoroughly legitimate and right. But on the other hand there really is a history of ideas, of dogma, of devotion, and it is not true that everything has always been the same. There are cases in which the old becomes new precisely in a manner for which there has been no previous precedent. In this sense Ignatius stands at a quite decisive turning-point, at *the* turning-point which absolutely divides the ecclesiastical history of ancient times and of the Middle Ages from the Church of the New Age. Of course he does not stand there alone. Of course the epoch which constitutes this turning-point is, from certain points of view, several centuries 'long'. It may be that we in the Church of today are in many respects still standing at the end of the Church of the Middle Ages, which only now is gradually realising and understanding precisely what was initiated with Ignatius, with Francis of Sales, with the whole New Age, with the Reformation, the Renaissance, the new natural sciences, the new technical achievements, the realization that the world is one single planet in place of the individual histories of particular regions taken in isolation one from another. But there is this turning to the subject, to subjective striving for salvation, to the subjective viewed as a task for the Church, to the attitude of reflection upon one's self, to that of 'sustained finality', to an existential ethic, to a 'choice' in which the subject in some sense exists by his own decision, chooses, transcends, reflects and is not merely, so to say, called by God in a manner which entails no self-reflection. This is, in short, a turning to self-responsibility. And although Ignatius stands in the midst of this revolutionary change he in turn is, nevertheless, the one who has already, to a certain extent, transformed something which was subject to the conditions of this particular modern world into something lasting. This appears for instance in the fact that in spite of his subjective approach to the salvation of souls, in spite of the fact that in his ideas the 'subjective' aspects of devotion outweigh the 'objective' ones, in spite of the fact that he founded an order which was no longer communal in the same sense as the orders of the Middle Ages, he is, nevertheless, the man of the Church, the man to whom the phrase 'sentire cum ecclesia' may supremely be applied. And if he is this, then he is this, in a true sense, 'in spite of' his subjective approach. For from the point of view of the history of ideas what provides Ignatius with his initial inspiration, what confronts him as unavoidable, is not the Church but modern man considered as personal subject. For Ignatius modern man considered in this sense is an ecclesiastical entity 'in spite of' his subjective aspects. The subjectivism involved here is not Calvinist or Lutheran, although Ignatius' approach to the subjective aspects of salvation is based on exactly the same experience as that of Luther, and although he raised the question of whether he was or was not confronted by a gracious God in a form every bit as radical as Luther, radical in a sense which would have been impossible in previous centuries. Perhaps it is precisely because Ignatius is *the* modern *par excellence*, as it were, in this unique sense that he sometimes gives the impression of being so archaic from one point of view, while from another he seems to figure simply as the representative of one unique epoch. Yet even while recognising this we must once more avoid exaggerating it to the exclusion of all else if we are to take seriously the historical influences to which a given man is subject, his recognition of the truth and his intellectual attitude.

It was necessary to make this third point by way of introduction in order to recognise at all that we are justified in supposing that there is something to be discovered in Ignatius or in his use of the motto concerning the 'Major Dei Gloria' which had not previously been recognised and expressed always and in all circumstances by everyone.

IV

The attempt must now be made, therefore – and it is here that we first touch upon the real problem at issue – to say something about the meaning of this saying. The particular factors in the attitude which finds expression in this saying must first be analysed. This brings us to one specific element among them which seems to us to be the definitive one and this definitive element must then be investigated more closely.

Anyone who says that he wills to live, act, suffer etc. to the greater glory of God thereby asserts first and foremost that he resolves to adopt an attitude of absolute self-surrender to the sovereign will of God, and believes that he has taken up this attitude. The first element in such an attitude, therefore, is obedience to God, and that 'indifference' or detachment which is necessary for this as it can be formulated on the basis of the Exercises. Man is ready to do God's will, and he knows that when he does it he is honouring God, his disposition of things, his position as supreme Lord. But anyone who explains that in this way he is being fundamentally obedient to God who reveals himself in his *doxa*, and anyone who supposes that in speaking of the greater glory of God there are inevitably matters which must be tested, selected and then put into practice on the basis of this, and that in such testing, choosing and acting the glory of God, or even the greater glory of God, is achieved – anyone who thinks this, I say, must not overlook the fact that dispositions have already been made to which he is himself subject. This is the second element. When the Exercises are made or given, when plans for life are projected and subjects for choice are put to the test, when we examine what we must do, then all too often we overlook the fact that we are already subject to pre-existing arrangements, that we are very far indeed from being simply those who make the arrangements. If we enunciate a maxim which is intended to govern our actions then we must at the same time admit that we are quite unable to take this maxim alone as the sole adequate principle by which we shape our lives. Any principle such as that of 'omnia ad majorem Dei gloriam' necessarily entails an attitude which is theologically *a priori*, and in dealing with such principles we must see that this *a priori* attitude must from the outset necessarily be supplemented and limited by an existential *a posteriori*. Someone who is sick cannot start questioning whether an activity which presupposes good health would not be for the greater glory of God in his case. When we set out to direct our lives to the greater glory of God the demands of God himself are not the sole considerations from which we start. In certain ways our lives have already been arranged for us beforehand. There is much that is totally excluded from the sphere of our choice. Freedom in the creature is already subject to pre-existing conditions. Man's freedom to act in history – and this applies to his strivings for salvation too – always takes the form of an obedient fitting in with situations which we can do nothing to alter. Indeed it always means accepting the fact that we have been made to fit in necessarily and inevitably with a given concrete situation. There is a certain priority of the actual over the merely possible, and this element of the concrete and the factual in us, in our life, in the span of life allotted to us, in our temperament, our hereditary traits etc., is, as it were, the woof which runs across the warp of the *a priori* principle 'Ad majorem Dei gloriam'. To put it better: this state of being fitted in with things as they are must from the outset be taken into our calculations if we are rightly to understand the maxim with which we are concerned. We are very far from being simply those who can arrange things for the greater glory of God. Rather God has – perhaps before any such decision on our part was possible – already made his own arrangements for us to act for his lesser glory. Now if we were to try to defend the principle simply by saying that humbly submitting one's self to this will of God is precisely acting for his greater glory, then it is true that formally speaking we would be saving the principle from being overthrown, but in fact this would do nothing to alter the situation. It can be seen, then, that when man enquires what he, as the disposer of things, can do for the greater glory of God, he is, even as he asks, already subject to dispositions superimposed upon him from without.

Now a maxim which is to be comprehensive enough to include both these factors must also implicitly express the fact that there is a certain fluidity in this state of being subject to superimposed conditions; that the obedience involved here has a special element in it, an element of changeableness, of being subject to the vicissitudes of history. To put it another way, and thereby to sum up the first three elements once more: in this statement, 'I will lead my life to the greater glory of God' man says: 'I await a command from God, and ask in all openness what this command is to consist in'. Secondly he says: 'In the most essential matters the command has already been issued. Whether I like it or not it has already been imposed upon me, so that I am very far from being in all respects the one who is summoned or the one who is questioned. The field available to me to choose from for the greater glory of God is already restricted from the outset'. And thirdly he says: 'This state of being called by God, whether the call has already taken specific shape or whether it still remains open and general, is subject to change. Now I am healthy; tomorrow I am sick. Now I must do this, tomorrow that'. Man's state of being subject to prior dispositions on God's part has a certain intrinsic fluidity in it. Obedience does not in the least imply that we have to work out a plan on the grand scale once and for all by some abstract principle. Rather in essence it implies that obedience must take place in the historical vicissitudes of our human existence, ever new, ever unanticipated and incalculable as these are. 'Ad majorem Dei gloriam', therefore does not by any means imply – at any rate in any adequate sense – that man can map out the course of his life once and for all on the *a priori* principle of the greater glory of God. It means that in essence he is not so much the author of projects as the one who has been 'projected', one whom God has already made dispositions for, and who is always only partially in a position to make fresh dispositions on his own account.

He who knows that God has already made arrangements for him, and that from time to time he must respond in all obedience to fresh arrangements imposed upon him by God, and must take these upon himself as they come upon him in a concrete historical situation, (one, therefore which cannot *a priori* be mapped out), such a one can *ipso facto* accept the vicissitudes to which he is subject. This 'letting things fall upon one' is an essentially Christian attitude. For only that freedom which, in spite of its power to dispose of things, and its capacity, so to say, *a priori* to map out the course of life, recognises that it is a creaturely freedom, i.e. a freedom subject to conditions superimposed from without, is a genuinely Christian freedom. And only the life which lets itself unfold in an uncalculating manner, stage by stage, here below is a truly Christian life, evincing the humility appropriate to a creature, trust in God, recognition that one alone knows what is adequate as the formula of our life and its reality, namely God and not ourselves. This acceptance of the fact that our life is arranged by God, and this obedient acceptance of the fact that our life is unforeseeable and subject to the vicissitudes of history, is an essential element in Christian life.

For all this man is capable – and here we touch upon the fourth element – of perceiving, realising, taking into his calculations in an extremely impressive way, the fact that this state of being subject to prior dispositions and the changeableness of such dispositions is under the greater, broader power of God to dispose of things – and at the same time in man's own power. Man is essentially the one who must simultaneously plan and live from day to day. The one who plans out his life and his activities beforehand, and yet must still accept what comes to him. If it be objected to this that planning consists precisely in the fact that man does accept what God sends to him – then we must reply that strictly speaking this is not planning at all. For when God sends some fate to us then we are no longer in a position to raise the question: 'Is it to the greater or lesser glory of God?' Instead we have quite simply to accept it. In other words in the concept of 'major Dei gloria' the explicit, reflexive conscious planning of life really is included, even though man is, and necessarily must be, the one who submits to being disposed of, who accepts, and in a certain sense, who is not capable of planning. It is in this explicit, conscious and constant awareness of man's own further openness to the possibility of having conditions imposed upon him either by God or by man himself that what is definitive in the fourth element involved in the 'major Dei gloria' really consists. In this saying we must realise what it means when it says '*ad* majorem Dei gloriam'. The 'major Dei gloria' is not so much that which is actually done, but rather that towards which our acts are orientated in order, as it were, that they may attain to it as their ultimate goal.

Let us now examine this fourth element somewhat more closely. First, what constitutes it is not found in every man or in all cases. This brings us back once more to the problem which was already adumbrated in the introductory remarks. It might be said that either the 'major Dei gloria' expresses something essential to Christianity as such, in which case it must always have been there from the first, and must be present in every Christian and in every Christian life, or it says something which does not belong to Christian existence as such, in which case it follows *ipso facto* that it is a matter of indifference – every bit as much so as for instance it is a matter of indifference whether Ignatius wore a woollen or a linen garment. But to say this would as we have seen be precisely to interpret the facts wrongly. There are factors which are essential to Christianity, which in a certain sense must always have been present wherever Christianity is found and yet which even allowing for this we have not always been used to adverting to so explicitly as real and vital factors present in our lives. Now the fourth element which we are considering is numbered among these real factors. Another way of expressing this state of affairs might be to say that the actual subjectivity of the subject here becomes the theme of the subject's investigations instead of being merely the mode in which his self-explication is realised in the concrete. This is something which is typical of the new age. The Christian recognises that what he is actually doing in the here and now, the conditions to which he is subject in the here and now, fall essentially short of what he is actually capable of in terms of the fulness of Christian existence. As a result of this realisation he constantly orientates his individual decision in the here and now towards the boundless range of other possibilities open to the Christian and will thus learn to regard himself as the subject not only of what he actually does in the concrete but also of what he is capable of over and above this. In this way he can assume possession of himself as a subject in this sense on his own account. Only on the basis of this attitude can he truly ask what in the here and now is or is not 'ad majorem Dei gloriam'. But just as it is not until the New Age that this sense of the self as subject is arrived at, so this saying 'ad majorem Dei gloriam', intended in the same sense and with the same depths of meaning, is likewise only arrived at in the New Age, and in fact only from Ignatius onwards. This 'selfhood' of the subject was not always a theme of investigation for the subject himself in the sense in which it has come to be so in the New Age. And therefore the wider range of possibilities over and above the conditions actually prevailing in the concrete here and now and ordained by God was not always a theme of investigation for the Christian considered as subject in this sense. But in order to avoid any misunderstandings on this point we must straight away add: this New Age is very far from being the age of unChristianity, though it is constantly being accused of this. This subjectivism is, in the last analysis, nothing else than the outcome of Christianity itself. It is true that we have become accustomed to regarding the New Age more or less as a falling away from Christianity; and in fact this is correct to the extent that in the New Age many individuals have fallen away from Christianity, and many legitimate developments both on the human and the Christian plane have emerged initially outside the Church's orbit. Nevertheless the modern age, in spite of its interest in the subjective, in spite of Descartes, Kant, German idealism and modern existentialist philosophy, is, in the last analysis, something which is there because Christianity is there. It has been thrown up by Christianity to provide opportunities for self-reflection and for the necessary unfolding of Christianity itself in terms of self-reflection. When, therefore, we say that Ignatius' formula, 'Ad majorem Dei gloriam', does not become possible until the New Age this does not mean: 'Sad to say' St Ignatius could only have lived in the New Age, and he has done or seen something in that Age which is not evil, but which, in the last analysis, would have been more or less superfluous in earlier ages. No, the New Age is an age which Christianity itself has ushered in in order to realise itself by way of self-reflection.[6]

This fourth element has, furthermore, a critical function to perform in relation to the actual concrete process of taking the decision. First an example may help to throw light on this point. In the life of St Francis of Assisi St Bonaventure relates that St Francis had the gift of tears, and in his mystical meditations melted, as it were, into tears to such an extent that a doctor drew his attention to the fact that if he wept so excessively he would

[6] These statements, and the special emphasis given to them here, are deliberately intended to bring out *one single* aspect of a more complex process. On the problem itself and its manifold aspects cf. the author's expositions in *Handbuch der Pastoraltheologie* II, 1/2, (Freiburg, 1966), 1, 178–726; 2, 35–45; including the observations of J. B. Metz, *ibid.*, pp. 239–267. cf. also K. Rahner, 'Der Mensch von heute und die Religion', *Schriften zur Theologie* VI (Einsiedeln, 1956), pp. 499–544.

become blind. To this St Francis of Assisi replied: 'What does it matter if I lose my eyes, seeing that these are things which I have in common with the flies?' If St Ignatius had had his attention drawn to the same danger he would have sought to stem his mystical flow of tears. Now we can describe neither the one nor the other procedure as 'the more Christian' or 'the more holy'. Moreover we should remember that we have no understanding of such mystical gifts, and that therefore we have no right to interpret St Ignatius' actions on grounds which make us far too ready to believe that we can reconstruct what Ignatius' answer would have been along these lines. For someone who really can weep tears of mystical ecstasy – for such a one the reply of St Francis of Assisi is really the obvious one. Of course if God had taken away this gift of tears from St Francis he would have submitted to this, and would have been content with it. But in the actual moment in which God, so to say, bestows himself upon him in this manner he looks neither to left nor right but uses to the full this gift of God's grace, this ordination of God – uses it, as it were, without reflecting upon it and, in a certain sense one might almost say, naïvely. In Ignatius' case it is quite otherwise. Here the subject is alive to himself in a much more intense and radical manner. Having become aware of all these factors he, so to say, draws back from them in a special way for which there is no precedent, withdraws himself in a certain measure from these concrete circumstances in which his own existence is realised, objectifies them to himself and asks: 'Now is this really and definitely the best course? It is certainly good – but is it to the greater glory of God?' The realisation of existence in the concrete – even when it is willed by God, perhaps when it is actually commanded by him, and at least when it is ordained and allowed by him – is explicitly measured against a higher standard, and inevitably in doing this the subject stands back from this concrete mode of his own existence. Not everyone does this, and indeed not everyone needs to do it. Not every saint has done it in this sense. In fact we cannot do it ourselves in all circumstances. This is not because, as Ignatius himself will say, many situations are simply as they are and cannot be altered, so that they are not subject to our choice at all, but rather because an attitude of absolute reflection upon one's self, an absolute transcendence of the self reflecting upon itself in relation to what can be chosen or altered would once more be the measure of a freedom and a possibility of decision which does not belong to the creature.

Everyone who has pastoral experience will have encountered this again and again in his life. Again and again he will find men who in their devotion have become neurotic from a reflection upon themselves which is excessive, because again and again they direct everything into the empty space of other, greater, ever-changing possibilities, and then want to make a fresh choice 'for the greater glory of God' for every step they take on the basis of this attitude. Men such as these forfeit a certain trustfulness, a certain immunity from the dictates of their own temperament and their own impulses. But this does not for one moment alter the fact that this fourth element does involve a critical function with regard to the concrete situation which already confronts us or the decision directly demanded of us in the here and now. To this extent the typical attitude of choice is implicitly contained in this saying, 'Ad majorem Dei gloriam', together with all that the Book of Exercises has to say about the three classes of men, the three degrees of humility etc. It might be objected to this that every Christian must freely work out and so choose his own salvation. And if he chooses rightly he has brought to bear the right principles of choice, with which, naturally, he must in some measure be acquainted, for the purpose. All this may be true, but nevertheless this peculiar attitude of choice, this withdrawal of one's self to an absolute point in order from *there* to reflect and to test what is to be done, does exist. And this existential structure involved in the act of choice does exist in the case of St Ignatius in a degree which the moral theologians right to the present day have probably not yet sufficiently grasped. Again and again it seems to be presupposed that the third kind of choice, the process of rational checking, or the element of the rational in the two other modes of choice and stages of choice in the Exercises and in the Christian life is absolutely *the* decisive factor. Now this is not true. On the contrary, Ignatius is the first – is, indeed, almost unique in this among the theologians – to have developed in his Exercises a logical structure of choice which is indeed applied in the practice of these Exercises to the extent that they are carried out because it *must* be applied. And yet no-one has really penetrated beyond the theological and metaphysical principles and presuppositions behind this structure of choice.[7] Ignatius does, in fact, envisage a Christian

---

[7] On this cf. K. Rahner, 'Die ignatianische Logik der Existentiellen Erkenntnis. Über einige theologische Probleme in den Wahlregeln der Exerzitien des hl. Ignatius', *Ignatius von Loyola. Seine geistliche Gestalt und sein Vermächtnis*, (Würzburg, 1956), pp. 343 ff. – K. Rahner, *Das Dynamische in der Kirche* (Freiburg, 3rd ed., 1965), pp. 74–148.

who – and this is something which carries immense dangers with it – as person, as 'self' in the New Age takes up a transcendent vantage-point from which to consider, test and choose what is and what can be to the greater glory of God. And this is precisely what lies behind this saying, 'Ad majorem Dei gloriam'.

This in turn throws light on a further point, namely the significance which this saying has for an existential ethic of the present day.[8] It is precisely not true that everything can be rationally deduced. It is not true that the individual in his individuality, in his decision, is simply the individual instance of more general, more abstract principles. We can realise how difficult and obscure these questions are by considering, for instance, the difficulties raised by the theories of J. Lahitton with regard to the recognition of priestly vocation. One may be quite ready to accept that this theory has its importance as a practical rule of thumb for ecclesiastical superiors in judging of a man with regard to his possible vocation to the priesthood. But if these principles are understood as having a theoretical, metaphysical, existential or ontological value Lahitton's theory is basically false. What would be the use of the whole process of choice formulated by St Ignatius, with all these subtle rules etc. concerning 'consolation without prior cause' etc. if, from the aspect of metaphysics or existential theology (or however we may wish to express it) the situation were such as that which Lahitton envisages for certain cases in which the presence of a priestly vocation has to be discerned. In such cases, indeed, one would only need to say: 'Dear friend, if you are a normal, balanced man, then you only need to have the right motives and your vocation is established. You can depend upon it that it is there. You have passed the entrance examination. You are an intelligent man who shows with ample probability that he can observe celibacy, and you yourself know whether you have the right motives'. And if the subject then replied: 'Obviously I don't want to be a rich man, nor do I seek for any special comfort in life. I want to do something for the good God', then one would only have to fall on his neck and say: 'You have a vocation!' One has only to compare with this the complex, intricate 'apparatus' for testing a vocation which St Ignatius sets forth in the Exercises to realise

---

[8] On this cf. the author's article, 'On the Question of a Formal Existential Ethics', *Theological Investigations* II (London & Baltimore Md, 1963), pp. 217–234; and further the articles collected under the title, 'Der Einzelne und die Kirche', *Schriften zur Theologie* VI (Einsiedeln, 1965), pp. 499–544.

that the saint had a quite different idea of the existential decision and the process of arriving at it than that implied by such rationalism. For Ignatius there really is something like an existential and ethical attitude on man's part, which precisely implies an openness to that which lies beyond the data which can be calculated and deduced on the rational, abstract and essentialist plane. And this existential and ethical attitude finds expression both in his Exercises and also, in brief, summary form, in the saying 'ad majorem Dei gloriam'. Now if one reflects that this 'major Dei gloria', if it is in fact to be made effective at all, is ultimately a gift of God and must necessarily be so, then one realises what really is implied in this saying: an openness to the direct personal love of God, which is no longer arrived at through intermediate causes, and, in fact, the end of legalism and the freedom of children of God in the Pneuma of Christ. It is here that what is proper to God's own sovereign disposition of his creatures comes, in a certain sense, into force; a disposing of things which is no longer mediated through worldly causes or through the Church's official direction, a disposing of things which really can and must be called 'the better' precisely because it is itself the freedom of God in his sovereign act of disposing. And it is only when someone knows himself to be called, and is open to this sovereign act of disposing on God's part that he is truly in the New Testament. This does not, of course, mean that it is only with this attitude proper to the New Age and subjective in a good sense, which is characteristic of Ignatius, that Christianity began. But something specifically Christian here becomes explicit and actual for the first time, so that it can be seen and apprehended as such.

v

In conclusion something must be said about the dangers involved in such an attitude. First this attitude is strongly self-reflective and subjective in character, not in the sense that the general rules of the natural and divine laws do not have to be observed, but in the sense that the personal self is in a position of almost radical withdrawal from every form of actualisation in the sphere of human living in the concrete, and this means that he evaluates, judges, criticises, transcends, rejects, makes fresh choices of, etc. the various concrete forms of human acts by the standard of the absolute possibility of giving glory to God. Such an attitude does, of course, carry with it the danger of being fatally damaging to that attitude of spontaneity and freedom from restraint and over-calculation on man's part which is necessary for his acts to be fully human and fully Christian. In his act of reflecting upon himself man cannot overcome his own radical inadequacy. If he sets himself to do this, if he wanted to do it in a manner that did go beyond this radical inadequacy of his, he would be going beyond himself as man, as creature. In the last analysis he would be presuming to be God. That which is unthought out, uncalculated, belongs essentially to man too, and to that extent the attitudes here described represents a radical danger to this spontaneity and freedom from restraint, to that basic peace in which man dares to live with himself. There are men who fail to achieve this, and who are not better but worse on this account. Viewed from this aspect one can exercise too much 'examination of conscience', self-control and self-criticism. Whether it can be stated as a general principle that we of today are in danger of gradually slipping into this is a question which need not be entered into here. But fundamentally speaking the attitude which we have been describing does entail this danger. He who is *always* asking 'Is this to the greater glory of God in these present circumstances?', he who, so to say, does not bring an immediate, spontaneous and unselfconscious enthusiasm to bear on his concrete actions *ipso facto* fails to perform them in a manner which is to the greater glory of God.

The Jesuits are often accused of being rationalists. This need not necessarily be a reproach. Rationalism may be no less justifiable than any other of the possible attitudes. But what is noteworthy is that on the basis of his deepest inspiration, his special brand of mysticism, Ignatius perceives the absolute sovereignty of God, measured by which any specific activity or non-activity on man's part must be totally inadequate. It is on the basis of this vision, then, this overwhelming experience of God as ever greater, that Ignatius feels himself compelled to ask in all that he does, however good it may be, whether something still greater, something less inadequate to God's immeasurable greatness, would not have been possible. This attitude, which, as it were, is the outcome of a mystical and non-rational approach, and at the same time of one which is existential in the right sense, can degenerate precisely into an over-cautious pseudo-rationalism if it is not spontaneously carried through. The true Ignatian scepticism, however, towards what is given and what we are confronted with in the here and now, has the function precisely of leaving the last word to God. Yet it is often invoked in order to reduce everything to shreds by rationalism, and to destroy an enthusiasm which is spontaneous, fine and, in the good and holy sense, naïve.

The attitude in question involves a third danger, which appears still more clearly. This consists in the fact that in the case of narrow-minded and petty people the 'aristocratic scepticism', as it might be called, can drift into something approaching officiousness and a 'managing' attitude, and thereby religion can actually become choked by legalism and institutionalism. One becomes sceptical with regard to particular details. One finds that this or that is not so important. One perceives that some particular point is still not the vital factor. But when we adopt this attitude the one factor which is vital, namely God who disposes of our lives in absolute freedom and grace, is no longer there for us. For instance one adopts a rather casual attitude towards liturgical practices because one feels that 'nothing is really and certainly achieved by all these externals'. Again in theology the smoothest and most harmonious opinion is sought for, one which upsets no-one etc. And why is all this? Man is, in a certain sense, sceptical towards everything, and because of this the temptation arises all too easily of erecting a voluntarist system in the proper and formal sense on the basis of established and institutional practices, not because one is prompted to do this from one's own interior convictions or from some interior inspiration, but really because, for want of this latter factor, one is afraid to lose even that which has gone before, unless one falsely 'rigidifies' it in this way. As a result of this we find that deficiency, which we have encountered often enough, of any genuine, spontaneous, living enthusiasm. How much in the way of a fruitful exchange of ideas, how much spontaneous love in this connection, how much apostolic zeal, which is overpowering in the holy sense, can still manifest itself or speak out today? How anxious we are to ensure that nothing of the love which we entertain in our hearts shall be noticed! All these experiences, instances of which are all too frequently to be met with, and which make life so impersonal, so drab and so grey, can of course be the sign of a fine and laudable attitude, the maturity of the saint who sees through himself to his depths. But they also serve to show what dangers are involved in constantly asking where the 'major Dei gloria' lies.

The motto coined by Ignatius expresses something quite simple but something new in the history of ideas, namely that man dares once more to measure even the element of the holy in what he does and in what he intends to do by the mysterious and immeasurable greatness of God, and thereby does not merely submit in all humility as a creature subject to historical limitations to the various dispositions which God imposes upon him from time to time, but actually collaborates in bringing this intervention of the ever-greater God in his life to fruition, though always, of course, in subordination to God himself, through him and for him. Thereby man measures what is holy in his own actions once more by the greater holiness which, in the last analysis, can only be God himself, and what God alone brings about by his own direct action as Ignatius says. 'Ad majorem Dei gloriam', therefore, signifies the attempt constantly to judge the glory of God actually achieved in our actions by that greater glory of God which could be achieved, in order that we may be always ready and open anew, and in a manner that cannot be foreseen, to try to achieve that other glory of God (as we may now better express it) which God demands of us at another stage in our lives.

'Ad majorem Dei gloriam' opens up to man in his personal and subjective life, so to say, the greater range of possibilities entailed by the ever-greater realisation of God's own greatness precisely at that point at which we, because we do act for God's glory, might suppose that we should thereby exchange this same glory as embodied in our actions, for God himself. Such a supposition would be utterly false. If Ignatius' attitude should be qualified as an awareness of God as 'Deus semper major',[9] then exactly the same is true of the saying 'Ad majorem Dei gloriam'. Likewise in a certain sense man has always been aware that God is ever greater than his creature's own apprehension of him, and yet this sense of the incomprehensible greatness of God as ever greater is, in a certain sense, something that belongs peculiarly to the New Age, but belongs to it in such a way that it is permanent. And just as all this is true, so too in the same sense it is true that there had always been a certain basic awareness of the truth which found expression in the saying 'Ad majorem Dei gloriam' even though it is to the New Age that this truth properly belongs. But when we say that it belongs to the New Age we mean that it belongs to it in such a way that it is permanent and enduring.

[9] cf. Erich Przywara, *Deus semper maior*, *Exerzitienkommentar*, 3 vols (Freiburg, 1938–1940); new and expanded edition, Vienna–Munich, 1964, 2 vols.

3

INTELLECTUAL HONESTY AND CHRISTIAN FAITH

On first reading the title 'Intellectual Honesty and Christian Faith' the somewhat over-hasty enquirer might feel that there was no problem at all as to what intellectual honesty really means. The only question to be raised in this connection, he might feel, is whether this honesty can be maintained in the context of Christian faith. Now it is certainly true that in the very nature of the case the problem of how the two are to be reconciled will be one of our major preoccupations. But the first point that we have to recognise is that it is by no means so clear as all that what 'intellectual honesty' really is.

I

In portraying the intellectually honest man we might say that he is one who does not delude himself. He faces fully and unreservedly the difficulties entailed in adopting any 'credal' position today. He is quite ready to concede that the upholders of other views have just as much intelligence and good will as he has himself. He has the courage to change his convictions as circumstances demand. He is resolved to be not fanatical, but rather 'impartial' and 'objective' in arriving at his conclusions. He constantly re-examines his own positions quite as critically as those of other people. He allows for the fact that in his case too, under the influence of the spirit of a particular age, a particular social class, a particular kind of upbringing, personal calling, or even temperamental or social bias, he himself may be subject to prejudices. He realises that he must do his utmost to overcome such prejudices together with the ideological presuppositions arising from them. And in all this he fully recognises that the truth may be not so much consoling as terrifying. Such a description of the intellectually honest man is certainly one which, seems acceptable – at least at first sight. But if we are really in earnest in seeking to understand what constitutes intellectual honesty we must take into account the fact that, great though this virtue is, all the dangers which it is intended to avert are in fact present in the very process of formulating the concept of intellectual honesty in this sense, and threaten to distort and even destroy the actual concept itself. For this reason an attempt must be made to say what intellectual honesty does *not* mean if the actual concept itself in not, once more, to be hopelessly distorted by some ideological prejudice and the spurious authority which this carries with it. In this connection two postulates seem to me to be of fundamental importance.

Intellectual Honesty and Human Decision

It is not true to say that intellectual honesty is arrived at only when the subject is unencumbered (or, better, believes himself to be unencumbered) by the burden of any radical human commitment. It is a great temptation to suppose that the intellectually honest man is the one who maintains a sceptical reserve; one who does not commit himself, and comes to no absolute decision; one who does indeed test all hypotheses but (the apostle's recommendation to the contrary not withstanding) does not opt for any one of them; one who seeks to avoid error by refusing to commit himself definitively to anything; one who makes the radical mistake of taking the weakness of indecision (though it may be conceded that when this is only temporarily or partially present it may be a virtue) for the courage of the sceptic who is devoid of illusions. No – intellectual honesty is not at all like this! Certainly there are cases in which men are so perplexed that they genuinely believe that they cannot truly proceed any further with a previously held position, as for instance in the case of an anguished atheist who in his despair can only see all existence as absurd, so that this absurdity hangs as a sort of Medusa's head before his eyes. Such a one must quietly reconcile himself to this position, and try to accept even this experience calmly. For even this, so the believer says, will be made by God to bring a blessing upon him. But he must not assert that this is the *only* proper attitude for the intellectually honest. How could he presume to know this? How does he know that no-one ever emerges from this *purgatorio* or this *inferno*? How does he know that no-one ever has the strength to experience all this and still to believe?

In any case, whether we regard it as a curse or a blessing, freedom is inherent in our very nature (for our purposes it makes no difference how one interprets this freedom so long as one recognises that it is inescapable). And this freedom of ours is such that it plays a vital part in even our most basic human decisions and attitudes. It is true of believers and unbelievers alike that there are no ultimate basic attitudes, no absolute standards of value or systems of co-ordinates for determining the meaning of existence such as might enable them to evade the struggles and hazards entailed in the responsible exercise of freedom. This is not because it is sheer blind caprice that rules at this level, but because at this level it is no longer possible to separate one's basic views from the exercise of one's freedom. Hence it is that one who seeks to set himself free by being a sceptic, who refuses to commit himself or to make any position whole-heartedly his own on the grounds that he is anxious to avoid all danger of error — such a one does not remain free but has actually committed himself in the worst possible sense. For he is living his life, living it once and for all, and thereby carving out a course that is irrevocable. In the very act of living his life he stands committed. If in spite of this he attempts to live without self-commitment, in a certain sense to remain in the dimension of 'brute fact' and the biological, and if he attempts by these means to return the 'entrance ticket' which admits him to the sphere of freedom and decision, to remain 'neutral', then this is itself in its turn a decision, and it is quite impossible to explain why there should be any better grounds for arriving at this particular decision than at any other.

Furthermore there is no such thing as remaining poised in some dimension which is *prior* to decision. The attempt to remain neutral, therefore, is in practice only the refusal to bring one's powers of speculative thought to bear upon the decisions entailed willy nilly in the fact of living one's life at all. For in this there is one decision at least which we must arrive at (even if our speculative thought upon the subject is only at the incipient stage): whether life is to be regarded as absurd or as filled with ineffable and mysterious meaning.

In short: intellectual honesty commands us to have the courage to take basic human decisions however weighed down we may feel by uncertainty, darkness and danger. For these obstacles are inevitably entailed by the fact that the minds with which we take our human decisions are finite and historically conditioned. And these minds of ours, while fully recognising the disadvantages to which they are subject, still must decide.

But once this has been said it must once more be reiterated: we have to allow for the case of one who, in all responsibility and in accordance with the ultimate dictates of his conscience with regard to truth, finds himself so perplexed that he believes himself bound in duty to remain undecided upon many questions, and indeed, as it seems to him, upon the most ultimate questions of all, in order to be true to that conscience; one who believes himself bound with all the resources of his spirit to keep an open mind and not to give any definitive answer in the sphere of speculative thought. Such a one may, and indeed must, remain open as his conscience dictates. The enlightened believer will have only two points to make about this: first that there is one thing that no one man can know of another: supposing a man takes up such a stand at some point, whether proximate or remote, in the course of his existence. No-one can know whether a decision made at that particular point does not *ipso facto* entail a definitive decision against the sacred as providing existence with its meaning. But neither does one man have the right to bow down in worship before that particular meaning, when it is still remote from his own experience, merely on the grounds that the other feels himself compelled so to bow down, from a similar position of remoteness. Secondly the believer, faced with the man who, in the name of responsibility to the truth and intellectual honesty, is maintaining with difficulty his openness to the question to which, as it seems to him, there is no answer, will draw his attention to the fact that even this decision, namely that he can find no answer, does in fact constitute an assent to that which the believer himself calls the divine and blessed mystery of his existence, and further that the one who finds himself unable to find an answer has simply not yet been favoured with the courage to define explicitly for himself that which he is already implicitly acknowledging in his life by the silent eloquence of his actions.

Intellectual Honesty, Responsibility in Faith and the Exploration of Ideas
In the concept of intellectual honesty in relation to the exercise of faith a second misunderstanding must be guarded against. This is the opinion that in order to remain intellectually honest while believing one would have to have thought out in a 'scientifically' adequate way all the presuppositions which such belief, and especially Christian belief, necessarily entails. Faith implies a whole wealth of material in the form of the facts, statements and ideas which go to make up its content. And this is true not

merely of that relatively early stage in belief in God at which one is able to explicitate one's belief in the form of a concept able to be reflected upon and investigated, but also, and still more, at that further stage at which one actually comes to believe specifically in Jesus Christ, in a concrete saving history and in the Church.

Now if it were in principle the case that in order to believe at all while still fulfilling the requirements of intellectual honesty, one would first have to have thought out in an adequate and scientific manner all these presuppositions objectively implied in the content of faith, then there would indeed be an almost unresolvable conflict between intellectual honesty and faith. For who could maintain that he would ever be capable of achieving such a thing in his brief life-span, with the limited possibilities of scientific investigation open to him, and with his lack of specialist knowledge in hundreds of fields?[1] Who could achieve a thorough grounding in all the following subjects at once: metaphysics, philosophy of religion, history of religion, knowledge of the religious and intellectual background of the period of Jesus Christ, exegesis and biblical theology together with the immensely complicated methods which have been evolved, and which are nowadays required for these, knowledge of the relationship between Christianity and the ancient world in which it emerged, history of dogma and of the complex idiom in which the dogmatic teaching of Christianity and of the contemporary Catholic Church have come to be expressed, a precise knowledge of the problems of theological controversy between the Christian confessions and the history of these? To have a knowledge of *all* these *at once*, and a *fundamental* knowledge at that? Never! No-one, not even the individual who is a specialist in theology! For even he, at any rate today, apart from the fairly restricted sphere of his own special branch of theology is for practical purposes a non-specialist believer and Christian in all other departments of his life which have a bearing on his intellectual responsibility for his beliefs.

A further difficulty in addition to the above is raised by the approach to fundamental theology usually adopted by Catholics.[2] Certainly funda-

---

[1] cf. the author's 'A small Question regarding the Contemporary Pluralism in the Intellectual Situation of Catholics in the Church', *Theological Investigations* VI (London & Baltimore Md, 1969), pp. 21–30.

[2] On these lines of thought cf. especially K. Rahner, *Im Heute glauben*, Theologische Meditationen 9 (Einsiedeln, 2nd ed. 1966).

mental theology has, of its very nature, the task of entering *ex professo* into all the relevant problems and investigating them to the utmost possible extent with a view to providing a rational justification for faith (for the purposes of the present argument it makes no difference precisely what we mean by faith here). But in doing this it gives rise to the dangerous impression that the individual Christian has the same responsibility as an individual, especially if he is 'educated', that namely of working out for himself in a similar direct and scientific manner the problems of fundamental theology; that he must himself as an individual have a competent scientific knowledge of all the 'preambula fidei'; that such a responsibility has to be undertaken by anyone who is endowed with intelligence and good will, at least if he is educated, and that only the 'uneducated' are in the nature of things excused from this responsibility. (In the case of these latter the special circumstances of their faith are a matter for independent investigation). Some such idea does exist, though as an implicit presupposition rather than as explicitly asserted 'in thesi'. On this showing faith does admittedly come into conflict with intellectual honesty in the educated man. If he wants to be intellectually honest he sees how impossible it is for him to achieve this, because he recognises the complexity of modern science, and because he himself experiences its fluctuations, its disappointments and its uncertainties. And he therefore supposes that he cannot and may not believe because the idea has been suggested to him that it is only possible to believe in a rational and responsible way if he has more or less adequately discharged in his personal and individual life the task of research which is the object of fundamental theology.

There are, of course, non-Catholic interpretations of faith which make this appear irrational from the outset, and which confine it in its content to a sphere which must be ruled out from the first as an area for rational investigation. In other words these are theories which right from the outset interpret faith in such a way that it seems of its very nature to be a totally irrational experience and irrational attitude, and so to be incapable of having anything to do with intellectual honesty. But for the Catholic understanding of faith there is no such easy way out of the problem. As Catholics understand the matter an intellectual element is of the essence of faith as such. It bears amongst other things upon historical realities of which it cannot be said that they are simply, and from the outset, incapable of rational investigation. The believer recognises that the logical and the existential factors in his awareness constitute a unity, and he cannot and will not schizophrenically divide them one from another. The totally irrationalist concept of faith turns it into an ideology — turns it, so far as the concrete existence of the realistic man, relying on his own experience of reality, is concerned, into a dream which has no validity except precisely in the realm of fantasy.

The believer, therefore, must justify himself by the standards of intellectual truthfulness according to his own Catholic understanding of his faith, and must tackle the question of intellectual honesty on the basis of his own resources, but this precisely does not mean that this honesty is only sufficiently achieved when every individual believer has independently, in his own individual mind, and by an adequate process of scientific investigation, fulfilled that task with which fundamental theology is objectively presented. As a presupposition this is false. So far from this, even by standards of truthfulness which are fully responsible one can and must believe without having scientifically investigated all the objective 'preambula fidei' for the purpose.

Why is this? It is because the intellectual life of man is always, fundamentally and inevitably designed in such a way that a perceptible existential difference (as we might call it) prevails between that which is implied in the very fact of living and that which is the outcome of scientific speculation upon one's life. Man cannot shape his existence solely and exclusively on the basis of factors which he has made his own by a process of scientific investigation, and which he has 'proved' to himself in *this particular* manner (which is by no means the only one). And because he apprehends with his reason the inevitability of this difference, because he knows that the act of living in a particular way is not merely the outcome of rational speculation, he is therefore justified by the standards of his own sense of truthfulness, in other words 'intellectual honesty', and for this reason has a duty to accept this difference and, in deciding the shape of his life, to commit himself in an absolute and definitive way (in our case by faith) to that which has not been 'scientifically proved' in any adequate sense.

This does not, of course, mean that speculative testing and criticism within the limits of what is really possible form no part of man's obligations. One of the factors which belong inevitably, and from the outset to the very mode of existence which man must accept in all obedience and trust is that there is an area of speculation and testing by means of the critical faculties, an area which is admittedly capable of broadening and development. So soon as the answer to one of life's questions has been found it *ipso facto* raises another one, to which there is as yet no answer, so that one has to bend one's self to the task of answering this one also. But it would be precisely not intellectual honesty but rather intellectual scrupulosity, destructive and incapacitating, to adopt the position that the life of the mind or spirit either could or should be constructed only from materials which have been submitted to the processes of scientific speculation for testing and proving. I love my mother and accept all the consequences which this love entails, even though I have no theoretical certainty whatever that Mrs So-and-so really is my mother. I have a manifest right and duty to take a political decision, possibly even to fight on one side or the other of the barricades, even thought I have no theoretical certainty that my decision is, objectively speaking, the right one. Nor could even the most advanced computer, such as those which our contemporaries attempt to employ in such questions, excuse me from taking this decision for myself. I cannot take refuge from this situation by defining some theoretical position of sceptical neutrality because this in its turn is precisely a decision too, involving just as many consequences for me as the 'taking of sides'. If it be asked how, in that case, and given the existential difference mentioned above, man can submit to the demands which this terrible situation makes upon him of necessarily having to take some decision, it would be reasonable to reply: 'It *is* demanded of him, and the protest against the demand takes place, in its turn, *within* this situation and does not escape from it. Those who, in all obedience and honesty, come to decisions in this way, even though the decisions themselves may be quite opposite one to another, are actually more closely and fraternally united among themselves in loyalty to their own consciences and in the courage they have shown in coming to a decision with regard to the truth than they are to one who, when faced with the demands of truth, attempts to maintain a policy of sceptical withdrawal. And this is true precisely in those cases in which both those who commit themselves and those who refrain are aware of how dark and how painful any such decision can be. Finally the actual decision when it comes may indeed be deficient in terms of objective rightness. But however much this may be the case it still remains true that in every such decision, involving as it does a spirit of responsibility and loyalty to the truth, the subject gives his absolute and definitive assent to the absolute and definitive demand presented to him by that mystery of existence which we call God. It follows that provided the heart seeks the truth in this mystery in all innocence, it remains within the orbit of his favour even when it errs.

We have been raising some points of fundamental importance with regard to the 'existential difference', as we have called it. Now these obviously apply also to the relationship between intellectual honesty and faith. Indeed they apply here most of all. For faith is primarily concerned with the all-embracing meaning of existence, and Christian faith (as the declaration that historical events have a saving value) makes assertions about human existence in *all* its dimensions. In this case, however, the 'existential difference' between the events actually pointed to and their significance on the one hand, and the conclusions arrived at in terms of scientific speculation and theory on the other is necessarily and inevitably at its greatest. One who both believes and is intellectually honest knows this, must know it and acknowledge it, and has no need to shrink from this state of affairs. Of course there is an almost incalculable number of particular questions which – taken all together – it would be quite impossible for the individual to work out for himself by his own personal scientific investigations for the sake of providing a rational justification for his faith. But this is precisely what intellectual honesty does not demand. Why should one not trust one's own living experience without prejudice in this sphere as in other spheres of life even prior to any theoretic evaluation of such experience? Obviously one recognizes that one's Christianity, one's Catholic faith, is conditioned by one's historical, social and psychological circumstances. One realises that in a vast number of cases these conditioning factors are not present. One can say to one's self in all calmness: Presumably I myself would not in fact be a Catholic if the factors conditioning my life had been otherwise, if I had not been born and brought up as a Catholic from my childhood.[3] One realises, and can readily concede, that even in ideal cases, where very far-reaching investigations in the field of fundamental theology are possible, one cannot really obtain any absolute certainty in the attempt to find a rational justification for one's faith as such. In other words one's ideas are,

---

[3] One can concede that one's personal faith is historically contingent in this sense, without thereby asserting that there are no objectively valid grounds whatever which – objectively speaking – should cause everyone to be a Catholic, and without contesting the real possibility that another individual can become a Christian and a Catholic from a non-Christian and non-Catholic background.

humanly speaking, always open and provisional, and capable of further development.[4]

All this may be demanded by intellectual honesty. But it does not imply any suspension of faith in weary scepticism. Faith as such, as an act of human living in which the ultimate meaning of existence is accepted and embraced as God's word to us, is endowed with that absolute transcendence, that freedom from all conditions, which is indispensable to it if it is to be faith at all. But for this it precisely does not need, over and above the word of God and his grace (of which we shall have to speak at a later stage), any comprehensive evaluation in terms of theory of all its implications and presuppositions. In the first instance faith is present simply as something given (or as a possibility actually pressing in upon us in the here and now). As such it finds sufficient initial justification by what it carries with it in itself. It is a fact of life which man commits himself to whole-heartedly and without prejudice as justified even on the rational plane, so long as the opposite of faith has not become certain to him. The reason for this is that man must give life itself the chance to justify itself. And this can only be achieved if it is lived in a spirit of trustfulness. A further reason is that faith as conceived of here gives reason and order to existence; that it opens up into that infinitude which alone provides the perspective in which meaning and mystery can be reconciled, and can permeate the whole of life; further that conscience and morality with regard to truthfulness (to the extent that this is identical with a feeling for word and freedom which is self-authenticating) commands us to hold firm to such awareness of ineffable mystery to the very last, and never to surrender it except if a greater, purer, more all-embracing meaning presents itself. Yet a further reason is that faith that is really committed feels itself protected and nourished by the experience of grace which precisely carries its own intrinsic justification with it. For such experience of grace, however subtle and indefinable the form in which it manifests itself, and however silent and interior the state of liberation which it brings, does point us on to the mystery of God.

Now for the act of faith to be justified in this way, and in a manner which, while prior to any formal theorising, nevertheless does fall within the purview of fundamental theology, what is required? Certainly not

[4] This means that the fact that the assent of faith is absolute does not for one moment imply that the rational justification of the 'preambula fidei' as such needs to be raised to a similarly absolute level.

that there should be any positive or explicit realisation at this level that the experience of the illumination of one's existence by the mystery of God, and of being enveloped in that mystery (the 'mystical' experience of faith, as it may be called), can only really take place in terms of that whole range of factors on the human plane which make up the manifold content of the Christian and Catholic faith. The requirements of intellectual honesty are fully satisfied so long as this is *de facto* the situation in which the experience of faith is located, and so long as this mystical experience of faith, as realised in the concrete in the actual believers, that is in ourselves, does not elevate us above these factors or invite us to depart from them. With this proviso we are fully justified in committing ourselves to this synthesis, which is prior to any theorising on our part, between the mystical and transcendental experience of faith on the one hand, and the concrete factors which make up the content of the Christian faith on the other as a *de facto* reality, and in realising it as absolute and irrevocable in the act of faith itself. For as conceived of here faith itself possesses an intrinsic critical element of its own. Faith itself, that is to say, actively explores its own content. Faith itself activates the critical and speculative faculties of the believer, causing him to put the vital question of what his conscience demands of him in terms of truthfulness to himself. But the process of reflecting critically upon his faith, and of putting this question to himself of how it is to be justified in theory, must be allowed to develop in its own way. It must be allowed time so to develop. In investigating these theoretical questions the starting-point must be precisely *those* factors with which life confronts the concrete individual in his own personal and unique situation, and in the particular development of his own ideas. These are the factors which are real and genuine enough to offer genuine possibilities of really mastering this problem of the theoretical justification of faith. This attitude of judgment and criticism in the true sense may or may not raise connected questions which it is indeed possible to conceive of as legitimate in their own right, but which need not necessarily present themselves to the given believer in the concrete as problems which he feels himself personally bound to solve. He may not feel himself so bound precisely because he may, in all reason, modesty and courage, feel compelled to recognise that he is not competent to solve them. It is not necessary for everyone to be a Qumran specialist in order to be able to be honest in his beliefs. Not every honest believer is bound to enter into the most recent developments (as instanced in the 'Spiegel') in the 'life of Jesus' discussion. It is strange. One so often hears mention of the nature of man as historically conditioned (*geschichtlich*) even in his recognition of the truth. Yet there is an unwillingness confidently to accept one's own real and personal history (*Geschichte*) as the basis for deciding one's existence. There is an idea that it is impossible to establish any absolute truth for those who remain *within* history, and are involved in it. But history itself demands this because truth does *de facto* arise in history, and without it there would be no history in the true sense at all.

II

Up to this point we have been attempting to consider the question of intellectual honesty and faith by seeking to investigate somewhat more closely the real significance of the concept of 'intellectual' honesty. The same attempt must now be made in the converse direction, in that we must ask ourselves what is really meant by faith.

Christian Faith Considered as a Whole

As a specific, total and fundamental determination of human existence faith is necessarily an entity which is as complex as human existence itself, and one which, like human existence, resolves itself into the mystery of God. If therefore, we are to raise the question of what is meant specifically by Christian and Catholic faith with all its essential content, and not merely what is meant by the assent to God involved in an abstract or merely transcendental 'theism', then we must turn our attention to the 'basic fundamentals' of this faith. This does not mean, however, that we shall be investigating more closely all the widely differing ways in which the particular assertions of Christian and Catholic faith are to be related to these 'basic fundamentals' (whether objectively by establishing an intrinsic connection between the actual realities referred to and these fundamentals or subjectively by examining the believer's own assent to these assertions). The fact that the Catholic understanding of faith does necessarily entail this difference between what is absolutely basic and what is derived is explicitly stated in Vatican II.[5] The fact that precisely for the sake of reasonableness and intellectual honesty it is necessary for the individual to draw this distinction for himself is immediately evident from what has been said in the first part of our considerations. While bearing

---

[5] On this cf. Vatican II, *The Decree on Oecumenism*, No. 11.

in mind the necessary sense of historicity and of community (even in the dimension of truth), and while bearing in mind the difference between the exixtential decision which is prior to scientific investigation on the one hand, and the speculative process of metaphysical and scientific examination on the other, it is prudent, and also intellectually justifiable for the individual as human and as Christian (to put it simply) ultimately to avoid dissecting the totality of his belief into its individual constituents, each one of which would require its own separate speculative investigation and justification. It is sensible, and also intellectually justifiable, to say that Christianity (precisely in all the variations of its content) can be accepted or denied only in its totality, only as a whole. 'There can be no leaving out of particular parts of it'. In this second part of our considerations, therefore, we shall be concerned to throw light upon the fact that this essentially total and single entity that is the Christian faith is of such a nature that it fully measures up to the criteria of intellectual honesty.

For the purpose of such a demonstration it must, of course, first be laid down what this essentially unified and single whole consists in. This is not easy, but it is necessary to demonstrate it, and in fact to demonstrate it independently of the main line of investigation which we have set ourselves. It is not easy because Christianity, at least at first sight, consists of such a wealth of statements, dogmatic and moral assertions and ecclesiastical directives that it is all too easy to fail to 'see the wood for the trees'. It is all too easy for man to gain the impression that an assessment of this sort, into which so many individual factors enter (all of which, however, must be accepted *in globo*) would inevitably entail far too many possibilities of error for one to commit one's self to it with a good conscience. It is necessary to raise this question of the 'ultimate essence' of Christianity because one must view the single entity that is Christianity as a whole, even when one is in no position in the concrete to reconstruct it synthetically out of its various parts by a process of speculative reasoning. Again independently of the question which we are posing here, Vatican II regards a global understanding of the faith of this kind as necessary. This is not only to the extent that a distinction is to be drawn between the basic elements of the Christian revelation and the rest of the truths which it contains, but also to the extent that the Council itself attempts a formula purporting to sum everything up 'in a nutshell' for the preliminary initiation of the catechumen, when it says that such a one must have understood that 'he has been snatched away from sin and led into the mystery of the love of God, who has called him to enter into a personal relationship with him in Christ'.[6]

Let us too, therefore, attempt to sum it up in a brief formula of this kind, so that we can go on to see how it measures up to the criteria of intellectual honesty. This, then, is how we should sum up Christianity as a whole: Christianity is the assent on the part of the whole community (Church) formulated and held explicitly by that community to the absolute mystery which exercises an inescapable power in and over our existence, and which we call God. It is our assent to that mystery as pardoning us and admitting us to a share in its own divinity, it is that mystery as imparting itself to us in a history shaped by man's own free decisions as an intelligent being; and this self-bestowal of God in Jesus Christ manifests itself as finally and irrevocably victorious in history.[7] I believe that what is definitive in the Christian faith is expressed here, and that too in a formula which, provided it is rightly understood and explicitated, will also be found to cover the further contents of the Christian faith as well, so long as these are not taken to include those positive definitions freely enunciated by the Church which belong to the dimension of historical and contingent fact as such, and which, moreover, do not represent any particular problem on any reasonable approach to the question of intellectual honesty.

God in his Divinity as the Mystery of Human Existence

Let us examine the formula we have constructed, bearing in mind the provisos mentioned above. What it asserts first and foremost about Christianity and about belief in it is that God is the incomprehensible and impenetrable mystery, and that God must be recognized as mystery in this sense. Christianity is not a religion which, in its evaluation of human existence, postulates the idea of 'God' as a recognised and acknowledged landmark, so to say, one factor among the rest, which can be manipulated and combined with them so as to produce a satisfactory final estimate. On the contrary, Christianity is a religion which projects man himself into the dimension of the incomprehensible surrounding and permeating his

---

[6] cf. Vatican II, *The Decree on the Missions*, No. 13.

[7] For a fuller exposition of this cf. K. Rahner, 'Kurzer Inbegriff des christlichen Glaubens für "Ungläubige"', *Gul* 58 (1965), pp. 374–379; expanded in the third number of *Concilium* 3 (March, 1966).

existence. It prevents him from falling on merely ideological grounds (for this is the ultimate significance of the Christian religion) into the mistake of supposing that there is a basic formula of existence which is comprehensible to man, which is available to man himself to manipulate, and on the basis of which he can construct existence. Christianity constitutes a radical denial of all such 'idols'. It aims at bringing man into contact with God as the ineffable mystery without any diminution of his own human freedom, and without the *hybris* of attempting to control God. Christianity recognises that man knows God only when he is reduced to silence and adoration by the experience of this mystery. All his religious utterances are true only in so far as they constitute the ultimate word introducing the silence with which he reacts to the presence of this mystery, in order that it may remain present to him in itself, and not be replaced by the mere idea of God. But Christianity knows that this mystery permeates its own existence as the ultimate reality of all and as the truth of truths; that the Christian in his thoughts, in his freedom, in his actions and in the conscious acceptance of his own death, always and unquestioningly goes beyond that which can be defined, comprehended and conceptually manipulated in the dimension of the concrete and the particular which he encounters in the sphere of life and knowledge. The Christian never simply 'comes across' God (indeed in that case it would not be God at all) as one specific phenomenon among others within the sphere of human existence, one, therefore, which falls within the limits of his ideas and his actions. He is in contact with the living God as the all-encompassing and the unencompassed, as the ineffable upholder of being such that to call him in question is to call everything in question also, ourselves included; one who is not, so to say, conjured up by our questioning, but is already there in that he himself makes it possible for us to raise questions about him by himself providing beyond all question the basis from which such questions can be put, opening the door to them and raising us to the level at which we can ask them.

Rightly regarded Christianity is not a fortress of truth with innumerable windows, which we must live in in order to be 'in the truth', but rather *one single* aperture which leads out of all the individual truths (and even errors) into *the* truth which is the unique incomprehensibility of God. But Christianity insists relentlessly, in season and out of season that this overwhelming brightness that is darkness and silence to us, which encompasses our life and permeates everything, that is all other lights and the darknesses that correspond to them, shall not be lost sight of by us, that in our existence we shall not allow our attention to be drawn away from this strange and unearthly brightness, but rather face up to it, trembling indeed yet resolute (in our commitment to it), calling it by its nameless name, never endowing our own idols with that name. But Christianity has something more to assert of this unearthly and ineffable mystery, and this is its real message. For the moment it makes no difference whether a man dares to learn of this real message of Christianity from the innermost promptings of his own conscience as moved by grace, or whether he has the impression that this message constitutes the basic motive force, purged of all extraneous elements, in the religious history of mankind (for in this too the grace of God is mysteriously at work), or even whether he simply receives this message from the witness of Christ and his apostles. In any case this, the true message of Christianity, has this to say to us: God is the incomprehensible mystery of our existence which encompasses us and causes us to realise, however painfully, the limitations of that existence, which he himself transcends. But he does not only present himself to us in this guise as the ultimate horizon of the knowable, towards which the course of our existence as spiritual beings is orientated and by which it is corrected, even while God himself remains remote and silent to us. He does indeed perform this function, setting us at a distance from himself so as to make it possible for us to 'return to ourselves' in knowledge and freedom, and thereby to give coherence and intelligibility to the environment of sensible experience in which we live, viewing it as a cosmic whole and as our environment; and in the very fact of doing this he makes us experience for ourselves our own finite state. But there is more to it than this. The mystery which we call God *gives himself* in his divine existence, gives himself to us for our own in a genuine act of self-bestowal. He himself is the grace of our existence.

We shall say, therefore, that what we mean by the creation is that the divine being freely 'exteriorises' his own activity so as to produce non-divine being, but does this solely in order to produce the necessary prior conditions for his own divine self-bestowal in that free and unmerited love that is identical with himself; that he does this in order to raise up beings who can stand in a personal relationship to himself and so receive his message, and on whom he can bestow not only finite and created being distinct from himself, but himself as well. In this way he himself becomes both giver and gift, and even more the actual source of man's own capacity to receive him as gift. Thus the finite, of its very nature as finite, finds its ultimate fulfilment in God as the mysterious infinite. The 'creator-creature' relationship belongs necessarily and indispensably to the very mode of reality as such, but does not constitute its actual content. God creates because he himself wills to impart himself by 'externalising' and so giving himself. The distance between him and us is there in order that the unity of love may be achieved. Creation, covenant and law are there (as providing a framework for the finite) in order that love may exist in boundless measure. Obedience is imposed in order that we may receive the freedom of God. We are set far from God in order that the miracle of his nearness to us to bless us and even to forgive our sins may be made possible. The purpose of all this is not that the mystery may be wholly penetrated and resolved by our minds, but rather that as mystery it may become the blessing of man's spirit, which possesses this mystery directly and in a manner that draws it out of itself in order that in total self-forgetfulness it may love this mystery as its only true light and life. This is the real content of Christianity: the ineffability of the absolute mystery which bestows itself in forgivingness and in drawing us into its own divine nature, and, moreover, bestows itself in such a way that we can sustain it, accept it and once more really receive the capacity to accept it from itself. It can be seen, then, that this self-bestowal of God (upon man in the history which he shapes for himself as a free and intelligent being) has a threefold aspect. Now the three aspects involved, inasmuch as they mutually constitute the *self*-bestowal of God, are inherent in the divine nature as such. In this self-bestowal on God's part, therefore, what we Christians are accustomed to call the triune nature of God is already present.

God's Self-Bestowal in History in Jesus Christ
A further factor which belongs to the very essence of Christianity is the person from whom its name is derived, Jesus Christ. But the mystery that is Jesus Christ is bound up in the closest possible manner with the one mentioned above. The mystery of God's self-bestowal, in which God himself in his innermost glory becomes the absolute future of man, has a history of its own because it proceeds from God himself as his free act, and because man, as existing in the dimension of history, is involved in the historicity of humanity considered as a single whole. Also because he has to achieve the ultimate transcendentality of his nature, 'divinized' as

it is by God's self-bestowal, in the 'space-time' dimension of history itself in and through a concrete encounter with the concrete world. For it is in this that he exists, is aware of himself and realises himself. The self-bestowal of God, even though it constitutes the innermost and transcendental basis for the world's existence and its history, even though it represents the ultimate *entelecheia* of the world – nevertheless has a history of its own, that is an inner dynamism such that it manifests itself, unfolds itself and achieves its fulfilment in space and time. We call this the history of salvation and revelation. There is a point, however, at which this manifestation of the divine self-bestowal as something offered on God's part, and as something freely accepted, even though accepted only with the help of God's grace, on man's, attains its acme and the stage at which it becomes absolute and irrevocable. It is the stage at which the dialogue between God and man which *is the* man, which becomes substantiated in him (so that it is not merely conducted by him as something distinct from his own existence) resolves itself in an absolute assent from either side, and manifests itself as such. In other words *the* man in whom this identity is achieved appears as God's absolute and irrevocable assent as uttered to and as accepted by mankind. And it is at this point precisely that we find what the Christian faith means by the incarnation of the divine Logos. It is *ipso facto* present when the divine self-bestowal appears in history as absolutely and irrevocably uttered, and absolutely and irrevocably received. Admittedly there still remains the irreducible factuality of the history which has really been lived through, the fact that this takes place and is experienced precisely in Jesus of Nazareth. What we mean when we speak of the 'Church' is the eschatological presence of God's truth and God's love in this entity by word and sacrament. And this means nothing else than that the historical facts are enduring and valid, that in Jesus of Nazareth the history of God's self-bestowal has manifested itself in an irrevocable form, and in this form remains present and remains the object of belief.

How the Theological Assertions are Rightly to be Understood

The question must now be put whether this message, in which man's ultimate understanding of himself is alleged to consist, is to be considered credible measured by the standards of intellectual honesty.

First, in dealing with such a question it must surely be pointed out that a complex made up of statements of this kind, expressing as it does in the most fundamental manner what constitutes the 'one and all' of human existence, necessarily presents the greatest conceivable difficulties in putting it into words. In the very nature of things this summing up of the whole affords no one fixed point of reference, no factor by which its nature can be unambiguously recognised, understood and determined, and on the basis of which it can be defined and expressed. It is precisely because it is the absolute truth that is in man that must find expression here (but that truth considered precisely as the original and indefinable mystery) that what is expressed is necessarily obscure. The only ones who could fail to be aware of this are those whose sociological and intellectual environment is so closed in upon itself that they cannot entertain the possibility of their own mode of expression being truly or effectively called in question by any other from outside that environment. Now today the field of discourse in which we move is no longer closed in upon itself in this way. For this reason we have a sense of the 'inexactitude' of all theological statements, a sense that all can be called in question as to their precise meaning by a thousand other ideas, approaches or fresh problems which they raise, and can thereby be assigned to the already immense class of ideas which have not been fully thought out or reflected upon. But the threat which this state of affairs in the field of communications entails vanishes when we go on from this to the further realisation that all these religious statements, whatever their particular material content may be, refer to this mystery, which as such is itself unthought-out and unreflected upon, and that they only achieve their true value when they point on to this mystery. One who takes all these statements in this sense thereby ceases to be anxious on the grounds that we do not have a sufficiently exact knowledge of what is meant by them, that no explanation of them turns out to be thoroughly clear and unambiguous, and on the grounds that perhaps it is precisely he who appears to contest them who succeeds in penetrating to their true meaning. All these statements, in fact point towards the one enduring mystery which *must* endure. Of course on the material level the actual content of the individual statements still remains a matter of dispute, both because some of the real factors which contribute to salvation do belong to the realm of the historical itself, and also because the movement which leads into the ineffable mystery of God (together with the historical media through which this movement takes place) is capable of right and wrong interpretations, fuller and more deficient ones. But even allowing for this the conflict between the various interpretations is, in the last analysis, less dangerous than it appears. For it is a fact of experience that even a formulation which is disputed can, without actually being a matter of indifference, truly direct us to the indefinable mystery of God, and that the truth of one's own tenets does *not* imply that the tenets of another, even when they are false, may not serve in the concrete to lead that other to a point at which he accepts the mystery of God in a spirit of adoration and love. For we can remind ourselves in all tranquillity (even if this way of putting the matter is unusual) that according to Catholic teaching there are indeed true and false statements about the realities of religion, that to formulate assertions which are false can endanger the salvation of the individual who formulates them, but yet that there are no such things as assertions which point, so to say, to an hypostatised falsehood. Such a thing would be totally incompatible with that event of salvation which leads us to the ultimate reality of God's truth.

The Qualifications and Criteria for Deciding How Faith and Intellectual Honesty Can Be Reconciled
It must be recognised that intellectual honesty requires us to avoid any tendency to identify the fulness of reality and truth with the sum total of those realities and truths which we have actually grasped, or which it is possible for us to grasp and to have at our disposal. In other words the mystery of which we are here speaking does not constitute a phenomenon appearing, as it were, on the horizon of our awareness as intellectual beings. It is not merely one further piece of data for our minds which still remains to be worked out and added to the sum total of our knowledge. On the contrary it is the enduring basis for that knowledge (that which initially sets knowledge in motion with all its subsequent possibilities of being shaped and formed by the human faculties). And if this is true, then what sort of intellectual honesty is it which could ever forbid us to believe in the experience of grace which precisely transcends the ordinary processes of human life, and in the message of revelation which provides the key to that experience? What sort of intellectual honesty could compel us not to believe that this sacred mystery wills to give itself to us in an act of self-bestowal which brings us forgiveness and raises us to the level of the divine, itself becoming an innermost and most sublime source of life in us? What kind of intellectual honesty is it which makes it illegitimate to accept the ultimate content of Christian belief with our minds? For my

part I see no reason for such a prohibition. For such belief, at any rate in cases which entail the conscious and mature acceptance of such a promise, a special grace of courage in a supernatural degree is required. For this faith promises to raise man to those inconceivable heights in which alone he really becomes infinitely more than a mere intelligent animal. But who is qualified to judge, and what criteria can be applied in order to prove that such courage is intellectually dishonest, unworthy of belief, not to be credited? This is especially true in view of the fact that every act of knowledge and every exercise of human freedom is a prelude to an opening of ourselves to that which is beyond words and beyond all human capabilities to apprehend or to control. The only question, therefore, can be whether the boundless range of possibilities which spreads before us, immeasurable so far as we are concerned, is filled with the self-bestowal of God as an act of his free love, or whether it remains for ever void. Have we not, therefore, the duty of allowing God to be greater than the meagre confines of our own hearts? Of believing that God can and will come down to us, and that we can and will come up to him? Of conceding that neither of these things are rendered impossible by the finitudes of our own existence?

The Credibility of the Dogma of the Incarnation
This brings us to the question of intellectual honesty in its bearing upon belief in Jesus Christ, the life of Jesus being here taken as the event in which the ultimate and most radical mediation of God's self-bestowal upon the created spirit is realised. This event, therefore, constitutes the ultimate concretisation of Christianity in 'this worldly' terms. There are two points to be made about it.

First with regard to the 'idea' of the God-man, the essential content of the teaching that the Logos became incarnate in our human mode of existence. To a conscience which is intellectually honest and truthful this 'idea' is worthy of belief. The only factors which it presupposes are these:– first that man understands himself as the being which constantly transcends its own nature and reaches out to the mystery of God even as this mystery bestows itself upon man. It must further be understood (and this has already been indicated at least in brief) that the idea of the God-man is already implied as the eschatological climax to that process of historical mediation and revelation in which the transcendental self-bestowal of God is realised. At any rate it is implied as a conceivable goal which this process is open to attain. It is vital, therefore, to rid this idea of all mythological misconceptions. The human side of the God-man is no passive puppet, no mask through which God makes himself known. It constitutes no fresh attempt on God's part in which he strives once more to achieve as redeemer in the world what he failed to achieve as creator of it. The God-man is truly man in that he is set apart from God as his worshipper, in that he is free and obedient, in that his human nature is subject to historical circumstances, progresses and develops (this applies to his religious experience as well, because nearness to God, personality and genuine creaturehood grow in the same, and not in inverse proportions). And the God-man does not represent a second intervention on the part of God as Creator, this time taking place in the already established order of the world, but rather the climax to a history of the world that is also the history of the spirit and the history of salvation. It is to this climactic point that God has ordered the whole of history from its very inception. He has done this through his own self-bestowal, which exercises a decisive influence upon all the constitutive factors in history, for this self-bestowal of God in history constitutes an 'existential', a fundamental orientation of history, which transcends all its particular modalities. Thus the incarnation, considered as the climactic and focal point of history in this sense, had already, by its redemptive power, more than overcome the guilt arising from the misuse of freedom even before it was incurred. The incarnation remains a mystery of the divine self-bestowal. If it is viewed in this context it is impossible to dismiss it as being a mere mythologem, even though, admittedly, it does not compel acceptance by the intellectually honest mind either. In spite of this it is credible, worthy of belief. Believers, therefore, and those endowed with a reasonable sense of history, are not disappointed to find that the incarnation, both in the manner in which it takes place in history and in the manner in which it is recorded in the New Testament (on a true reading of this), is just as hidden and unremarkable, considered as an event, as the deed of grace in general by which man is made a sharer in the divine. This is what one would have expected *a priori*. Both the incarnation and the deed of grace in history as a whole are accomplished in acts of practical and 'down-to-earth' compassion performed in the context of everyday human life. And yet even in this context this deed of divine grace bears a wonderful witness to itself if we can only view this plane of human existence with minds that are willing to believe.

A further point that is essential is that this 'idea' of the God-man has been realised in concrete objective fact precisely in Jesus of Nazareth. It is essential that we should accept it as concrete fact at this particular point in space and time. Admittedly this means relying on the information that a particular fact has taken place in history, and for man's pride in his own capacity to transcend particular historical facts this is always a scandal. Man is tempted to hold *a priori* that there can be no question of a truth that is merely 'historical' providing the explanation of his own existence. But it is precisely the intellectually honest who can be self-critical enough to understand that real history cannot be dismissed in favour of theories concerning historicity. History in the concrete, the deeper meaning of which is never sufficiently realised, is necessary as the medium in which man's nature as a free and intellectual being can operate on the spiritual and transcendent plane. And again it is precisely the intellectually honest who can understand that man must commit himself to the finite dimension of space and time in order to render the eternal present to himself not merely as an abstract concept but as a reality actually present within him. It must be admitted that the courage to commit one's self to the concrete in this way is indispensable for faith. It must be unreservedly conceded that even to prove in terms of scientific exegesis that Jesus himself understood himself to be the Son of God in the metaphysical sense of the Christian dogma is far from easy. But one who can read, interpret and translate will not expect Jesus himself to express himself in the formulae of theological metaphysics, and will not feel this to be necessary in order to say what such formulae mean. And given the recognition of this it is not in principle impossible to supply such a proof. While this remains a difficult task for the individual in the concrete, with all the possible or impossible conditions to which he is at present subject, it is not the sole means to which the intellectually honest can have recourse in order to establish how Jesus thought of himself, and to justify his interpretation on this point. If the idea of the God-man is worthy of belief, if in fact in the history of human thought intellectuals have had the courage to believe in the concrete embodiment of this 'idea', yet solely and exclusively as realised in Jesus, if we have not, so to say, artificially constructed the circumstances of his life in the laboratory of our own minds, but rather found ourselves faced with them as pre-existing facts, and if we commit ourselves enough to give these facts a chance to prove themselves sound and valid, if finally we find ourselves already belonging to the community of those who believe in Jesus, and if we find God in that community, what reasons could validly be advanced for holding that we were unjustified in doing all this?

Belief in the Resurrection as Reasonable for the Human Intellect to Accept
We Christians experience man as indissolubly one and whole, and on these grounds we can hold that our existence achieves its radical fulness and wholeness only when we believe in the 'resurrection of the body', and understand this formula to express that which is to be man's absolute future. In doing this we do not follow the Platonists in thinking of man as a compositum of previously separate elements. Nor do we seek to know *how* we should picture to ourselves this attainment of total perfection in man through a process of total 'transformation'. Now if we apply all this to the life and death of Jesus on what compelling grounds can it be shown to be unreasonable for the human intellect to accept the experience of Jesus' disciples when they say that he rose from the dead? (Notice that this does not, in any sense, constitute a return to this mode of existence!). Is it not, on the contrary, more reasonable to believe for ourselves in what has been believed throughout two thousand years with might, light and strength, that is in the resurrection of Jesus? It is not only the sceptics, but the believers too who recognise that the disciples' experience of their risen Lord is incommensurable with any other experience in space and time, and must in the nature of things be so, since the reality which is the subject of this experience is one which is not subject to the limitations of our mode of existence in space and time. But to say that it is not so subject is not to deny it. It is possible to misunderstand this incommensurability of the disciples' experience of the resurrection, and to relegate it to the realm of myth. But we must avoid this danger. Our own personal experience of the enduring effectiveness of the one man must be fused with the Easter experience of Jesus' disciples, these two experiences mutually complementing one another so as to become absolutely and indissolubly one for us in the actual concrete situation in which we now exist. Where this is achieved the Easter experience does indeed become for us worthy of belief. Rightly understood, the Easter event does not merely bear an external witness to the role of Jesus as Saviour. It is in the Easter event in itself that that role is revealed. In this sense the Easter event coincides with Jesus' own interpretation of himself, and together with it constitutes a unified message which is worthy of belief.

At this point we must break off. We are conscious of having failed to touch even in the most cursory manner upon a great number of questions. Thus a whole complex of questions arises in connection with the bearing of intellectual honesty on that communal and visible reality of the Christian faith called the Church, together with the claims it makes in questions of truth and moral guidance. On these questions, however, we must here confine ourselves to pointing out that in an epoch in which man's responsibilities and duties as a social creature are being ever more deeply realised it would be old fashioned and anachronistic in the extreme to adopt an individualist attitude; to suppose that man could or should attempt to preserve or to realise the ultimate 'ideals' of Christianity as an isolated individual, shrinking even as he made the attempt from that historical and social phenomenon in which alone we encounter these 'ideals' as historical realities, and find ourselves confronted by them in our concrete lives.

To sum up my conclusions:– Provided one does not make an idol of 'intellectual honesty'; provided one does not suppose that the sceptic is most likely to be preserved from mistaking error for truth, provided one does not imagine that one can extend a theoretical suspension of judgment into the sphere of one's practical life as well, then intellectual honesty certainly does not prohibit one from the act of belief, from deciding that one's whole life shall depend on that supreme reality which Christianity possesses and avows. Certainly this great virtue of intellectual honesty does not compel one to believe, but it does make it justifiable for one to do so. For even this virtue achieves its ultimate and unique significance only when it arrives at that supreme point (a point beyond all merely intellectual prudence) at which it finds the courage to face up to the mystery of existence, and to love.

4

DO NOT STIFLE THE SPIRIT!

As a title to the brief contribution which follows, delivered as an introductory discourse on the occasion of the 'Katholikentags' conference[1] his Eminence the Cardinal chose a motto which runs as follows: 'Do not stifle the Spirit!' This quotation from scripture is found in the earliest of the New Testament epistles, the First Epistle of Paul to the Thessalonians, chapter 5, verse 19, in a verse, therefore, in which the apostle is expressing his concluding exhortations to the community he has founded. If we take the verse in this sense it may seem, on the first hearing, to be expressing something obvious. Who would take it upon himself deliberately: obstinately and of set purpose to oppose the workings of the Holy Spirit? And if this saying is indeed addressed in the first instance to the actual community of the faithful as a whole and not to the individual with his personal problems of salvation, then as an exhortation it seems to be almost superfluous. Is the Church not the temple of the Spirit, the Body of Christ which is vivified by the Spirit of Christ? Does not the Spirit preside in this Church with the power of the eschatological victory of the final age, never abandoning her, always making her the holy Church? How could the Church ever stifle the Spirit of God

[1] This festal lecture, delivered on the occasion of the Austrian 'Catholic Day', June 1st 1962, has deliberately been left unaltered, even though in certain of its ideas it may perhaps be less immediately relevant to the particular needs of the present moment in history. The period leading up to the Council was different from the present one. Nevertheless those factors which were essential then do still retain their validity for the work of the post-conciliar period as well. Moreover, it may well be that it is actually more necessary now even than before to draw the correct distinction between foolish 'enthusiasm' on the one hand and the prudent and sensible application of charismatic qualities on the other. For this reason it has been felt right to leave the text in its original form. For a right understanding of what is required in this respect for the post-conciliar work that is needful cf. the author's 'Kirche im Wandel', *Schriften zur Theologie* VI, pp. 455–478, and *Das Konzil – ein neuer Beginn* (Freiburg, 1966).

DO NOT STIFLE THE SPIRIT!

And yet we have only to ask ourselves what Paul actually had in mind in the concrete when he exhorted his hearers in these terms to see that his exhortation both to individuals and to the Church as a whole is far from superfluous. When we first read this exhortation we should tremble at the idea that it is possible for man at all actually to stifle the Spirit, the burning fire of God, at the idea which the apostle presupposes, namely that we ourselves – at any rate in a very broad sense – are actually in a position to do this. If only we reflected upon this what a change it might bring about in our lives! *We* could stifle the Spirit! We could frustrate his movements in us and in the world! He has been given into our power, made subject to the inertia of our spirit, brought under the control of our cowardice, placed at the disposal of our empty, earthly, loveless hearts! Not only are we able to be false to ourselves and to betray the dignity and destiny of our own nature. We can block the Spirit who wills ever to renew the face of the earth! We can kill the life of God in the world, render the spheres of life Godless, empty and meaningless! Furthermore what a terrible danger there must be, a danger that we are too stupid to notice! How easy it must be for us to bring it about, almost without noticing, that the flame of the Spirit is prevented by us from doing its work! How easy it must be evidently to act like this in all 'good conscience' if the apostle feels himself called upon to exhort us: 'Do not stifle the Spirit!'!

In point of fact, if we think of the gifts of grace bestowed by the Spirit as Paul sees them which must not be brought to nothing we shall find it easy to understand that the object of Paul's exhortations is far from obvious. For such gifts of grace are first of all distributed among many in such a way that no one individual possesses them all, and that they are given as the Spirit himself decides, and not according to the will and pleasure of any one individual, nor even to that of the authorities in their designs. And yet how difficult it is for one man to allow that the other possesses something important, something God-given, which he himself does not have, which he himself can never altogether understand; something that one's own nature tells one is alien, and which perhaps seems strange and even shocking. How easily man concludes that the divine is to be identified with that which he himself possesses, and which is accessible to him precisely because it has entered into his life. And further, for Paul these gifts are of such a nature that to the worldly individual they seem folly (1 Cor 2, 14). They can be manifested in the community in such a way that to the profane they are the occasion of derision; that those endowed with the gifts of the Spirit appear psychologically unbalanced or, to put it plainly, are out of their minds (1 Cor 14, 23). In dealing with his communities Paul presupposes that the Spirit blows everywhere, and in the most varied ways: as a Spirit of witness, of loving service, of instruction, consolation, helpful exhortation, alms-giving, understanding, compassion (Rom 12, 4–8), wisdom, knowledge, the prayer that moves mountains, the power of healing, acts of power, prophetic utterances, the discernment of spirits, ecstasies and the interpretation of utterances arising from these, service of others and leadership of the community (1 Cor 12, 4–11; 28–30). According to him the Spirit of Christ is active in a thousand forms and in no one individual are all of these present, because it is only all individuals taken together who constitute the one whole Body of Christ. All must take place properly and in order (1 Cor 14, 40), but this order in the manifestations of the Spirit is an order which does not restrict these manifestations in any way, which is aware of, and acknowledges the fact that these gifts are inconceivably varied in kind, and quite incalculable. It is an order which lets the Spirit move where and as he himself wills; which admits neither of merely human judgment nor of any hybris on the part of the authorities in the Church in seeking to reduce everything to their own plans. The order of which we are speaking does not allow such people to stifle the Spirit, the Spirit which can be uncomfortable, which always remains fresh and unfathomable, the Spirit which is that love which can be hard, which leads the individual and even the Church herself in directions which they had not planned, leads them always into that which is new and unknown, that which is only seen to be in conformity with the one eternal Spirit, ancient yet ever new, when it has actually taken effect; that which the Spirit himself has intended, and which is beyond all human wisdom.

The Church knows as part of her conscious faith that the Spirit too actually belongs to her, that he is indispensable to her. She teaches explicitly that it is not only her own official organisation, institutions, traditions, the rules of life which are permanent and immutable – in short that which is planned, that which can be foreseen that belong to her as the Church of God. The Church knows that the element of the unexpected and the incalculable in her own history does not consist solely in the incomprehensibility of the circumstances to which she is subjected *ab externo*, circumstances which she controls by applying her own internal **and** immutable principles to them. The Church knows that the Spirit of

God has been projected into her innermost nature, the living Spirit still actively present and at work in the here and now. The activity of the Spirit, therefore, can never find adequate expression simply in the forms of what we call the Church's official life, her principles, sacramental system and teaching. These can never be the sole or exclusive forms in which the Spirit has, so to say, made himself available to the Church. Pius XII has expressly laid down that not only the institutional factor, but the charismatic one too is of the Church's essence. According to Pius XII those who are charismatics in this sense are not simply at the disposal of the ecclesiastical authorities, nor are they mere recipients of directives. It is true that in the exercise of their charisms these charismatic individuals must submit their lives to the general 'order' of Christ's Church, that it is important for them not to break out of the confines of that Church, which is also, though not exclusively, a Church whose authority is vested in her official ministers. But even though all this is true, still the charismatics can be men endowed with such gifts of grace that Christ can lead and guide his Church quite 'directly' through them.

All this is a recognised fact. But it is a fact that is too often not recognised clearly enough in theory, and not acted upon vigorously enough in practice. Often the awareness of the role of the charisma of the Spirit in the Church remains at the level of mere theoretic knowledge, which has of itself no charismatic vitality. This is not merely due to faults of self-will and ossification on the part of the Church's authorities. There are other and weightier reasons why the truth of the Spirit and his charisms in the Church should be rendered ineffective in this way. It could be said that from this aspect it was easier to be a Christian in the early Church which Paul knew. The communities were small; their standard of living was simple and easy to understand. There was a place for that which had not been planned for or foreseen, as well as for that which was the outcome of policy and design. Moreover the world in which such movements took place was for its part reliable and comprehensible. Today, on the other hand, we live in an age of industrial societies on a massive scale, an age in which the histories of all the nations have been drawn together into a unity, in which all have achieved a degree of communication with one another which, whether it be friendly or hostile, is in any case extremely real and direct; an age of automation, of cybernetics, of a demand for security which is already becoming neurotic in its intensity; an age in which the aged in the community constitute a far higher percentage of its members than in earlier times; an age in which the needs and opinions of the masses are manipulated; in which the machine has grown immensely in significance as a factor in society, for it is to a large extent inevitable that the circumstances previously mentioned should conduce to this effect. These and similar factors in the contemporary situation apply not only to society in the worldly sense, but also the social entity of the Church, and they are from first to last hostile to all that is charismatic. In other words they have the effect of making it seem as though the only effective and valid factors are those which are the outcome of plan and design, that only the power of the masses has any prospect of success, that the lives even of individuals are more and more dependent upon the great social institutions of the state and its authorities, organisations, ruling officials with their official enactments, five-year plans, subsidies etc., all of them aids to the machinery of propaganda.

If we are honest we shall recognise that this danger in the present age is undeniably a danger for the Church as well. We say that we have entered upon the age of the world-wide Church. That is true. But we have also entered upon an age in which every regional movement in the Church almost inevitably takes place under the eyes of the Church as a whole, and in dependence upon the central machinery of the Church. It is judged according to its real or supposed effects upon other countries and other areas of the Church's influence. There is a danger that no such movement can hope to be taken seriously unless it very quickly wins the support of public opinion in the Church throughout the world.

This is the danger that threatens the charismatic element in the Church from the external situation in which she is placed. But it is intensified by the presence of a further danger, this time arising from the interior situation of the Church. For even today the situation of the Church is still – unhappily is still – one of defensiveness against the powers that threaten her from without, of a unity indeed, but the kind of unity that belongs to a faction closed in upon itself so that watchwords are needed to enter it. It is a situation dominated by a spirit which has been rather too hasty and too uncompromising in taking the dogmatic definition of the primacy of the pope in the Church as the bond of unity and the guarantee of truth, this attitude objectifying itself in a not inconsiderable degree of centralisation of government in an ecclesiastical bureaucracy at Rome, so that regulations governing the life of each and every individual are issued from the Church's central ministries, and no-one can be sure that, despite all intentions to the contrary, the approaching Council will not have the effect of strengthening this tendency. For a Council is expected to produce regulations covering a wide area of life, and it is almost impossible for it to avoid prescribing that its regulations are to apply in a univocal sense to the entire Church. In short, the fact that there is a charismatic element in the institution of the Church is recognised. It will not be denied by anyone. And yet because of the contemporary circumstances of the Church, both external and internal, this fact fails to make its due impact both in theory and in practice.

It can be seen, then, that in general the saying 'Do not stifle the Spirit' has the force not merely of an obvious and universal principle, but of an urgent imperative precisely for us in the here and now. As an exhortation, indeed, it has so urgent an application to the contemporary scene that its proclamation must take priority over that of many other principles. But precisely as a most earnest exhortation this saying applies supremely to us central Europeans in our relationships. Let us be honestly and calmly self-critical. What is the state of the Church in the particular sphere to which we belong? Are not weariness and mere routine far too predominant as factors in our lives? When new 'movements' arise or new enthusiasms which set us fresh goals to achieve, or seek to arouse support for new ideas, are we not all too fond of preaching balance and deliberation in applying the Church's principles, instead of boldly translating them into imperatives – imperatives which are not indeed necessary everywhere and at all times, but which certainly are so for us in the here and now? Are we not all too often lacking in the courage to say an unambiguous 'no' or an unambiguous 'yes'? And this applies not merely to those basic principles which are immutable, and which no-one seriously wishes directly to challenge or to deny, but also to those watchwords and slogans of controversy which summon us to a decision in the concrete. Do we know what to reply when someone asks: 'What concrete objectives have you Christians set yourselves to achieve in the next ten years? What is it which does not yet exist, but which, according to you, must exist and which you are currently aiming to achieve? And that too not merely in eternity, but in the here and now? Do we not all too often claim to be adopting an attitude of detachment towards the various factions, whereas our real reason is that we are unwilling to expose ourselves to any demands in the concrete? Where is the courage we need really to become engaged in the questions of the time, really to face up to them, really to feel the burden of them? Are we not all too ready to suppose, in our weariness and anxiety for peace, that our minds are already clear on all points, equipped with all the answers to all the questions – questions which are, in any case, not all that important? Among us, as in the Church in general, is there not a phenomenon which might be called the 'Church of officialdom'? In other words is there not an intermediary class of official administrators which (almost inevitably, so far as we are concerned, and yet how dangerously!) comes between the Christians and those who are their real shepherds, really called by God to their ministry, and really responsible to him for their flocks? Is not our preaching, the expression of our Christian faith, too traditionalist in character, too second-hand? Does not far too little of it well up spontaneously from that experience of grace, that awareness of being touched by the authentic word of God, which is utterly our own, and which has its source in our innermost nature? Where in the life of the Church do we find its members really initiating an 'experiment' which is not smothered over right from its very inception, so that after all everything remains as it was? Let us face up to the fact that from the point of view of cultural and social history we are passing through a revolutionary change in the times, a change which we certainly do not over-estimate, but rather under-estimate. Let us then take this revolutionary change in all its breadth and depth as a standard by which to measure the vigour, the courage, the breadth of vision which we bring to bear upon the radical change which we ourselves are undergoing in the Church. When we do this are we not compelled to fear that at this turning-point of the times we have proved ourselves still more inadequate than did the Church of the time when the feudal society of the eighteenth century was transformed into the society of civic liberalism of the nineteenth, or the time when the workers emerged as a new social class? Must we not say at this point that our response has been far too hesitant and lame, that we have merely allowed ourselves to be forced bit by bit by the sheer weight of the facts, and that for all this we have lagged pitifully behind the times? In a word where is that bold, powerful, creative 'self-confident' movement of the Spirit among us in the Church?

There may be some who take these remarks of mine merely as so much facile criticism; who refuse *a priori* to let themselves be disturbed, who proceed from the tacit assumption that all must be well, since they themselves are honest men who do their duty even though they too know of no remedy for the ills of the time and of the Church. But such people have failed to understand the true purport of what I have just been saying. These remarks of mine are not intended to lead up to the recommendation of any facile 'cure-all', which according to my ideas needs only to be adopted for the Church and the world *ipso facto* to be delivered from their ills. I too have no such prescription to offer. And it is extremely painful and bitter to put forward accusations when one does not know how to alter the state of affairs which is being complained of. Nor do these observations of mine imply that everything in every department of the Church's life is in a bad state. On the contrary there is much that is filled with the Spirit and alive with divine life, love, faithfulness, patience in bearing the Cross, apostolic work which is full of self-sacrifice, youthful courage, theological acumen, a determination to tackle fresh problems and much else besides of which the Spirit is the prime dispenser, so that without him none of these factors would be present in the Church at all. But should all this, for which we do indeed thank God, make us blind to those other factors of which we have been speaking? Are we on this account to be excused from facing up to the real question of which of two alternatives is more characteristic for our particular age and for the Church as it exists in our particular countries? These alternatives are on the one hand the average and the stereotyped, the bureaucratic and over-officialised, the stale and the dull which refuses to commit itself to any form of attack, and on the other the fire and energy of the Spirit, the charism of life that comes from heaven, though again only in the measure in which it can be permitted to exist in this world of the mediocre. However thankful we may be for the Spirit who does not forsake us even in this age, are we not still faced with the responsibility of being honestly and severely self-critical, and saying that it is through our own fault, the inertia of our own hearts, that we feel too little of the movement of the Spirit as guider of the Church, and that too at a time when the impetus of the Spirit was never so sorely needed? In view of this, then, should we not all conclude in fear and trembling that evidently the saying of Paul is addressed to us not merely as a permanently valid principle, but as an imperative for our own particular time, disconcerting, accusing, shocking us out of our complacency?

But if this imperative has, in this sense, a particular application to us of the present age, then the question does become urgent for us: What must we do in order to avoid stifling the Spirit? This is a dark and difficult question. If it could ever be thought easy to answer it would be no question at all. The real answer to it is itself a factor in the movement and guidance of the Spirit, who himself ensures that he shall not be stifled. It can be found, in the last analysis, not by the reflexive processes of theory and speculation, but rather, at basis, through the sureness of instinct to be found in Christian living. And for this reason the poor stuttering schoolmaster can only say very little, and that in very inadequate and halting terms, on this particular question. And what he says, in so far as anything can be said directly and explicitly on this point, is once more only a part of the theoretic statements which, as we have pointed out, cannot be any substitute for the Spirit, his power and his inalienable and uncontrollable grace. Only with these provisos can there be any right understanding of the few modest observations which follow.

The first thing that we could do, and do with all our hearts, would be to acquire an attitude of *caring*; of recognising with anxiety that it is possible to stifle the Spirit. The Spirit can be stifled not indeed throughout the entire Church, but still over so wide an area, and to such a terrible extent that we have to fear that judgment which begins with the house of God. And for this reason we must all face the possibility with fear and trembling that *we* could be the ones who stifle the Spirit – stifle him through that pride in 'knowing better', that inerita of heart, that cowardice, that unteachableness with which we react to fresh impulses and new pressures in the Church. How different many things would be if we did not so often react to what is new with a self-assured superiority, an attitude of conservatism, adopted as a defence not of the honour of God and the teaching and institutions of the Church, but of our own selves, of what we have always been accustomed to, of the usual, with which we can live without daily experiencing the pain of the new *metanoia*. But if we realised, and with burning conviction, that we can also be judged for our omissions, for a general obtuseness and inertia of heart which, though indefinable, extends over all spheres of our lives, for our culpable lack of creative imagination and boldness of spirit, then we should lend a sharper ear, a keener eye, a livelier anticipation to the slightest indication that somewhere that Spirit is stirring whose inspiration is not merely confined to the official pronouncements and directives of the Church, or to the holders of official positions in her. Then we should be eagerly on the watch to see whether charisms were not appearing, of which only a glimpse and a feeling can initially be obtained. Then we would not make it a condition for admitting those charisms which the Spirit wills to impart (a condition to which, however, we do not subject our own lives and activities) that such charisms must have no element of the human in them, nothing which has not yet been purified out. For this is not possible in view of the fact that even the fire of the Holy Spirit burns up from the thorn-bush of our human – all too human – nature.

The second requirement is the courage to *take risks*. Let us permit ourselves to reiterate most strongly what has just been said. We live in an age in which it is absolutely necessary to be ready to go to the utmost extremes of boldness in our attitude towards the new and the untried, to that point at which it would be, beyond all dispute, simply inconceivable for one who accepts Christian teaching and has a Christian conscience at all to go any further. In practice the only admissible 'tutiorism' in the life of the Church today is the tutiorism which consists in taking risks. Today, when we are struggling to solve the real problems which confront us, we should not, properly speaking say: 'How far *must* I go?' because the very nature of the situation itself absolutely compels us to go at least as far as possible. We should be asking ourselves, rather: 'How far *can* we go by taking advantage of all the possibilities in the pastoral and theological spheres?' The reason is that the state of the kingdom of God is certainly such that we must be as bold as possible in taking risks in order to hold out in the manner demanded of us by God. For instance in œcumenical questions we should not ask: 'What do we have to concede to the separated brethren?' but 'How can we create, in every conceivable way, the conditions which make possible a fruitful encounter with them, provided only that the measures which we take are reasonable, and are in any way reconcilable with the Christian and Catholic conscience?' 'How can we be sufficiently bold and unreserved in doing this, for today it is simply out of the question for us to do anything less in order to bring the unity of Christians at least one step nearer?' It appears to me that this kind of 'tutiorism' should be applied to these and many other questions. In other words one should take as the motive force of one's actions the conviction that for these particular times of ours (the principle does not apply permanently to all times) the surest way is the boldest, and that the best chance to gain all, or at any rate something is not caution, but the utmost boldness in taking risks. And if we do adopt this attitude, then there will be a radical change of policy in many of the questions now being canvassed in the Church.

What is needful in order for the Spirit not to be stifled is a true and bold interpretation of what *obedience* to the Church really means. It is a holy virtue. The Spirit of Christ in the Church manifests itself in obedience to the established authorities of the Church. That is no true Spirit of Christ which leads us outside the Church of the bishops, the Pope, the official ministers of the Church. But it is important to recognise the truth that the work of the Spirit in the Church takes effect not only through these official ministers, but through those over whom they preside as well; that his influence also extends in the inverse direction, from the ministered to the ministers. And if this is true, then the individuals upon whom God bestows the grace, and also the burden of charisms (and it would be better if more of the Church's members would commit themselves to accepting that the Spirit might be entrusting them with such gifts and such responsibilities) have also a right and a duty to avoid simply hiding behind an attitude of dumb obedience – in truth not in the least because it is a humble attitude, but because it is a comfortable one. Rather they must speak out – proclaim what they believe to be true, for it is quite possible that this may be the truth of the Spirit of God himself. They must be tireless in testifying to it even in the presence of the established authorities in the Church, and even when it is inconvenient or unpleasing to those 'authorities', even when they themselves have to endure the sufferings of the charismatic for doing so, in the form of misunderstanding and perhaps even disciplinary action on the part of the authorities. The spirit of true obedience is present not so much where the official machinery of the Church is running smoothly and without friction, not so much where a totalitarian régime is being enforced, but rather where the non-official movements of the Spirit are recognised and respected by the official Church in the context of a universal striving for the will of God, while the 'charismatics' for their part, while remaining faithful to their task, maintain an attitude of obedience and respect towards the official Church. For it is God and God alone who builds the one Church, shaping the true course of her history as he himself wills out of the materials of the multiplicity of spirits, tasks and ministries in the Church, and out of the ensuing tensions and oppositions which are so necessary. And further this course may seem quite different from the one thought out and planned in the official councils of the Church's ministers, even though these are quite right and are only fulfilling their bounden duty in so planning a course for the Church.

A further prior condition which is necessary if the Spirit is to become a vital force in the Church is the *courage* to endure the *inevitable antagonisms* in the Church which we have just mentioned. The Church is not 'one heart and one soul' in such a way, or to such an extent that there can be no controversy, none of the pain of mutual misunderstandings in her. There are, in fact, many charisms in the Church, and no one individual possesses them all. Nor is it given to any one individual to have all the various kinds of charisms at his disposal. For even though the authorities of the Church are united, and even though they are at one in their care to ensure that there shall be one faith and one love in her, this does not imply that the official Church exercises any real controlling power over all the charisms. On the contrary many different opinions are upheld among us Christians, and this is as it should be. We should manifest many different tendencies, and there is no necessity for each to be positively suitable for all. The sort of love that might be designed to weld all into one uniform whole would be all too easy. But in the Church it is the Spirit of love who must reign, binding the many and divers gifts in their very diversity into a unity. One who possesses this love recognises and accepts others too according them their due value even though they are different from himself, and even in cases in which he no longer 'understands' them. The principle which is given to the Church as a concomitant of the love she has to preserve in all her actions lays down that everyone in the Church must follow his own spirit, so long as it is not established beyond all doubt that he is in fact following a pseudo-spirit. In other words it must be presumed, until the contrary is proved, that he is orthodox in his beliefs, that he is a man of good will, and that he has a right to his freedom. To proceed from the opposite assumption would be contrary to the principle mentioned above. Moreover, while it is once more true that it rests with the official authorities and not simply with those subject to them to judge whether in the individual case it has been proved that a pseudo-spirit is being followed, it is no less true that those authorities themselves have the sacred duty, for which they will have to render account at the Day of Judgment, of examining themselves in a spirit of humility and self-criticism, to see whether such proof really has been put forward, or whether they have been over-hasty or self-willed in their judgment, judging merely by the standard of their own spirit and their own lights. Patience, tolerance, according to others their due freedom so long as it has not been proved beyond all doubt that their actions are wrong (and not the contrary of this: to forbid all personal initiatives until they have been explicitly proved to be orthodox, the subordinate sustaining the burden of proof here) –

all these are specifically ecclesiastical virtues, which flow from the very nature of the Church. For she is not a totalitarian organisation. Such virtues are the necessary conditions for ensuring that the Spirit shall not be stifled.

It is no spirit of indifference to the Church's authorities which leads us to presuppose these virtues in the authorities and to act accordingly. On the contrary it is itself a Christian virtue. One can take for granted that there will inevitably be antagonisms in the Church, for this is something inherent in her very nature as formed by the will of God. There is no need, therefore, to wait for a formal and positive expression of consent on the part of the ecclesiastical authorities for each and every enterprise in order to be able to say: 'We too have the Spirit of Christ'. But if anyone were to conclude from what has just been said that each and every movement in the Church must be allowed to have its head, that no-one should really take it upon himself to appraise the movement of a different party within the Church, to issue warnings against it or to demand genuinely and in all sincerity that it should be resisted, then such an one would have misunderstood what I have just been saying. For to impose this interpretation on what has been said would be precisely to deny that the various movements, tendencies and charismatic impulses, in so far as these are genuine, really do develop within one Church, and that they must really be experienced as the counterpoise to corresponding movements, tendencies etc. in others. Besides such a one would be maintaining by implication that no movement could develop within the Church without the gift of the Spirit from above. Now this is not true. Neither the faithful in general nor the holders of official positions in the Church in particular are equipped with any such *a priori* immunity to the innate promptings of the spirit of this world. We must therefore be able to summon up the courage or charism – for this can, in fact, precisely be a gift imparted to one particular member of the Church – to say 'No!' as members of the Church. To take up a stand against particular tendencies and outlooks, and that too even before the actual officials of the Church have been awakened to the danger which threatens. For to say 'No!' in this way can be the means of rousing the official Church to perform its function. But it is precisely when we do find the courage to accept these conflicts and tensions within the Church, this real multiplicity of gifts and charisms, of tasks and functions, that we draw the sting from the struggle between opposing tendencies which always and inevitably do occur even within the Church, that we transform that struggle into the strivings of love, and that we set the Spirit free, who would otherwise be stifled.

A further factor to be numbered among the necessary prior conditions for ensuring that the Spirit shall not be stifled is that all members of the Church, whether high or low, must be convinced of the fact that of the various movements which arise and which should arise in the Church, not all of them have necessarily to be initiated by the officials and authorities at their head in order to be legitimate. These authorities must be neither surprised nor reluctant to find a movement of the Spirit manifesting itself prior to any plan or design on the part of the Church's official ministers. Nor must the faithful suppose that there is absolutely nothing for them to do until some directive has been issued from above. There are actions which are, under God's will, demanded by the conscience of the individual even before the starting signal has been given by the authorities, and furthermore the directions in which these actions tend may be such as are not already approved or established in any positive sense by those authorities. It would be necessary in such a case for the individual to think out afresh, and on the basis of this charismatic element in the Church, what place should be accorded to 'canonical approval' and to legitimatised custom *contra* or *praeter legem*.[2] By introducing such concepts as these the canonists leave room not merely for legitimate developments in the sphere of what is reasonable and just at the human level, but for the impulses of the Spirit as well. Those, therefore, who have the power to command in the Church must constantly bear in mind that not everything that takes place in the Church either is or should be the outcome of their own autocratic planning as though they belonged to a totalitarian régime. They must keep themselves constantly alive to the fact that when they permit movements to arise 'from below', this is no more than their duty; it does not constitute an act of gracious tolerance on their part. They must not seek to retain all the threads in their own hands right from the first. They must recognise that the higher – and precisely the charismatic – wisdom may quite well lie with the rank and file, and that charismatic wisdom as applied to the Church's official ministers may consist in the fact that they do not close their minds to wisdom of the former sort. The authorities in the Church must always be aware of the fact that neither the obedience which the rank and file owe to them as a

---

[2] For a fuller exposition of this cf. 'Die Disziplin der Kirche' I, *Handbuch der Pastoraltheologie* I (Freiburg., 1964), pp. 333–343, especially pp. 336 ff.

matter of duty on the one hand, nor the supreme juridical authority vested in themselves on the other render the rank and file devoid of rights in relation to the authorities themselves. Nor does this relationship provide any guarantee that every measure adopted by the authorities in every individual case is necessarily in conformity with what is right and pleasing to God, or that they must *a priori* be preserved from extremely catastrophic decisions and omissions.

All must pray. Each one must have an anxious conscience about his own poverty and deficiency in charismatic gifts. Each one must be ready to pay heed to the gift of another, even when he himself does not possess it. Obedience must not drive out the courage of self-responsibility, nor, conversely, must the courage of one's own convictions drive out obedience. We must be resolute enough to try out even the most radical projects in the recognition that in our situation, so extreme as it is, it is no longer tolerable merely to carry on prudently along the same lines as before. And if we do all this, then perhaps we may clear the ground – even to do this much would be, once more, a grace of God – for the Spirit to quicken us, this in turn being due solely to God's grace. Then we shall have no need to fear that at the judgment of God the reproach will be levelled against us that by our inertia and cowardice we have stifled the Spirit and that we were unwilling to admit it even for a moment.

In the last hundred years the proportion of Catholics relative to other denominations has in practice failed to increase. Instead, despite all the struggles of the missions, heroic as these may appear, it has remained the same. And all this even without counting the shocking extent of the apostasies within the Church in the midst of the so-called Christian peoples. Even if the increase in the world population explosion, as it has been called, merely maintains its present rate, by the end of the present century, which some of us may yet live to see, there will be six or seven billion human beings – in other words twice as many as are living today. Now this increase will take place to far the greatest extent in that section of humanity which either in practice or as a result of an absolute political prohibition lives outside the Christian sphere of influence. In view of this fact it may be presumed that in the next few decades the Catholic element in the population of the world will diminish rapidly and perhaps even startlingly. This is only one of a hundred considerations which might be advanced in order to illustrate the seriousness of the global situation in which, even from a merely secular point of view, the Church finds herself.

This is the situation of the world, and it is also our situation in the present, because it is no longer possible for any country to stand apart as an autocracy in the circumstances of the present time. Have we the courage and hardihood to say to ourselves: 'Do not stifle the Spirit!'? have we the unshakeable faith to trust, in spite of these warnings and exhortations to ourselves, that the Spirit of God will not let himself be stifled because he is the Spirit of him who has conquered the world upon the Cross? With this sort of sincerity and this sort of courage let us go forward as believers to the decisions which we have to make from day to day.

5

THE CHRISTIAN IN HIS WORLD

'THE Christian in his World' – an inexhaustible topic, upon which only a very few stammering remarks can hesitatingly be offered! For the 'world', as envisaged for the purposes of this discussion, is incomprehensible and indescribable. It is the world of a human race that is growing gigantically and at a terrifying rate; a world which has developed into a unified compositum made up of originally distinct cultures and peoples, so that today everyone has become everyone else's neighbour and the history and destiny of every nation has become the history and destiny of all the others as well. It is a world of rationality, of technical achievement, of atomic power, of automation, of the 'A B C weapons', of the media of mass communication, of nomadic wanderlust, of militant ideologies on the grand scale, of mass hysteria, of propaganda, of the artificial manipulation of human needs, of organised enjoyment; a world which, the more it is subjected to rational planning, the more incalculable it becomes; a world which is no longer something ready given by nature to provide a secure habitation for man, but which constitutes, rather, the material for man's own creative planning; a world the tempo of which is accelerated by man himself. But it is also a world which, after all, never ceases to belong inalienably to what is permanent and immutable in man's nature: his love, his all-transcending questioning, his longing, his loneliness, his demand for happiness and eternity. It is a world of unfathomable anguish and of death; a world that is at once terrifying and familiar to us, and which, in spite of all, we love. It is our world, our fate that we accept, for we know no other besides it. It is in this bewildering world that we live. We must see it as it really is. Let us therefore ask in all honesty: What part does the Christian play in this world?

I believe that the first point to be recognised is this: the Christian shares this world of today, just as it is, with all other men in a spirit of brotherhood. He does not flee from it. He is willing neither to live in a ghetto, nor to take refuge in history. He neither takes flight into a romantic past, nor does he confine himself to one particular small group in society, in which alone he can feel happy. He accepts the world in its worldliness. He has no intention whatever of changing it back into the vanished world of the Middle Ages, in which religion exercised a direct influence upon all departments of life. He makes no pretence of knowing of some prescription, ready-made or even better than the non-Christians, for each and every problem that arises merely on the grounds that he knows that this world is encompassed by the power and compassion of the incomprehensible mystery that he calls God, and upon whom he dares to call as Father. He knows as well as anyone else that his world has been caught up in a movement the effects of which in terms of concrete living in the world no-one sees clearly, since all calculations serve only to increase the element of the incalculable. The Christian accepts this world as it is: a world of human power, and at the same time of human anxiety and utter impotence. He neither idolises it in terms of ideological dreams of utopia, nor yet does he condemn it. It exists; and the Christian, true realist that he is or that he should be, accepts it without question as the sphere of his existence, his responsibility and his proving. He can afford to be a hopeful realist because, even while remaining loyal to this world and its tasks, he is journeying towards the future that is absolute, which God himself has ordained for him, and which is coming to meet him through and beyond all the victories and defeats of this world and its history.

The second point is this: the Christian recognises the diaspora in which he has to live today, wherever he may be, as the setting of his Christian life as something in which an ultimately positive significance is to be found. When I use the term 'diaspora' I am using it in the biblical sense in which it is currently employed, not in the sense ascribed to it until recently, in which it designated the situation of a Catholic minority in the midst of a majority of Protestants. This nineteenth-century idea may still have a certain validity in the field of pastoral care, and still point to certain needs which have to be fulfilled. But this meaning is more and more receding into the background, and the term is being applied more and more to a fresh phenomenon, which we now have to examine. This is the society which is based on a multiplicity of ideologies: the society which, taken as a whole, and from the point of view of its constitution, its special patterns and its culture, bears the stamp of other influences besides the purely Christian one. In this society Christians, whether Catholic or Protestant, live, provided they are true Christians, in common as brothers in the diaspora. It is the diaspora in this sense, in which non-Christian liberal humanism, militant atheism and the atrophy of religion are everywhere apparent, that is referred to when we use the term 'diaspora' here; the diaspora which all Christians have in common, in comparison with which the differences between the various Christian confessions seem not indeed unimportant, but historically speaking secondary. This diaspora must be seen by the Christian of today as the divinely ordained 'situation' of his own Christianity. It is the setting in which his free and personal act of faith is posited, a faith which cannot be overthrown in favour of any social ethic, the situation of free decision, of personal responsibility, of personal avowal of one's faith. And all this gives a fresh application to the old adage that Christians are not born but made. This is the situation which had to arise as a necessity of saving history. Christians know than on the one hand, if their own theological expectations of the future are to be fulfilled, they will always exist as the creed that is under attack, and on the other that when all kinds of far from homogeneous cultures are permitted to exist each in its own sphere as parts of one and the same world history, an attack on any one of them will only come from without, from those who do not belong to that particular culture. We Christians accept this situation. Certainly, in common with all other citizens we want to have the right to co-operate in the sphere of public life. Certainly we also demand that in cases in which, in spite of all variations within the community, the unified political system makes it quite unavoidable for all to have one and the same form, the Christian history of our people and the fact that the great majority of the people want to be Christians even now shall be respected. We demand in the name of freedom and tolerance that he who, in effect, gives the casting vote shall not be the one who is most radical in denying Christianity. But we Christians have no interest in maintaining Christian façades behind which no true Christianity is alive, and which serve only to compromise and to discredit such true Christianity. On the other hand it does not seem fair to us either than non-Christians, while secretly conforming to the ancient heritage of Christian culture in their private lives, nevertheless believe that they must attack Christianity in public. We Christians are not to be numbered among those who suppose that their beliefs and their conception of the world can only be rendered attractive if our faith enjoys the special protection of the state. But we do not, on that account, need to suppose that the prevailing political system must be constructed according to rationalist formulas out of a few abstract principles of freedom and equality, and that it must eliminate every element of Christianity which has contributed in the course of history to the make-up of this political system. We accept the situation of a society made up of a multiplicity of cultures, in which Christianity exists as a diaspora. But it is to the society so constituted that we ourselves precisely belong, the masses of our own people together with the heritage of a tradition that has lasted more than a thousand years. This is no mere ballast, but rather genuine riches, carrying with it responsibilities for the future. We recognise that we must genuinely accept this situation. In other words we must be prepared to be critical of ourselves, and to maintain a constant awareness of the fact that on our own principles we ourselves in turn have to accord to others their due meed of freedom even when they use this freedom to come to decisions which run counter to Christianity itself. But while recognising this let us add in all honesty in our dialogue with non-Christians that the formal rules of the game of democracy are not sufficient of themselves to make it possible for all to live together in peace and freedom. For a society or state to exist it is indispensable that there shall be a single common basis of ultimate moral convictions, whether this be the natural law or whatever we may like to call it, or whether the state itself has a code of laws already drawn up in the concrete and conditioned by its own past history. Furthermore, where necessary this common basis in moral law can and must be defended by the power and authority of the society and state itself. It is not easy to accord due value to all these principles at the same time, and so to arrive at a firm conclusion as to what is right for us of today. We are quite ready to enter into discussion, are anxious for a fair and open dialogue with all, and are even ready to entertain reasonable compromises. On the other hand we refuse to be intimidated when we are stigmatised as bigots, narrow-minded reactionaries, or intolerant, merely on the grounds that we hold that Christian ideas too must be allowed to exert their due influence in the sphere of political life. We have only to compare our position with that of that false liberalism which maintains that political life can and must undergo an ideological process of sterilisation, and that creeds and conscience should only be allowed a voice in the churches or the clubs of the humanist society. Is not this too an ideology, and a bad one at that? Since every fresh claim to freedom on the part of one involves an alteration in, and a restriction of the sphere of freedom hitherto enjoyed by another even before his consent has been obtained, no one member can be allowed an absolutely unrestricted sphere of personal freedom. Hence too not all authority is *ipso facto* and of its very nature hostile to the very essence of freedom. Such authority may be exercised to ensure that all have a reasonable share of freedom in the one sphere of freedom that is available, and to guarantee and maintain a due share for each individual. We Christians are guilty – unhappily this is all too obvious – of sins of our own. For this reason it is difficult to say which of two sins is the more widespread among us: the sin entailed in a reactionary clinging on to Christian forms and customs in the political sphere when these have become obsolete, or the sin of being too cowardly to stand up for what is genuine and new. Perhaps the situation is even such that both sins are often committed at once, and by the same individual Christians – even, it may be, those who occupy high offices and dignities. However this may be, we Christians are willing to accept unreservedly the situation of our diaspora in a pluralistic society, and in doing so to guard against the error of taking refuge in the ghetto of a reactionary defence of the traditional for its own sake, or in the comfortable cowardice of renouncing all claims to influence the course of political life.

There is a third point to be made. It concerns the Christian community. In the situation of a complex society made up of heterogeneous elements and of a diaspora extending through the whole of that society, the Church necessarily changes from a Church of regional and national communities to a Church of believers. What we mean by this is that the members of a Christian community constitute this community not solely in virtue of the continuity of office and the stability of the institutions governing the relationships between those members, though these factors can have a decisive influence upon the lives of the individuals even prior to the personal decision of faith which each one takes for himself. A further factor is precisely this free personal decision of faith which each individual member has won his way to in striving to come to terms with the pluralistic environment. Without impugning the sacramental significance of baptism (including infant baptism) it can be said that for the purpose of the concrete social realities of this environment the Christian community no longer depends (or at least depends less and less) upon baptism and the ecclesiastical institutions as such, but rather on the free exercise of faith. We are, of course, living through a period of transition from the regional or national Church to the Church of believers, and the Church cannot, in her solicitude for the salvation of all, use her official institutions arbitrarily to accelerate this process of transition. At the same time she must recognise that in this situation one new member who decides to join her from his own genuine decision of faith carries more weight than three who, while belonging or seeming to belong to her, really do so only because of the weight of social tradition.

In this situation two points of importance emerge with regard to the community, and therefore with regard to the task of the individual Christian in the Church as well. On the one hand there must be a continual emergence of genuine new communities. The Church must be manifestly seen to be sustained by the faith of all not merely in her institutions and her official organisation, for this depends upon itself and regards the Christians merely as the subject of its own salvific activities. Church means people of God. Church is identical with ourselves – all of us who believe and bear witness to the world as a community of faith, of eternal hope and love, to the grace and pardon of God in Christ. If such a community is to exist and to constitute a living representative of the Church at one particular place, then the bond of brotherhood between all the members of the community must transcend all differences of individual functions in the community and all distinctions between those who hold official positions in it and those who do not, necessary though such distinctions may be. This bond of brotherhood must overcome and endure through all such distinctions. It must be possible for the established authorities and the ordinary Christians to communicate with one another. All must feel personally responsible and be ready to give their active participation, their hearts and, where necessary, their material resources too in order to ensure the vitality of the community. We must come to know each other and cohere, must play our part in maintaining the liturgy and the attitude of neighbourliness. We must not be willing merely to receive the Church, but must be ready to give; we must positively want to make contact, to get to know people, to help and to serve. The community must recognise that it, and in it the Church, is not merely an organisation based on religious techniques with the function of satisfying individual religious needs, but the community of those who, because they are united in Christ, are also united among themselves. They must be united in such a way that their communal life signifies not merely philanthropy or benevolence towards their fellow men, not merely orthodoxy or reception of the sacraments, not merely a willingness to pay the Church's dues, but truly that love which, confronted in the concrete with a 'neighbour', a 'fellow worker in the household of the faith', does not fail, but rather proves itself. The educated man who is, in the nature of things, an individualist, and who thereby becomes all too easily an egoist with his head in the clouds, has a special responsibility and special tasks here, always provided that he is in earnest in wanting to live a Christian life. He must not, in the first instance, ask: 'What has the community to offer me', but rather, 'What can I myself give to it in the form of active participation, example and help'. Certainly his most important 'lay apostolate' will be found in the sphere of his life 'in the world', his profession, his specialised knowledge, in the secular and civic community, among his fellows at what seems to be the merely human level. Certainly as a Christian too he will have to prove himself here first, in the sphere, therefore, in which there is no need whatever to try and stick a Christian label on his life so that everyone else, wherever he may be, can at once notice what he is. For even such virtues as goodness, faithfulness, courage, a manifestly reasonable attitude to the problems of life and death, self-discipline and a readiness to take responsibility together with other human virtues – these do not cease to be Christian virtues merely because they are sometimes practised in an exemplary manner by those who do not consider themselves to be Christians at all. And even such virtues, provided they are exercised and lived to the bitter end, to the point at which they become incapable of being merely 'profitable' any more, of themselves lead man to the silent mystery in which the ultimate meaning of existence consists, which alone provides it with its ultimate reason and significance, to God himself. But all this should precisely not be taken to imply that the Christian in the diaspora has not also the task of helping to build up the Church of God, the community of faith, hope and charity, in his own region, in order that it may bear witness to all to the fact that the ultimate meaning of human existence is not emptiness and absurdity (it makes no difference whether a man shouts his doubts aloud on this point, or maintains a discreet silence) but the absolute future that is God himself. And both factors, the task of the Christian in the world which he shares with all men of good will, and his vocation to build up the Church in the community, are ultimately one and the same. For the consecrated reality that is the Church is precisely a visible sign of the fact that the world, even in its secular aspect, and even when it is at its most worldly, is sanctified by God's grace. And when this world, together with all its sublime, its questionable and its worthless elements, is accepted without reserve and as an act of deep personal decision right to the last, it shows itself to be based on the unfathomable depths of the divine.

The other point which is relevant to the contemporary 'diaspora' situation, and which concerns every Christian in his task as a Christian and as a member of the community of the Church, is this: The community for which each one is responsible must not on any account become a ghetto. This is easy to say, and sounds obvious, yet it is difficult to put into practice. There is no need here to enter into a discussion as to whether the Church of believers, the future community of the believers which has already begun to exist, should be regarded as already and inevitably having the sociological status of a 'sect', (taking this term in a completely neutral sense, and as it is used in the sociology of religion), or whether it is too misleading to formulate it in this way, since it suggests one specific state of affairs. At any rate the community, both in the present and in the future, must be a community of brothers who know one another and love one another, a community that coheres, that creates the kind of environment which is so necessary of common convictions, common aims, mutual help and mutual love, an environment in which Christian faith can develop without restriction, and can exploit all the possibilities so as to become a vital force. But then the danger inevitably arises of a community of this kind becoming a 'sect' in the bad sense, of it forming a ghetto, living as a sort of religious 'back to the land' community. This makes it all too possible to arrive at the unfortunate situation of withdrawing, from an intellectual, cultural and social point of view, into a sort of 'hole-and-corner' existence, having too little to do with normal life, feeling that one belongs to an esoteric and exclusive club, in which the members mutually confirm one another's positions. All this on the grounds that the estimate which the world, the public at large, makes of the Christians is that they represent a *quantité négligeable* of harmless religious ideologists or fanatics whom one does not have to take seriously because they are incapable of coping with the realities of life. This is not how it must be. The Christian community must not be a fire that warms only itself. It must not be a preserve for life's inadequates, or a rosary confraternity for harmless souls who can achieve nothing more than to be pious, and to make this piety of theirs their sole contribution. An analogy may be drawn between the Christian community and a modern family with a healthy outlook and attitude towards life. A family of this kind is no longer willing to exist in all departments of human living as an autonomous clan, withdrawing in its self-sufficiency from all others. Rather such a family comprises the concrete realisation of a personal independence and freedom which is completely and fully developed in all departments of human living. So too it must be with the Christian community. It must be open to influences from outside itself. Its members must maintain a genuine and unreserved contact in their lives with the world, its outlook, the problems that occupy it and the tasks with which it finds itself confronted today. They must not imagine that the Christian community of today can be an intellectual autonomy in the social, cultural or political spheres, or that the Church has to have an exclusive monopoly of all values and all that is important in life. What has been said of the Church as a whole at the Council must be applied to every regional Church as well. It cannot and will not continue any longer to act as an impregnable fortress with small arrow-slits in the walls from which the defenders shoot at their enemies. Now it is rather the spacious house with the large windows from which one looks out upon all spheres of humanity, all of which are encompassed by the creative power of God and by his compassion. And the altar that stands in the midst of this house is consecrated to God as a sign of grace, not only for those who actually live in the house, but for all who, in a spirit of good will and good conscience, seek to find the way to fulfil their existence. In accordance with this the preaching and teaching in the regional Churches must be of such a kind that as far as possible outsiders too, the onlookers at the divine service and those who merely take an interest, can understand what is being thought and said there. The message must not sound esoteric, as though it were aimed exclusively at a club of privileged members. Rather it must be presented as the mystery of what is manifest and the manifest in what is mysterious, for in reality everyone encounters this in his personal experience of life, even though not everyone is able to recognise it – at any rate sufficiently distinctly – as a factor which deserves to be examined and pronounced upon in its own right. If the Christian Churches of today want to enter into discussions of an ecumenical kind, or on subjects of theological controversy, then they must make sure that this discussion does not sound like a discussion between two ghetto-like ideologies. Rather it must be conducted first and foremost as a general discussion among Christians concerning the possibility of a more genuine encounter with the world which is not Christian or which has not sufficiently realised its own Christian depths. It must be an attempt undertaken in common to think out afresh the eternal validity of the Christian message for the world and its future. I believe that ecumenical discussions of this kind will, in the long run, only be fruitful if they are, at the same time, discussions with the world of today, which has quite different questions to put to Christianity than those which the confessions are accustomed to put to each other. In its struggle against everything that smacks of a sectarian mentality or of the outlook of the ghetto the Christian community must make sure alike in the presentation of its services, the expression of its faith and its community life that it spares no effort to banish and to keep banished every element of the old-fashioned, the prudish, the 'old-world', the bigoted – everything, in short, which derives merely from one specific social group, and one specific historical tradition. This does not mean that the Church needs to deny the folly of the Cross, the high ethical standards of the Sermon on the Mount, the need for discipline and the courage of non-conformity. In the heritage of its own past it has preserved sufficient in the way of human and cultural treasures to be able to present itself to the world even today. And that free and unconstrained discipline in moral matters which it stands for and wishes to practise will once more always evoke a response from what is best in the hearts of others also – providing only that there is no attempt at evading the full rigour of contemporary moral problems by failing to face up to the dire needs which are with us every day, or by withdrawing ourselves from these in our thinking and living alike to areas where life has already passed us by. More than ever before the Christian community must always be developing fresh points of contact, which eliminate that feeling on the part of the so-called 'outsider' that he is an alien and is viewed with distrust, or else is merely the object of a plot to win converts. The Church must give these the chance to feel themselves to be close friends even though they may not always be able to share in all her dogmatic or moral principles.

For the community of the present day to reconcile both of the tasks confronting it, to be truly a family united by one faith, and at the same time an open missionary community, venturing boldly on intercourse with the world, is not easy. It is not easy to ensure that the nucleus of the community shall not be made up of individuals who have nothing else to do than to be pious. This is not to say anything against those individuals who, in the wisdom of old age and under the shadow of approaching death, are pious in a very true sense, and are so precisely because to be anything else in this situation would simply be cowardice and a flight from reality. But in its more active sections the community must be made up of those who recognise that in the celebration of the mystery of the Lord's death it is the focal point of their own lives that is made sacramentally present. They must be coming fresh from their work in the world precisely to the recognition of this fact: to find in the dead and risen Lord the ultimate outpouring of grace upon human existence in this present world, and so to go out once more from the experience of, and the act of receiving, this grace to joy and confidence in the fact that their worldly life has been redeemed in its worldliness, and while remaining worldly. But it will be necessary to construct far clearer and more convincing concrete prototype examples than hitherto of what the way of life and social patterns of such communities must be in order for the men of today to feel immediately at home in them. These examples must include preaching, confession, liturgy, work for neighbours in the parish, the charity of the community as a whole. When all this still leaves so much to be desired it becomes absolutely the first duty and task for the Christian of today to collaborate patiently and unselfishly in the construction of such communities, and not to take the lack of them as an excuse for holding himself dispensed from selfless service of this kind.

The fourth and final point is the most difficult, and at the same time the most attractive. Christianity, always ancient yet always new, as it always has been, is and will remain, is, even in these 'diaspora' conditions, and even today, the grace bestowed upon Christians and at the same time the task with which they are presented. We are moving on in ever-increasing tempo to the world of tomorrow, to the unification of world history; to a world oppressively closed in upon itself by the increase of world population; to a world of technical achievements undreamt of as yet, and social patterns of a still more complex character. But at its ultimate roots it still remains the world which everyone has already experienced in the depths of his own heart, and it is inevitable that it should be so. It is the world of happiness and doubt, the world of innocence and guilt, the world of life and death, the world of loneliness and freedom, of love, of faithfulness, of service – that world which, in virtue of what it is, in virtue of its movement outwards and forwards and its terrible imperfections leading to its final collapse in death, raises the question inexorably of the ultimate mystery of itself, God. And why should this be so? It is because in its unfolding process this world is encompassed and upheld right to its innermost depths and in the course of its history by a greater movement, in which God himself encounters it to judge it and to endow it with grace. It is because in the long run no one can fail to hear the ultimate all-embracing question silently put to him, even if, in his own thoughts and in his own life he wants to deny that one should entertain the idea of the incomprehensible. This is the situation that is old and ever new, the truly Christian situation which transcends from the outset all lesser situations, whether old or new which are confined to a particular epoch. We recognise, therefore, that our lives depend in the most radical, and yet in the most obvious sense, upon God; that we are hidden in the absolute mystery which receives us, and in receiving us forgives the sinfulness of our lives and endows us with the grace of itself. Everything else which contributes to our lives is included in this. This assent on God's part is present in Jesus Christ in the dimension of our history, and in that he has shared in our common human lot (not only, therefore, in the labyrinthine depths of our own consciences). We celebrate the death of this same Jesus Christ as our salvation, and in so celebrating it accept our own death also as the drawing of our existence into the immediate ambience of God. In doing this we seek truly to endure that death in this life in such a way that we feel ourselves to be truly the Church, the community of those who have ceased to value this life for its own sake. And all this too remains, even today, that which is old and yet new, and always the same in Christianity, and at the same time that which corresponds to the contemporary situation in which we find ourselves. We must never lose sight of this fact when we ask ourselves anxiously how the Christian should appear in his contemporary environment, and what he ought to be doing today. Much that concerns this problem must be raised in fresh forms and answered anew, and much must remain open. But the innermost and ultimate meaning of the question and answer is still always to be found, even if the finding of it is constantly and indisputably conditioned by the problems and vicissitudes of the particular situation in history that is ours as distinct from all others. For even in this environment, the ultimate question is this: Whether in the midst of the tasks and struggles of this life we respond unreservedly to the call of him who is first and last, present from the very origins and still present in the most distant future, committing ourselves to him in faith, hope and love, in the act of believing that this First and Last has made himself known to us and borne witness of himself to us in the love that is in Jesus Christ, the crucified and risen Lord.

6

'I BELIEVE IN THE CHURCH'

Dogma and dogmatic definitions are always a scandal. Let us admit this much to ourselves; many of the statements included in the Church's 'dogmatic definitions' are repugnant to us at the first hearing. *All* assertions which are intended to be more than the mere temporary expressions of positions which are being maintained in the living context of some discussion are somehow *ipso facto* strange and unpleasing to us of the present day. It is only with an effort that we can entertain them, and, as it were, not without a struggle to overcome our repugnance. We may recall our reactions when we hear pronouncements concerning personages of the past, concerning 'heaven', 'the resurrection', 'original sin' and many similar topics. Is not this reaction of ours rather like that of a man who, when he is already exhausted and wearied to death, has to listen to a lecture on the technique of how to calculate a matrix of the metaphysics of being? We hear these statements and know what they are intended to convey. We have the impression that we know just as well as the speaker himself what he means, and yet we do not really take it in. Indeed, in our innermost selves, so filled are we with leaden depression and sheer desolation, we have the feeling that there is one thing that we actually know better than the man who is addressing us on these topics. We feel that we know that he does not understand what he is saying, that he does not notice how inappropriate it is at this stage to speak in these terms, even if it ever was appropriate. The effort of will required of us by those who thus address us seems too great, and in any case meaningless and superfluous. We must have patience here. It is impossible to make everything clear and intelligible all at once. All that we intend at this point is to remind ourselves of something which the Catholic Church recognises and acknowledges as self-evident for its own faith. Such a reminder may well be useful for many in the contemporary situation, who already know it all in principle, or ought to know it. For him who cannot tread paths such as these this article can serve as a quiet exploration of his own convictions. It is precisely this kind of individual who must reflect that much still remains to be said in other contexts, for instance about the sinfulness of the Church, the limits of the Church's authority etc. (on this cf. the relevant articles in *Theological Investigations VI* (London & Baltimore, 1969).

We are not unbelievers. Oh yes the earlier 'attitude of unbelief' familiar to us from our fathers' time — that is something that we could not revert to even if we wished. The only real practitioners of this who still survive are those who are behind the times (admittedly there may be many of these). How insolent it was, and how exaggerated were its claims to knowledge, this unbelief! It is no credit to us that we can no longer entertain it. Our minds have encountered too many factors which are obscure, and which cannot be dismissed as mere fancies such as might be expected swiftly to dissolve before the light of our intellect. And our heart has felt too much in the way of sorrows even to death through these incomprehensible factors for us to imagine that we could not believe because we know too much. But it is precisely at this point that *our* difficulty arises. We are, as it were, susceptible to an overdose of the light of faith. Faith is not difficult to us of today on the grounds that we can explain things sufficiently without it, but because faith itself seems to us to be trying to explain more than we can bear. A given statement — e.g. that concerning the bodily assumption of Mary into heaven — seems to be asserting almost too much. It seems to have a clear and happy knowledge of what is meant by the body and its resurrection, by 'now', and by 'heaven'. Yet our faith, so difficult and arduous as it is, yet so tough, so wholly devoid of false pathos or exhibitionism, consists in a constant 'Lord help thou my unbelief!' It takes the ultimate reserves of strength in our hearts to sustain this appeal and at the same time in any one individual it is the ultimate strength upon which his heart can call. For this reason our faith is not curious, eager for novelty. It appeals to God and finds him on the Cross of Christ, tortured to death by us. It reaches out to the sacramental life because it seeks to meet the word of grace in that context in which we find ourselves on this earth and at this particular stage in earthly history. It knows that faith means *faith in the Church*, and that scripture and oral tradition have been transmitted in the Church. For the monologue which we conduct with ourselves, and in which we are on our own, turning things over and over in our minds, would finally have driven us into doubt if it were not for the fact that this doubt had been transformed by God's own grace into a readiness to hearken to the word that has been sent down with full authority from above in the Church of Christ.

If we want to hear the message that has an absolute value for us, i.e. that decides the ultimate meaning of our lives in our earthly here and now, and in human words, then it cannot simply be left to us to work out for ourselves, but must confront us as the word of authority handed down by God himself, which does not bow to our will, and yet which must at the same time consist in something more than mere abstract or transcendental truths, i.e. statements of universal principle which are so general and vague in their application (however important they may be) that they still manage to survive and to carry some kind of force and authority even when they are denied. Without this kind of message, brought to us in this way, we would either be alone and defenceless, or at most our only weapon of defence would be mere 'metaphysics', and this would be like a net the meshes of which were so hopelessly wide that they would let the concrete reality of our own being, the life we have to live and for which we are responsible, slip through and escape. What is needed in view of all this is a declaration that is authoritative and concrete, and that we encounter as binding upon us. And this is given to us in the word of the Church, which itself encounters us and addresses us as the active mediator of the message, whether we hear it or not. So we are believers, hearers of the word of God as found in the mouth of the Church. What the Church says is our light and our strength, the love of the living God in spite of all the darkness, the word of forgiveness in spite of the experience of our own sins, the word of the Holy Ghost which has been poured out into our hearts in spite of all that they have experienced in the way of weariness, feebleness and emptiness – in short the word of Jesus Christ, the Son of God and at the same time truly man, crucified and raised from the dead into the eternal life of God, he who has plumbed the depths of human destiny, the presence of God in this world, the source of salvation and of peace, Lord of those who believe in him and recognise with trust that their destiny is hidden in him, the head of those who have been called and redeemed, who together with him make up that fellowship of truth and love and mercy which we call the Church, visible for what he is in himself in the authority which has been handed down to its official ministers in the word of God, both written and proclaimed, and in the visible sacraments of the Church.

Now if it is true that we are confronted with a message from this Church, how is it that it appears so new and (at any rate in some sense) unaccustomed, 'hard' (Jn 6:60) and forbidding?

Let us gradually get down to work. We are not concerned here to examine the content of such a message. We ask only what the *attitude* is which we ourselves must adopt in order to hear such a message aright at all.

Undoubtedly it is quite possible to fail to experience something because one is not listening – not listening because one is too indolent or too proud. It is possible to misunderstand something because one takes the initial difficulty of understanding as an excuse for impatience and impertinent contradiction. All new knowledge is intended to change him who acquires it, but it is only with reluctance, or at any rate not with any great eagerness, that we allow ourselves to undergo the painful process of being changed in this way. We want always to remain just as we are (however unhappy we may be in the circumstances in which we find ourselves). What is new is always unfamiliar and frightening. The only thing we hope to gain from the acquisition of any 'new' knowledge is to confirm ourselves in our existing position: 'That is precisely as I had already thought. That is right' (In other words it agrees with my own preconceptions; although we do not actually say this). Real truths, however, when they make their initial impact upon us, make us shy away. They carry further implications beyond themselves; they threaten us, change us, compel us to enter areas of thought in which we can no longer take custom and habit as a substitute for insight, in which we no longer feel ourselves at home, and in which reality appears in a guise which is not yet faded and subdued by familiarity, where that which seems so terrifying and so dangerous now has not yet become a part of our everyday lives.

What an experience it must be when it is a truth of God that is making its initial impact upon us! What ought our attitude to be to such an occurrence in order not to deny it from the outset? If we are sinners (do we admit this or not?), if we always have the sinister inclination to suppress the truth of God (Rom 1:18), if we are tempted to reduce the truth of God in its greatness to the petty dimensions of human 'truth', then it is obvious that when we first encounter the word of God we are always at first blinded and dazzled by its brilliance, bewildered and upset by the fact that it is so immeasurably above us. And because of this it is to be expected *a priori* that we should be vexed and out of humour because the message sounds so hard to our ears. We are always tempted to believe that God's word is improbable and complicated (In spite of the fact that because of its immeasurable depths it is divinely simple). We are always inclined to explain away the message as not in conformity with God's nature, and therefore as false and erroneous. But in reality what we mean by this is that it is not in conformity with our own prior conceptions of God, which we presume to be correct, with that particular element of the divine which we have contented ourselves with recognising. It is to be expected from the outset that we shall find reasons enough for taking scandal from the lowly guise in which we encounter the message. It will appear utterly and hopelessly foolish, 'primitive', so far removed from anything sublime or wise that to the world, that is ourselves, it appears as folly and scandal, especially if we are encountering it for the first time. We have heard the old message so often that it sounds familiar to us. We only give half an ear to it, and we are, so to say, 'padded' against the scandal of it by custom (just as in fact we have become accustomed to our own sins and our liability to death, so that the most terrible things strike us as entirely 'natural'). Thus the incarnation of God, the Cross on which God was abandoned by himself to failure make the same kind of impression upon us as a long-familiar piece of furniture in our own houses. We no longer feel either astonishment or exaltation as we look upon it. It is simply 'there', and it is taken for granted that it is right. Let us simply leave it as it is! But if a message of God makes a fresh and unwonted impact on our minds, ill-prepared as they are for it, then this lack of prior dispositions on our part causes us to react with explicit hostility. Our minds, under these circumstances, cannot fail to be kindled to resentment at it. In such a case it is no longer possible for us to apply the tactics of a studied lack of attention. It is no longer possible to continue to wage merely a cold war that is beneath the surface against the truth of God. Man's contradiction of, and revulsion against the truth of God comes to the surface and is made explicit. A thousand reasons for objecting to it will suggest themselves to us. The first will be that it is new. The second that we have enough to believe in as it is without this. The third that we have to be suspicious of those who convey the message to us on the grounds that they are exaggeratedly pious, or else over-zealous enthusiasts. The fourth will be that in any case the matter is unimportant. And so we go on. All these can be real reasons, and are not necessarily false in themselves in every case. Only they do not constitute any genuine grounds for resisting the truth of God. Rather they are human objections, deriving from the guise of lowliness and abasement in which the word of God has become incarnate and human, and in which it still continues to do so ever anew.

There is nothing to be particularly ashamed of in the fact that we, or rather sinful and earthly man in us, do take scandal in this manner at the truth of God. It is predictable from the outset that we shall do so. Indeed, if we were to find the truth of God too easy to accept (as do many of the 'devout'), then this rather would be a sign that all was not well; that we had so radically misunderstood this truth that it was no longer the truth that God wanted us to have at all. The truth of God never comes as a kind of poetic consolation or a devotional story for children. But even though it is never this in reality, it can be misunderstood in this sense. And when it is so misunderstood it can be degraded into a sedative to soothe the nerves; in which form it enters easily into the disposition of a 'devout soul'. But this is not a sign that there is an especially firm faith at work here, and that the light of God is shining especially brightly. We have no need, therefore, to envy those endowed with 'spirituality'. If God performs miracles of grace in their case, and the new knowledge is born in them without any birth-pangs, let them have the honour and glory of it! But the grace of faith can work in an obstinate spirit and a rebellious heart as well, and usually this is the way in which God performs his greatest miracles.

As we have said, we have to reckon with the fact that the truth of God, even when it really is the truth of God, does not necessarily 'suit' us. It does not suit us because we do not suit it until we have altered ourselves in order to do so. We must protect ourselves from ourselves. The humility of a sensitive spirit, readiness for change, the courage to take the pain of a new idea, prayer for light from above – these will achieve what is necessary. We do not need to be alarmed when we find that at first a new message shocks us. But we must take care that this initial scandal is made to conduce to our salvation. Now it does this when it startles us and stimulates us into adopting an attitude of patient attentiveness, of enduring the toil involved in learning something new (how hard this seems to us 'old' men!), of praying for light, for the sincerity and readiness to receive which one owes to any word if there is even a chance that it may turn out to be the word of God.

Now that we have sketched in a few rough general outlines, indicating the inner attitude which we ought initially to adopt, we may go on to say something on a further point, namely on the objective sphere outside ourselves in which alone all our efforts can be brought to their true fruition. This sphere is the Church and the Church as object of faith. It is strange. As believers who receive the word of God from the mouth of the Church as God's own truth and as the good tidings of our own salvation, we feel ourselves to be faithful children of the Church. We feel ourselves to be so and indeed we are. And yet when we are confronted by this same Church with a truth that is new and startling – we do not merely have to think of the definition of the glorification of the Blessed Virgin, there are plenty of other examples – then we shrink into ourselves. Then we are startled out of the slumber of habit and custom, which we confuse with the quiet confidence of real faith, and we recognise that after all we do not belong so manifestly and so unreservedly as we had somewhat complacently supposed to the sphere of faith that is the holy Church. We suddenly realise that the reason why we had found it easy to accept the earlier truths was that they were *our* truths, our habits of mind, and not because they were those of the Church. But now we have to take ourselves in hand, abstracting wholly, in the initial stages, from the actual content of the new message of which we have become aware, and we must ask ourselves: 'Where do I stand, where do I want to stand in order to hear this message aright, to heed it and to believe in it?'. And our answer will be: 'In the faith of the Church'. What, then, does this mean? What do we mean by that acknowledgment which we have made innumerable times with heart and lips from our youth upwards: 'I believe in the holy Catholic Church'?

The Church is the object of our faith, and, in a mysterious manner, at the same time the dimension in which it exists. In this dimension alone is it possible to have anything like the fulness of Catholic faith. These two aspects of our faith are mutually complementary, and it makes no difference to our present argument at which of the two points the actual act of faith on the part of the individual is initiated in the concrete: whether he believes in the Church first and then in the rest of the matters proposed for his belief because these come from the Church, or whether he first attains to belief in Christ and his word, and goes on from there to belief in the Church as founded by Christ. In any case, where faith is found in its Catholic fulness and its inner firmness, both aspects are present. On the basis of his faith in Christ the believer includes the Church too in his faith in such a way that it immediately becomes the direct medium and rule of faith as such.

As Christians we believe in that word that comes to us from the incarnate Word of the Father. We live and die on the basis of *his* message to us, basing everything with hearts and souls and with all our strength on the fact that there is no other name in heaven or on earth in which we could be blessed than the name of our Lord Jesus Christ, crucified and risen. But he is at once the head, the foundation stone and the architect of that entity, visible yet so mysterious, which we call the Church. Like her Master and Head she extends her influence throughout reality in all its dimensions. To her belongs the Spirit whom he has poured out upon all flesh when he departed to the Father at his death, in order that he may come in the Spirit of his Father, who is his Spirit also. To the Church belongs the incarnate Word himself, with the flesh which he took from the Virgin Mary, when, as a son of Adam, he became a member of our race in order that he who sanctifies and they who are sanctified may become a single family, in order that he may sanctify those who are his brethren according to the flesh precisely because she, the Church, has extended his compassion to these, his brethren. This Church is constituted by those whom he has sent into all the world and to all peoples to preach his word. He did this in order that what took place in the very depths of reality (whether we realise it or not) through the incarnation of the Son, his death and his resurrection, may be rendered present to the spirit of man also through the word of his messengers, and may be received in a spirit of obedience and faith into the very centre of man himself, into that dimension in which he is free to be whoever he will be, and so who he ought to be.

This divine reality, Spirit, grace, truth, compassion and love of God, which is the most real factor in the world, however much it may be hidden, is brought about by God through Christ, through his Body, through his word and his commandment, through the authority derived from him, through his sacraments in their palpable and physical reality, their concrete apprehensible presence in the here and now. It is brought about in such a way that (in a manner similar to that in which the body renders the soul present) this reality is at once made present and apprehensible and unambiguously *there*, and at the same time veiled in the lowly guise of the form of a servant. The believer, therefore, possesses the grace of God in this form, and at the same time it is only to the believer that it is recognisable as the true presence of grace. This means that the Church (just as with Christ) is God's eternal compassion and his Body as it exists in space and time, both aspects (again as with Christ) being inseparable yet distinct. Considered as the sphere of grace in this sense, and simultaneously as an historically apprehensible entity, the Church is the sole dimension in which, in the last analysis, anything like the phenomenon of the Catholic faith is possible at all. The Church is the bearer of the message of faith. She has been entrusted with the word of the Lord in the person of the apostles whom Christ sent. She hands it on faithfully to all subsequent generations. It is not handed down simply in the form of literature (not even through scripture), for even scripture is not self-authenticating, but is rather the book of the Church's memories of her own experience, so that the only one who really understands it is the Church of the origins, because she has written it with the assistance of the Holy Spirit within her. The word of God in history, which went forth once and for all in Christ and his apostles, does not drift on aimlessly, and, so to say, without an owner on the current of secular history down the centuries. Rather it is carried down in a responsible manner by those who are empowered to uphold it, and who derive their authority from the apostles. As it proceeds down the centuries it is preached, expounded and preserved by the Church, administered by her official ministers in dependence upon the bishops and upon the bishop of Rome as the concrete focal point which binds them together and welds them into a unity, and who is capable of acting in his own person. The Church is the sphere of our faith because in the plenitude of power and the authority imparted to her by Christ, (a power therefore which we, the hearers, are bound in conscience to obey) she testifies to the true doctrine of the word of Christ, and only so makes it possible for us to obtain a clear and unambiguous understanding of it. The fact that we do hearken to this word is not due to any personal initiative on our own part, by which, having found this word lost and drifting somewhere or other in history, we grasp hold of it, but rather due to the fact that it comes to us through its own movement, borne up by those who can trace their mission and the responsibilities and powers with which they have been entrusted in an unbroken chain of authority back to Christ himself. When we speak of a word we mean a word as it exists on the lips of men. When we speak of the word of Christ we mean a word as it exists upon the lips of the Church authorised by Christ. It is because *she* utters it that it is proved to be *his* word.

But this is not the only sense in which the Church is the sphere of our faith. The Church has a priority in belief. The life of God brought to us through what we call faith and love, is first bestowed upon *her*, and upon the individual *in* her. It is not as though she had a separate existence as a mythical entity behind and beyond the individual believers. She is the Church because individuals have taken it upon themselves as an act of personal responsibility and decision to believe. But do not let us forget this: it is precisely this decision that is the act and the work of God, and only truly the salvific act of man when it is faith in Christ as the Word of God already present and real in history. And hence this actual act of faith in the concrete on the part of the individual presupposes that the divine reality is already present in the world. Now this reality is presented to mankind not as a unified group of individuals, but to man as the brother of the Son, one brother among many, as a member of the people called to believe, to man as already inextricably involved from the outset in a *common* destiny of sin and of salvation. The community of those who have been called out of the world, all of whom are in Christ Jesus, the Body of Christ, the house of God which the Lord has built – this community, therefore, is a reality, and can be so (however many further 'fellowships' there may be apart from it, and indeed, all the more so because of them) which has, at least in a certain sense, a priority over the individual, so that it sustains him, and without it he himself would not be what in fact he is, and could not act as in fact he is able to act as a member of such a community. The Church, therefore, as the fellowship of the faithful, is not merely the sum total of those who believe, each one on his own responsibility, and who are united to Christ by this fact. Rather it has a priority over the belief of the individual. It supplies the support and the basis of that belief. Certainly that belief is brought about by the Lord of grace and truth, and his act of grace is aimed at *those* men, the community of those joined together in one flesh and in one Spirit. Belief, therefore, is indeed a matter which is utterly personal to each individual man, and yet it is not simply his own 'private concern'. It follows that faith is only completely and truly possible in the community of the faithful, in the Church. Faith, therefore, always includes the act of trustful and loving surrender to the faith of the Church, active participation in the faith of the divine community of truth, for which the Lord has supplied the basis by giving of his flesh and his Spirit, and by being its true founder. Faith does not only mean accepting what 'I' as an individual believe that I have heard. It also means accepting what the Church has heard, giving my assent to the 'confession' of the Church. The Church is not merely the upholder of the message of Christ in the sense that she extends it to the individuals (only to disappear once more after the manner of a postman). Rather she is the enduring and abiding medium of faith, that in which faith is posited in order that one voice of praise of the living God may resound as from one mouth and one body, to give glory to his compassion.

However much, therefore, the individual may be sure that 'his' God has bestowed a special revelation upon him, and in a manner exclusive to him alone, he must make sure that in his faith he believes that which all believe. He must always be ready to give his mind in a spirit of submission, humility and obedience to the recognition of faith and the progress in faith which belongs to the Church as a whole. He cannot act as an 'heretic', choosing only that which pleases him as an individual. Always he must submit himself trustfully to the faith of the community of believers, which is always greater and more comprehensive than his own as an individual. Heresy is always more than merely an error concerning some specific point of faith, but rather, prior to any such deviation, error and apostasy from the Church herself, and from that insight into the inscrutable mystery of God which is bestowed upon her as the one recipient of his favour. This mystery is revealed to her as the bride of the Lamb. It is the mystery of the love of Christ made known to her in water and in the word of truth – to her, and to each of us only in so far as we are members and participants in this bride of the Lord. It is of no avail for the individual to try to rearrange and adapt his own personal ideological presuppositions, and so to arrive at Christianity by putting his own personal house in order. He can only be a Christian by entering into that house that is wide enough to shelter all, into the temple which God himself has built from living stones, and upon the rock that is Peter, the foundation of the apostles and prophets, as also of their lawful successors.

The Church, therefore, is always the measure of our faith, the measure and not that which is measured. Certainly she is the one who hears God and obeys him, the one who herself only receives the measure of her faith from the word of revelation, the word of scripture, from that understanding of her faith which God has bestowed upon her in earlier ages. Certainly she humbles herself ever anew in order to hearken to what God is saying to her in his revelation. But it is not for me as an individual to put the Church to the test to see whether she does in fact conform to the measure of her faith as thus conceived, or whether, measured by the standards which do apply to her, she is indeed hearing the word of God aright. If this were the case I would in fact be setting myself up as the standard by which the Church should be measured, raising my personal understanding of the faith and my insight to be the norm of the Church. I would no longer be the one who hearkens to the Church herself. The fact that the Church does indeed hear the word of God aright is guaranteed by the Spirit who is promised to her. In the last analysis there are no norms, rules or principles for determining whether the faith of the Church herself is correct, such as I, as an individual apart from the Church, could use or apply on my initiative, regarding her, as it were, *ab externo* and as an objective entity. Certainly there are standards which do apply to the Church. But the fact that she submits herself to these standards, and applies them correctly in order to arrive at a true explication of her faith – that is the miracle of *her own* Spirit. What these standards are and how they should be applied is something which I as an individual learn precisely from seeing how she, the Church herself, does in fact apply them. And this is the only way in which I can learn this. There is no absolute standpoint apart from her affording a perspective from which she can be rightly regarded. It is only in the Spirit of God himself that she can be judged. Now the moment one decides to stand apart from her in order to judge her, and precisely to the extent that one does this, one has *ipso facto* lost this Spirit. The only objectivity that can be achieved in faith is the subjectivity of the Church. For the objectivity of faith is guaranteed by the Spirit of God who judges all things, and is judged by no-one. But this Spirit is present in the Church as her subjectivity, and is present nowhere else. No-one can attempt to measure this, the ultimate standard of all measures. This ultimate standard, in so far as it is apprehensible at all, actually is the Church, since the Spirit of truth has united himself inseparably to her, and to me, the individual, only to the extent that I am standing within her, and have given her the allegiance of my faith by believing what she believes. The Church is simply she who is always at the service of God, and who remains always encompassed by the power of God's truth even though, humanly speaking, she is always on the point of rebelling against the truth of God, even though she remains 'infallible' only by a miracle performed by the Spirit and constantly renewed. But it is precisely because, while remaining free, she is so possessed by the Spirit that she becomes the ever-obedient servant of the truth, it is precisely for this reason and for no other that she becomes the mistress of our faith too. But she becomes this in a manner that is absolute and unconditional.

From my point of view also – where else could I find the firm concrete criterion which I need, one which is not subject to the vagaries of my own spirit and opinions, to judge whether I as an individual and in the personal allegiance of my faith, really do stand in the truth of God? Do my conscience and the inner experiences of my spirit supply such a criterion? No! – For it is precisely this conscience of mine that attests that what my spirit demands is that faith which comes from hearing and obeying, the faith which listens and does not speak itself. But when I believe *in* the Church this does not take away from me the reality of my own inalienable decision of conscience in faith and for faith. I would not in fact be in the Church at all if I had not, of my own free choice and in the grace of God, given her my assent. But what I am seeking is a quality inherent not in the believing subject, but rather in the object of belief; a quality which assures me that I am not mistaken as to the true content of my belief. It might be asked whether God *has to* supply me with such a criterion, or whether in fact he *could have* contented himself with assuring me in the witness of my own conscience that what I had heard was in fact *his* truth and not simply the voice of my own heart, so disposed as it is to evil and error. But this question may be left on one side. It is enough that God has, in fact, of his mercy, given me such a criterion: he who hears you hears me. For the fact, therefore, that it is he whom I hear I do not rely merely upon the content of the message or the overwhelming impression which it makes upon me and upon my conscience, but rather upon the fact that this message is spoken precisely by those who have been sent by the Christ of God. According to the word of the Lord himself it is the messenger who provides the guarantee of his own message by the fact that he has himself authentically been sent. And in this sense too the Church is the guarantee of her own teaching and not, *vice versa*, the teaching (judged by *me* to be correct) the guarantee of the Church.

The teaching of the Church is inherent in the Church, and it may seem to authenticate itself by the very fact that it shares in the nature and spirit of the Church, in which humility and freedom are combined. But this is true only because this teaching is precisely an integral element in the Church herself, who can bear witness to herself because she has received her mission from Christ. Only in virtue of this fact is scripture the word which can command obedience. I cannot decide to check the Church's credentials, as it were, by taking scripture away from her (even though it properly belongs to her) and by invoking it against her as a criterion apart. It is *she* who submits herself to the guidance of scripture. But it is not for me to check or to verify whether in fact she is doing this, for in attempting such a thing I would be setting myself up apart from the Church in order to judge her and to see whether in fact she was really doing this. The only guarantee that she is allowing herself to be guided by scripture is her own Spirit. If I wanted to take scripture alone as the sole concrete embodiment of the word of God which commands my allegiance, then, whether I realised it or not, only two alternatives would be open to me: either I would be entering into dialogue with a book which as such was incapable of defending itself against my wrong ideas or of offering any resistance to my false interpretations, and in relation to which I must in the nature of things have the upper hand, *or* (the second alternative) I would have to have recourse to the Spirit of the Lord which gives this book its life and defends it. But in that case, once more, the question would have to be raised as to whether in the last analysis it was the book upon which the Spirit had descended and not rather the men whom that Spirit had sent to proclaim his message and so, amongst other things, to attest *a priori* to the fact that what they wrote had come from the Spirit himself. And when the question is put in this form as to whether the inspiration of the Spirit bears in the first instance upon the book or upon the men sent by that Spirit, the answer can only be: upon the men.

The conclusion of all this is that he is truly a believer who hearkens to the Church and believes in the Church.

In our attempt to define what the right approach should be to the problems which arise when some specific dogma is defined in the Church one further point remains for our consideration, that namely of how the faith of the Church makes itself clearly perceptible to us in the Church.[1] A doctrine of the faith can be made explicit simply by the fact that it is preached by the official teachers of the Church universally throughout the world, and that it is believed by the hearers of the word. Those properly authorised to perform this duty of the 'ordinary' proclaiming of

---

[1] On the whole range of questions connected with this problem cf. especially K. Rahner – K. Lehmann, *Mysterium Salutis* I, J. Feiner – M. Löhrer eds. (Einsiedeln, 1965), pp. 622–707, esp, pp. 639 ff., 692 ff., 769 ff., 7774 ff. (with extensive bibliography).

doctrine are the bishops as successors of the apostles in union with the bishop of Rome as the successor of Peter, the head of the apostles. What these bishops preach with the assistance of the Spirit as the one faith of the Church as a whole and as the word of the living God who reveals himself *is* the word of the Lord, and as such is binding in conscience upon us to believe. But the proclamation of the Church's teaching can also take other forms. Prior to a new and more emphatic promulgation of teaching the Church can give added strength to her own teaching and her faith in general by bringing together the official teachers of the Church, the bishops together with the Pope, and thereby providing an assurance that what the individual official teacher is teaching and what his Church has learnt from him and holds to be true is in fact the teaching and the faith of the Church as a whole, and is thereby confirmed by the witness of God himself. In this way the teaching and understanding of the faith on specific points can acquire an intrinsic certainty, and the council can then go on to proclaim it solemnly by an extraordinary act of the teaching authority of the Church. Yet a third course is conceivable, one which, so to say, constitutes a middle path between the ordinary and extraordinary acts of the Church's teaching authority. In conformity with the position enjoyed by the bishop of Rome among his brethren, in virtue of which he is the teacher in an immediate and direct sense of them, the bishops, and all the faithful also, and in virtue of which he has the task of strengthening their faith, he, the bishop of Rome, as the successor of Peter, and as the chief teacher and shepherd of the whole Church, can lay down authoritatively what is in fact the official teaching of the Church and the faith of the Church as a whole. The Church can reflect upon the tenets of her own faith and define her position in regard to them as binding in conscience upon the individual, and when she does this the Spirit of God does not permit her to fall into error. Furthermore, as the chief teacher of the Church the Pope occupies that position in the Church as a whole at which, even if only in principle, this infallibility of hers acquires its concrete embodiment. For these reasons, when as shepherd in this supreme sense he promulgates his teaching in a definitive manner for the whole Church he enjoys that immunity from error[2] with which God willed his Church to be endowed in her knowledge of him. His *'ex cathedra'* definition is

---

[2] For the differences of opinion on this 'freedom from error' cf. K. Rahner, 'The Church and the Parousia of Christ', *Theological Investigations* VI (London & Baltimore Md, E.T. 1969), pp. 295–312.

infallible. It is this because the Lord ordained that his *Church* should act as the foundation and the support of truth. The Pope is equipped with this freedom from error to the extent that he is on the one hand a member of the Church and on the other as such precisely the visible head of the Church. And in virtue of this his decision is 'of itself' binding upon all the faithful in such a way that if it were false the whole Church would fall into an error of faith.

The manner in which a conciliar or papal definition of doctrine of this kind comes into existence in the concrete can assume the most varied forms. It can be developed in the midst of fierce controversies or against a background of peace. It can be directed against some heresy that is in process of arising or it can constitute the peaceful culmination of a process of self-reflection by which the Church discovers her identity anew in the developing awareness of her faith. Viewed in terms of practical human expediency it can be evoked by the most varied situations in the field of human thought: by developments in theology, by certain attitudes arising in the realm of spirituality, by experiences, whether good or bad, which the Church undergoes in the course of her history, or by a thousand other factors. It is conceivable that these human situations, which in practice have acted as stimuli and so contributed to such a definition of faith, were of a nature that was anything but pleasant or welcome: the rivalries of opposing schools, political influences, unenlightened devotionalism, reactionary tendencies and resentments – all these can be, and have already been, contributing factors in this sense. As such their influence can be discerned right from the outset of the history of dogma and of the councils.

It is perfectly possible that – if we may put it in this way – the divine logic in such events may be far from simply coinciding with what human logic and human designs would have suggested in arriving at such a decision. The theology arising from the prior deliberations which, at the human level, constituted a contributing factor towards an eventful decision of this sort can in historical terms be ill-informed. Technically speaking it may have been far too limited in its outlook. Humanly speaking it may have been grossly inadequate and lacking in vitality. Such a decision may – viewed purely historically and from a 'this-worldly' standpoint – have been taken in an intellectual atmosphere which later turned out to be unfortunate or at least overtaken by historical events, and which therefore disappeared. Such considerations may even strike the contemporaries of those engaged in making the decision and those actually involved in the conflict of ideas which precedes it. It may fill such people with anxiety and fear, and, from the human point of view, make it immeasurably more difficult for them to give their assent of faith to such a definition. Such a definition can, however true it may be, be in a certain sense 'one-sided'. I mean by this that there may be other truths, no less true than the one actually defined, which it may be necessary to set alongside it in order to provide a counterpoise to it, and so to ensure that it is the truth in all its aspects and as a balanced whole that is actually proclaimed. Yet in the actual definition which is produced these further supplementary truths may fail to be expressed at the same time and with equal clarity. All this is part of the human lot to which we are all subject; our experience of the divine truth necessarily takes place in the history of the Church, in our own human history. Yet in all the vicissitudes of that history it never ceases to be the word of God. It can be degraded; it can be circumscribed in the interests of human – all too human – ambitions, feelings etc.; it can be unworthy in its formulation through human short-sightedness and narrow-mindedness. Even to the view of a Christian – for this too is subject to human limitations and short-sightedness – it may seem inexplicably bound up with, and conjoined to error, to the point of being logically speaking hopelessly paradoxical. As a result every instinct, and even the conscience of such a Christian may be in revolt against it. But there is one thing which it cannot do: cease to be what it is, the truth of God in the mouth of the Church. But this is precisely what would be the case if what the Church with her ultimate teaching authority, proclaimed as her faith were in fact to turn out to be error. The divine truth has an extremely human history. This may be. Blessed is he who is not scandalised at the servile guise in which he encounters it!

Such a truth, defined as doctrine by the Church, may have a psychological background as avid for new ideas as that of the Greeks, as enthusiastic as that of the Romans, as complicated and recondite as that of the Germans. It may have all the limitations of 'primitive' (i.e. held back from developing) theology. We may have the impression that those who formulated it had no profound understanding of the restrictions imposed upon those who were 'against' this doctrine in the period when the faith of the Church was first achieving its self-awareness. It may be that the theologians who were 'for' this doctrine achieved a most unjust victory in influencing the Church's official teaching in this way, yet believe that it has thereby been confirmed that they are the 'better' theologians. All this may be the case, and much else besides of a similar nature. But this does not mean that one should allow one's attention to be diverted from the ultimate reality and the profundity of what is taking place when the teaching of the Church is made explicit in its authentic reality as the outcome of her reflecting upon herself. One who does allow his attention to be diverted in this manner is like the man who will only allow that something is alive when the life in it can be defined in terms of 'organic chemistry', one whose idea of the things pertaining to the spirit is limited to those phenomena which can be tested by the methods of association psychology or behaviourism. It must be insisted once and for all that it is not theology *alone*, whether in its philological or its historical branches, nor is it personal logical deductions *alone* that define the limits within which we must remain in order rightly to understand the Church's teaching. Rather the Church herself, who possesses the Spirit, defines those limits. This Spirit and his power cannot be translated in any adequate sense into the work of the exegete with his philological investigations, or into the work of the theologian with his researches into history, or into that of the logician with his methods of speculation. Certainly the Spirit does work in all of these fields, but he is always more than the sum total of this work. Any other interpretation would draw the knowledge which faith brings down to the level of mere secular knowledge. No-one can test out this working of the Spirit in his own person. No one can say 'See, it is precisely *there*, and what is there is nothing else than this working of the Spirit'. All that one can do is as a Christian who believes in the Church and in her Spirit to say: 'If the Church speaks so solemnly and definitively then the Spirit *has already* performed his work: in the work of the theologians, in the prayers of the devout, in the researches into scripture. The Spirit works through all this, and – a little perhaps – in spite of all this, and certainly his working extends beyond all this. He who entertains reservations with regard to this Spirit, he who wants to subject his power to criteria which he himself can apply is, in effect, denying the true nature of the Church. (He might seek to use criteria in this sense by attempting, for instance, to establish whether the historical method really has been properly applied – obviously according to his own personal judgment – or whether the scriptural exegesis on which the official teaching is based is up to the standard of modern criticism – again, obviously according to his own judgment, or up to the standards of 'science', of which, of course, the individual himself is the authentic representative). When the teaching authorities of the Church require the assent of faith to some defined doctrine, then there are no precautions or safety measures (whether in the writings of the Church or in any *a priori* established methods of theology) to ensure that the Spirit of the Church is not making any mistake.

All this should not be taken as implying that the Church should either underestimate or neglect either honest exegesis, genuine historical theology, true logic or information of all kinds and ranging over as wide an area of human knowledge as possible. For the Pope, the Council and the theologians alike it is a solemn duty conscientiously to avail themselves of all these means. They cannot leave it to the Spirit as though he were present for the purpose of dispensing them from what they can and must perform for themselves. If they neglect this duty either wholly or in part then God has means enough and punishments enough in his providence and judgment to teach the individuals concerned that they must not tempt God. But even when those actively engaged in preaching and developing the Church's teaching (or alternatively reducing it to stagnation) must be condemned as sinful and stupid men, still even in this case – indeed more than ever in this case – the faults of men remain encompassed by the pity and truth of God, and cannot escape the truth of God. When a man acts and speaks definitively as the Church's official representative, and in the name of God, then however sinful his way of exercising his responsibilities may be, he will never succeed in changing the truth of God into error. In certain cases proof, whether real or supposed, may be adduced that the human element in the process of arriving at a doctrinal definition on the part of the Church is vitiated by the faults of wrong information, over-hastiness, narrow-mindedness or theological over-traditionalism. But this is never a proof that in such a case God himself has allowed human error to be promulgated in place of the attestation of his own truth. In the proclamation of the Church's truth the guilt of the human instruments is no criterion for denying that what she proclaims is true and binding and sublime.

PART TWO

Mysteries of the Life of Jesus

7

CHRISTMAS, THE FESTIVAL OF ETERNAL YOUTH

As the festivals return each year in their inexorable rhythm it is difficult to speak of them in a way that is worthy to any extent at all of the eternal youth of the mystery that we celebrate. Preacher and hearers alike are weary in heart and spirit. The gospel words, consecrated as they are by a holy tradition, are in their effect upon us, like window panes that have become misted over. They actually obscure our vision of the reality that lies beyond. The words fall from the pulpit like dead birds from a wintry sky. And all this is only one symptom of the general weariness that pervades our hearts, a weariness that comes from the experience of disappointment and futility, and which is our silent companion as we journey towards death.

But it is precisely because of this that the festival has so vital a contribution to make for us of today. It is the festival of the birth of him who is the Son of God and true man, of him who, in his creaturely being and activity, was so totally and radically given over to God right from the outset that in very truth his life in its creatureliness is the life of God. It is not a festival which is held in celebration of a past that has long since vanished, but one which celebrates a present, this in turn constituting the beginning of an eternal future that is even now approaching. It is the festival of the birth of eternal youth. A child is born to us, but not a child who simply begins to die from the moment when it starts to live. This child is rather one in whom the eternal youth of God breaks in upon this world definitively and victoriously; into this world, which seems only able to go on living in that the death of one of its inhabitants makes way for another to be born. To that extent this world of ours cannot escape from the despairing cycle of birth and death. What we celebrate today is the advent of that child whose true youth is not restricted merely to that meagre stock of life which is allotted to *us* at birth and which is slowly but inexorably used up in the course of our lives, but is rather the eternal youth of God himself, the youth of God who, eternally ancient yet eternally new, is the endless fulness of eternal life. This eternal youth has taken root in that sphere in which we, who are under sentence of death, still live. Thereby it has not simply abolished death, but has undertaken the higher enterprise of making life victorious, of submitting itself to death in order to make death itself a means by which we ourselves can make our own this eternal youth of God. At Christmas he whose death was the birth of our eternal life himself already began to die. It was on this day that it was revealed for the first time that the life that is allotted to us on our pilgrimage is not merely something that we inherit from former generations, not merely cosmic energy, not merely the spirit which, in itself, is free from earthly limitations only to the extent that it can be painfully aware of its own finitude. The life of which we are now speaking is rather the eternal fulness of the life of God himself, which knows no death, offered to us as free creatures, so that when we accept this life of God himself it may bring about eternal life in us. Right from the very origins this life too has been made present in the world, and it drives the history of the world onwards with a speed that grows ever more daring so that its progress is accelerated not by terror of death and the void but by that life which lies at the very heart and centre of it, and which God himself has decreed. So has it always been. But in the child who has been born today (we can say 'today' because his birth at that point in history is precisely not something that belongs to a vanished past) something has been revealed for the first time upon the visible surface, so to say, of historical reality. And this is that God, whose glory transcends all transient things is himself, as an act of his own free grace, the ultimate power which lies behind the world. Or let us see this same truth the other way round. It is precisely in our minds and hearts that the experience of the history of the world can properly take place. And when in our minds and hearts we experience this ultimate and intrinsic dynamism in history, tending towards the infinite, we can in all confidence give the name of 'God' to the goal towards which this dynamism is tending, and to the interior power of it. Thereby we can actually perceive for the first time what the word 'God' really means. This is something that was initially revealed and initially brought to its fulness in the Christmas child. For this is the child who today has entered upon the journey of his own personal history, a journey which leads through death right to God himself. And when this child arrives at that point his whole being is totally transformed, for the end of this journey is that state which we are accustomed to call the resurrection. In him the world has won its first definitive victory. For the first time it has achieved its predestined transformation into the life of God himself. For the first time the high points of its history have been plunged into the unapproachable light. Today that victory has commenced which proceeds from the innermost depths of God's own eternal nature, to seize the world at one single point, the point that is called Jesus, and to take it up into the innermost life of God, full of eternal youth.

How frigid and artificial all this sounds – what we can say of Christmas as the birth of eternal youth! Words such as these have to be turned by the individual into the life of his own heart unless they are to remain at the level of mere rhetoric. But how can such a transformation of words from without into the reality within one's heart be possible? For this there is no blueprint. But at the same time we can say this much: Act first and foremost as he who has been born today acted in his own life. He had to do with the lilies of the field in all their beauty, with the sparrows, with the fresh green ears of the growing corn, with his mother, with the malice of his enemies, with hunger and thirst, with the bewilderment of his friends, in short with life just as it is lived from day to day in its bitterness and its beauty, without any falsification, without exaggerating either the good or the evil in it. When you accept *this* life, opening yourself simply, trustfully, obediently and without protest to its single ineffable meaning, a meaning which pervades it throughout in all its incalculable complexities, then you have begun to celebrate Christmas as the festival of eternal youth, for then your life will keep flowing, ever open to fresh experiences which will not be frozen either by that obtuseness which kills or by some obstinately held ideology which seeks to act as schoolmaster and so to provide a wise guide to life as it leads on to ever-fresh surprises. But you, when you open yourself to the inner meaning of life in this sense, do not give life its meaning *ab externo*, but rather let that meaning that is already present, even if mysteriously, in its innermost depths, rise up from the roots of your nature, endowed as it is with grace, in a quite simple and unremarkable manner into the sphere of freedom, where it finds expression in the so-called everyday virtues. We are concerned here with the God-given meaning of existence which is intrinsic in those acts which are performed in freedom, and thereby given finality and permanency. It is this meaning that becomes the mystery which you now accept and which you entrust yourself to for guidance.

Listen, then, to the quiet of your own heart. The message of Christmas's eternal youth must come from within in order that the message which comes from without, from the pulpit, can be understood and translated into living reality. Perhaps then you will first hear many terrifying voices, the words of which seem to be running into each other in confusion: the voices of everyday cares, of the disappointments of life, of secret longings and many others; a strange choir! They are like an orchestra in which the instruments are first trying out their powers independently, and in which no kind of harmony seems yet to have been achieved. Rightly understood, however, all the voices of the heart which one can hear if one keeps quiet enough, speak of the youth of eternal life, however complex and confusing the manner in which these voices seem to break across one another. For the voices of love, of peace, of trust, of protection, of the blessings of a life that is exalted above the common, speak explicitly of a youth that endures for ever, and is subject to no limitations. And the voices of disappointment, of emptiness and of doubt are in fact once more simply protests against death, and as such themselves bear witness to the life of which we have been speaking. For a death that was more absolute and more comprehensible would simply be accepted in its own right. Such a death would give rise to no protests. Those subject to it would simply accept it for what it is, and want to die. Death is in no sense a counterpart to life, on an equal footing with it. The effect of grace upon us is that we experience an absolute and unconditional longing for eternal life. And in the light of this all experience of death and all sense of protest against death arising from it is seen to be simply something secondary and derived. It is there merely because life has not yet run its full course in freedom through history.

But when all the voices of this life blend into a single basic harmony in the quiet of one's heart, and all the movements are combined in the one single movement which is basic and primary, when this single basic movement of life is neither interrupted nor held back by any attitude of mistrust or any secret doubts, then it can, on the contrary, achieve the fulness of its nature as sheer infinite freedom. Then all the forces which are innate in man, and which have their ultimate source in God himself, speak together and say: 'I believe in eternal life'. But when the inner man trembles and quails before the utter boldness of his own demand for eternal life, when all this seems to the heart in its poverty almost too good to be true, then the voices of the heart must hearken to the message of the child that is born today, and in the harmony of both these voices together the miracle of a sure faith in eternal life, that is in the birth of Christ, our eternal youth, can be worked in our own hearts. Both voices together, that of the spirit and that of history can become one, do actually become one, because one and the same deed of God has created both voices and sustains them in being in a single act of God's bestowal of himself upon the world. This one word formed out of two separate words promises the youth of eternal life, and it effects what it proclaims, for it is the creative word of God himself. And this word has fashioned the void that is in our life, dedicated as it is to death, only in order to fill that void by imparting to us the plenitude of its own infinite and boundless life. Let heaven rejoice, let the earth exult – so we sing today. A child is born to us. Today the day of the new redemption has dawned. Who, then, has come? He who will accomplish what is new in the old, for the old is still there. What does he accomplish? He accomplishes his own presence in us. Who is he? The unique and ineffable mystery which, nevertheless, we really do apprehend. *How* has he come? The answer came in the form of a question; God came as man in order that we might understand that by the power of the grace which is in it the question, even as it is put, contains its own answer within it. But even then how has this ineffable mystery actually *come* to us, when already and at all times it pervades our existence? It is because it is with us now not as something that is remote and that judges us, but rather as something that is unspeakably near to us and that brings us pardon; something by means of which all who love sustain their lives. And this ineffable mystery has also come because it willed to come in spirit and flesh since man as a unified compositum can be redeemed only in both of these. But what *effect* does this ineffable mystery have, which we call God? It brings us the youth of eternal life in the midst of our mortality, our blindness and our futility. Do you believe this? Lord I do believe, help thou my unbelief! If you believe you have eternal life. And if you think that you do not believe have trust! God will bestow belief upon you, that belief that is recognisable to him. A child is born to us. The eternal youth of the immortal God has appeared as the true interiority of our own life.

PRAYER

God, the eternal mystery of our life, by the birth of your own word of love in our flesh you have made the glory of your life in its eternal youth into our life, and have caused it to appear in triumph. Grant us that when we experience the disappointments of our lives we may be enabled to believe that your love, which you yourself are and which you have bestowed upon us, is the eternal youth that is our own true life.

8

HOLY NIGHT

EVERYWHERE in the world and every year when these days come round the talk is of the 'holy night', that is the night of *Christmas* (= German 'Weihnacht', literally 'consecrated night'), and everywhere 'Silent night, holy night' is sung. This way of referring to Christmas is simply an echo of the liturgy. For the mystery of the birth of the Lord and his resurrection are the only two mysteries the liturgical celebrations of which begin during the night. And the liturgy calls this night of Christmas the 'nox sacratissima', the night of supreme holiness and consecration. The Epiphany, the Ascension and Pentecost are festivals of the day. But at Christmas and Easter the night is the time in which the divine mystery of salvation enters into our lives. As the reason why this should be so in the case of Christmas we might be tempted to suggest that it was from considerations of fittingness and privacy for these are necessary at any birth. But the fact that Christmas and Easter are sacred *nights* shows that something more is intended by the celebration of night as holy in this case than simply the quiet and privacy which should attend upon the beginning of any human life. And this serves as an indication to us that there is some common factor which applies to both festivals.

Taken together these two festivals are the festivals of the beginning of our redemption. Taken together they give promise of that day for which we are waiting in faith. It is because both of them celebrate the beginning of the victory of a day that is eternal, because, taken together, they signify the victory of a new beginning – it is for these reasons that both of them take the form of celebrations of supremely holy nights.

There is a strange ambiguity about the phenomena of our human world which serve as the symbols of salvation (or the loss of salvation). This is not because it is possible for man, faced with these simple things of the earth, to 'get everything mixed up'. Where genuine signs and manifestations of God's salvation are concerned man does not 'get mixed up'. The real reason why these symbols should be ambiguous is that these things, which are the signs of salvation, are subject to change as the history of salvation unfolds, for this history is also the history of the world, and these signs are themselves drawn into the history of salvation as it unfolds from Adam right up to the second coming of Christ, in which salvation comes into the world (and not simply into the spirit) in its full actuality. The relationship in which these symbols stand to the history of salvation is not that of static and immutable entities. They are not simply 'used' for the purpose of pointing to something outside themselves that has nothing to do with their own intrinsic natures. It is because the world itself has been drawn into this process of change which is taking place in the 'now' of the period since Christ, and which is to issue in a new heaven and a new earth, and it is because this change is still continuing, that these things, considered precisely as signs, are so strangely ambiguous. This is why they speak to us of both the old and the new.

The symbolism of night is a case in point. Is night not the symbol of that time when no one can work (Jn 9, 4), of darkness and of the shadow of death, in which we sinners are imprisoned (Lk 1:79), of that sinister darkness which overtakes us, and in which we cannot remain (Jn 12:35 f., 46)? Is not every night a reminder of that night in which *he* was betrayed, and in which Judas went out (Jn 13:20; 1 Cor 11:24; Lk 22:53), of that night in which the most that can be hoped for is that it is already far advanced and that day is coming at last (Rom 13:12), that night in which a man's soul will be required of him (Lk 12:20), and which threatens constantly to become fixed and permanent in the form of the 'exterior darkness'? And yet ... Night is also the time when the Lord comes (Lk 12:38), appearing at midnight as a bridegroom arriving at the nocturnal marriage-feast (Mt 25:6). Night can be the time of heavenly visions full of consolation and divine guidance (Acts 16:9; 18:9 etc.), the time when the Son raises his heart in prayer to his Father (Lk 6:12). And was not that night when he came to his own, to the dark stable of the world, filled with heavenly song (Lk 2:8 ff.)?

Our night is on the point of becoming a holy night. The day has not yet come to which there is no longer any evening. That time still prevails which holds all things in bondage to the law of death; that time which dissolves things, deprives them of their firm outlines and draws everything back into a darkness inhabited by the ghosts of the past. One can utter lyrical praises to this night of ours as the time of stillness and unity in which all things are gently reconciled; as that which provides a basis for a general stillness, rest and harmony which embraces all things, and yet which is pregnant of all that the future contains as well; as the time when everything returns to itself once more, in order to begin afresh to achieve a brighter future. One can praise the night on the grounds that it is richer than the day, for day makes things clear only by separating them off one from another. One can imagine that it is the night that is the time that is full of mysteries and that by comparison with what it promises day is a mere disappointment, for night does not yield up its hidden riches to the day. But all these experiences of what night means would be so much false romanticism, or else the faint afterglow, as it were, of our enjoyment of day; for night is that which issues from the death of day, and in itself it is really nothing more than empty darkness. It would be false romanticism in this sense if it were not for the fact that into our night-time one has been born who is more than merely one element among the rest, caught up in the despairing cycle of day and night. This cycle consists of an incessant alternation of these two elements, in which neither can prevail over the other. For each of the two elements, day and night, as its turn comes round, must perforce call the other into being and give way to it, and thereby the radical insufficiency of each is revealed. But it is not in virtue of its very nature that night becomes Christmas night. In itself night is simply empty darkness, and it would be false to the facts to pretend that this intrinsic emptiness of night could ever be a hidden fulness. The reason that our night can become, in the deepest and most all-pervasive sense, Christmas night is that he has been born who, as Son of the Father and Word of the Father, is above all time and above the world itself. It is because he who has been born in the time of night is, from his very origins, not a child of time at all, that is of day and night. Every night can be Christmas night because he was born into our night, and thereby filled it with every kind of promise and every kind of miracle; because God has sent down his grace upon the emptiness, the poverty and the darkness of night, and because he has predestined it to issue into the day of his own light, a day to which there shall be no evening. It is in virtue of this, and only in virtue of this that night becomes the promise of that true day. Only because of this is it that day which is already on the point of dawning, the time in which the light shines darkly because the fulness of it is already so inexpressibly near. Saving history as Christians understand it is not simply an interpretation of the natural order such that even without any such interpretation the order would still be just the same; rather it is the process by which the natural order itself becomes radically and all-pervasively transformed into something which only the eye of faith can recognise for what it is, because only to the eye of faith is it apparent that nature too is involved in the order of redemption. It is only in virtue of the fact that the Word of the Father has entered into the world, and has become, in the power of his Spirit, the law which lies at the very roots of the whole natural order, that these things which are in the world can be symbols of that which is to come. Yet they are this in objective fact. And this is why it is precisely the believer, and, in the last analysis, only the believer who can afford to be a 'romantic' as he is, for instance, precisely when he sees every night as the promise and the image of the holy night of Christmas.

In that one night every night, night as such, is redeemed and consecrated. Henceforward there is no longer any darkness upon this earth which may not turn out to be the shadowy womb of eternal light. Henceforward when any man closes his eyes he cannot be sure that he will not open them again upon a greater light. Henceforward there is no *de*scent into formless darkness which may not become blessed and fruitful by leading to an *as*cent into everlasting light. There is not a single day upon this earth which, as it fades quietly into its evening twilight, cannot speak to us of the promise that a day will come to which there is no evening. That future which we await in a spirit of faith and hope as already coming to meet us we call after the day, the light, and other phenomena associated with these. And in this we are right. For these phenomena associated with light are the prime witnesses of the fact that God is pure luminous affirmation, and that the things which God has made, and which are still in process of developing, will not always be caught up in an endless cycle between two equal poles, day *and* night, light *and* darkness, yes *and* no. But is there not some special time – Christmas, for example – when the 'no' which we choose to say to this world can become a 'yes' in the language of heaven? Let us remember that it is the things that *are not* that God has called, that it is through death that life has been given to us. And again we have to recognise that *all things* come from him who is above *all things*. He cannot be expressed, therefore, even by the phenomena of this world associated with light. And yet night too is worthy of our praise. We have to recognise that this too belongs to God (Ps 74:16), and so that to the eye of our faith the light of eternity is already visible even in it, while our ears already hear the hymns of the heavenly choirs with which it is filled.

But in doing this we are acting as sober watchmen who know that God has come into our night in order to lead us forth from it into his eternal day. Christmas night (Weih*nacht*) is celebrated as the beginning of that day in which the sun will never more go down. The reason that the Christian can make the night a festival in this way, and celebrate it as supremely holy, is that he is a child of the day. Only he can look into the darkness without perverting his own nature who knows that the night is already on the point of drawing finally and for all time to its close. The Christian does not, so to say, become intoxicated with a morbid love of the night, as though it held a poisonous sweetness for him. Rather in the boldness of faith he walks bravely through the night which God has made, but which he has also transformed when he brought Christmas into being. We keep a sober watch through the night like the shepherds in the fields. And like them too in the night of our present lives we perform our everyday duties quietly and without question. And then still in the night we hear tidings of the light. There shall be no more night there (Rev. 21: 25) because *here* night has become Christmas night. This is why we can praise the night in our Christmas celebrations: 'Silent night, Holy night'.

9

PEACE ON EARTH

It is customary to speak of Christmas as a festival of peace. But if we are thinking of the Christian meaning of Christmas, and not merely of how it is celebrated in the family and the broader social units, it is not immediately obvious why it should be thought of in this way. For why should the coming of the Word of God in human flesh as an act of compassion simply in itself and as such signify peace? While it is true that scripture itself contains references to the peace which Christ brings, still this is more often and more explicitly associated with his death on the Cross. *Prima facie*, therefore, the only biblical text which seems to provide any justification for this idea is Luke's reference to the angelic choirs which appeared at Christmas and sang: 'Peace on earth to men who have found favour with God'.

Before we invoke this text, however, or before we wrongly take it as a palliative for the anxieties of life on this earth, turning Christmas into a festival of peace in the secular sense, it is fitting to give some initial consideration to what peace really means as referred to at this point in scripture.

For a point that immediately strikes one is that what the angels tell us here about the peace of Christmas follows upon what they have just said about the glory of God in the highest. And this in itself transfers us into a quite different world from that of the politicians and philanthropists who have so much to say on the subject of peace, whether sincerely or merely rhetorically according to circumstances. Peace as conceived of here in the bible is the outcome and the reflection of the glory of God. But what is this glory of God? Viewed precisely in the context of Christmas it is not primarily or initially something that *we* pay to God. It is that glory which God himself makes to shine out by performing a deed of his omnipotent compassion in the world of darkness and guilt. It is because he himself comes, therefore, because he himself condescends to us, coming to forgive us and redeem us, that God is present in the world in his glory. And it is this that makes that glory manifest to men. It is for this reason too – this is the message of scripture – that there is peace, peace at least for those who accept this glorious and saving deed of God in a spirit of faith, for those whose inward eyes and hearts are open in love to perceive and to receive what God is offering them at this point: redemption from their sins. Even so, however, the question still remains, how does peace come to him who accepts this glory of God in a spirit of faith?

Let us put the question once more: What is it which takes place at Christmas? Our reply is that the Word of God has become flesh and dwelt among us. But what does this mean? This is that inexpressible mystery which we believe because in the last analysis the only possibility open to man is to believe *either* in the abyss of emptiness and nothingness *or* in the incomprehensible mystery of hidden blessedness. All *intermediary* positions between this immeasurable abyss on the one hand, and this utter sublimity on the other, cannot in the long run be maintained. So far as we Christians are concerned it is the incomprehensible mystery of hidden blessedness that we believe in. But what we mean by this is not some kind of utopian ideal which is to come at some future point, but which has nothing to do with the present world in which we live. No, the incomprehensible mystery of blessedness – we call it God – has already entered into this world itself. God has fashioned this world with its terrors, its conflicts and its ultimate and profound instability only with the proviso that he himself will accept it just as it is, that it belongs to him, that he will endure it and bring it to its due consummation by his own power and by his own fate. That consummation, namely, which a created being can only attain to if it is supported by the reality of God himself or the environment of being which is proper to God, and not merely by the perishable beings which he has created. The eternal rejoicing of the eternal God has itself been made to become the heart of the world. Within the indissoluble unity of his own life he has enclosed all its conflicts, all the onslaughts of its denizens one upon another, internecine in intensity though they are, and has managed so to contain them that they do not break out of this unity of the divine life in which all things remain unified and tend towards the point of reconciliation as the one end of them all. The mystery of Christmas has a twofold message for us. First the conflict between creatures which are mutually opposed is taken up into the unity of the one God and Creator who is over all things. From this position of his, high over all creatures and unaffected by the opposition between them, he has created light and darkness, heaven and earth, the visible and the invisible. But there is more to it than this. Even though this conflict may be allowed to take its course and in fact be given free rein, still it is contained and already, even as it rages, it is transcended by the fact that God himself has taken into himself all things even in their conflicts one with another. This is what has taken place in Jesus. It might seem that this is too little; that such a process of reconciliation, in which conflicting creatures are taken up by God into the peace of his own unity, should take a quite different form, one in which the power and brilliance of such a deed would be made fully manifest. But to expect anything of this kind could only lead to disappointment. The reconciliation must take place in the Son of Man; in a single human life, in its pettiness, in its brevity, in its ordinariness and poverty, with its death. For if God really does accept that which we ourselves are, endures that which takes place in the internecine strife which is waged in the world outside us as well as in the interior of our own hearts, then this must be the form in which he does so accept these things. It must be small, average and unremarkable precisely in this way. Otherwise he would not in fact once more be truly and precisely in that position in which we ourselves find ourselves.

By the fact of Jesus becoming man the one who is unity itself has accepted all the complexity and conflicts of human existence and truly identified himself with them. But this cannot derogate from the ultimate reconciliation achieved by the unity which lies at the roots of his own being. Moreover this One who is unity itself has endured all this conflict, and has thereby brought it to its ultimate point of reconciliation in his own history. And it is for these reasons that what lies at the very heart and centre of all reality is peace and not that state of inward contradiction which dissipates and annihilates. Conflict there still is in the world and in the heart of man alike. Strife there still is, seemingly internecine in its intensity. All things still seem to be irreconcilably at war with one another. But however much we, caught up as we are in this disharmony and agitation, may sigh for peace as for a distant utopia, still reconciliation is already there at the heart of things. We must make sure that it is believed and accepted in that God-in-creaturehood, the glory of God, comes to be accepted. Things are at enmity one with another so long as they have not discovered the greater unity which transcends them all and at the same time unites them. The all-encompassing which already belongs to the encompassed, the reconciler who already belongs to the contradictory opposites – he is there, since God himself has become incarnate. He who does not accept this unity in a spirit of faith must not complain that his heart, his life, the world, are torn apart in conflict and devoid of peace. But the reason that we can accept God in this way is that he has come in the flesh that belongs to our world, and precisely because he has accepted all the anguish generated in this world of fleshly creatures who tear one another apart and are torn in their turn. He has accepted this in patience, in longsuffering, in endurance, in hope because he, who is our peace, has created peace by accepting flesh in its sinfulness, and by being obedient even in the midst of this internecine conflict, even to the point of death itself. Thus at that point at which patience and resignation begin to evince themselves in the heart, where there is assent to one's lot even though it is incomprehensible and crucifying, the unreserved acceptance of opposition, endurance, the humility which does not seek to understand or to control – where there is a certain sharing in the achievement of that event which took place at Christmas by the power of God: all is accepted and all has the promise of peace.

The only way in which man can have peace is to accept the incomprehensible God in the incomprehensibility of our own existence and lot. But one can accept both of these because God himself has accepted us when he himself came in the inward conflict of our own flesh. Would not the beginning of eternal peace be there if at Christmas we were to say a quiet 'Yes' to God who came, accepted us, divided and broken though we were, and in his own person brought us reconciliation and unity?

10

SEE, WHAT A MAN!

Man is a complex and changeable being. It is no blame to him not always to be the same, nor is it demanded of him that he shall be so. For this reason it is difficult to define who and what he really is. There is much that he himself cannot speak of with any willingness. He flees from himself. He is able to do this because it is only possible to reflect upon and speak of one's self when one has time and leisure to do so. But among the factors which are intrinsic to his make-up there is one in particular, that he finds it impossible to speak of, one that reduces him to dumbness. How might a portrayal of man be expected to appear if it were designed to throw precisely this element into relief? The element that makes him what he is, yet what he is unwilling to admit that he is, and is not prepared to be.

It would have to be the picture of a dying man, for though we are indeed unwilling to die, we are nevertheless given over to death to such an extent that death pervades all things for us even in this present life as a sinister power. The dying man would have to be suspended between heaven and earth, for we are not fully at home either here or there. Heaven is too remote from us, and earth too is far from being a dwelling place in which we can feel ourselves really secure. The man in our picture would have to be alone. For when we arrive at our final hour the impression is that our fellow men feel shy and embarrassed (because they, in fact, are not yet ready for that stage in their lives), and that they leave us alone. The man in the picture would have to be depicted as though two intersecting lines, one horizontal and one vertical, were passing through his body. For the heart of man is, so to say, bisected by, and becomes the point of intersection for two such lines. The horizontal one extends out on either side of him as though striving to include the whole world within its ambience. The vertical one points sheer and undeviatingly upwards as though in an effort to concentrate the whole of man exclusively upon him who is uniquely one. The man in the picture would have to be nailed fast to these. For our freedom upon this earth extends only to a certain point, the point at which it becomes limited and circumscribed by the inescapable necessities of life. The man in the picture would have to be represented with his heart pierced through, for at the end everything has been transformed into a lance which spills our heart's blood to the last drop. He would have to wear a crown of thorns, for the deepest pains come not from the body but from the spirit. And finally, since all men are in the same condition as this one man, this solitary figure would, in spite of his solitariness, have to be flanked on either side by other figures, the exact replicas of himself. We might go on from this to represent one of these figures as despairing and the other as hoping. For we never know altogether for sure whether there is more hope or more despair in our hearts as we draw nearer to death. This would more or less complete the picture. It would not represent all that is in man, but it would show what must be shown of us precisely because we are unwilling to accept this particular aspect of ourselves as true (to entertain doubts on this point is simply another way of shrinking from the recognition of this truth). All the other truths which also apply to us do not need to be represented in the picture, because we are ready and eager to recognise them as it is. Our consideration of what such a picture would reveal to us about ourselves poses a question for us which we must answer. And yet this is a question which we are unable to answer by ourselves.

This picture of ourselves which we view so reluctantly is the picture which God has set before our eyes in the death of his Son on Good Friday. And when this picture of man was to be set up before us one of those taking part in this drama said: 'Behold the man!' (Jn 19, 5). Again, in his writings Paul says of the Christians that they are those before whose eyes Jesus Christ was portrayed as crucified (Gal 3:1). To some it is a stumbling-block, to others folly, but to those who have been called the power of God and the wisdom of God (1 Cor 1:23 f.). Now if God thus sets before our eyes the picture from which we have been copied, then as we view this picture, we are not looking merely at the radical instability of our own existence. Then, in the very act of forcibly confronting us with *the* question that *we* are, God also gives us his own answer to this question. It is only because he knows the answer that the drama conjured up by his unfathomable love has brought home to us the question that we ourselves are. And since his eternal Word has itself become man and, in the fulness of his human nature, has died upon the Cross of our existence, he has spoken his answer to us, and thereby given us the initial spark of courage which we need in order to look upon this picture of ourselves, which was concealed from us, to hang it in our private rooms, to set it up by our waysides and to plant it over our graves.

To what extent, then, is this the answer of God to the question that we ourselves are?

The answer to this question might be stated in a single sentence which the Fathers of the Church have repeated again and again: 'All that was received and accepted is redeemed'. All that he accepted is redeemed because thereby it has itself become the love of God and the fate of God. He has accepted death. Therefore this must be more than merely a descent into empty meaninglessness. He has accepted the state of being forsaken. Therefore the overpowering sense of loneliness must still contain hidden within itself the promise of God's blessed nearness. He has accepted total failure. Therefore defeat can be a victory. He has accepted abandonment by God. Therefore God is near even when we believe ourselves to have been abandoned by him. He has accepted all things. Therefore all things are redeemed.

Does this pass unnoticed by us? Do we feel ourselves imprisoned in the stifling incomprehensibility of our existence, brought up against a blank wall, and unable to find any escape? Do we find ourselves quite unable to feel that everything is redeemed? Do we imagine that the darkness of Good Friday has in reality lasted continuously ever since the first Good Friday of all? Do we believe that we could accept him, the crucified one, as the image of our existence, were it not for the fact that we do not know how this man, so surrounded by pain and the darkness of death, can also be the salvation and the light of God for us in the extended death that is our life? How is the miracle of Good Friday faith brought about? It is the miracle of grace. No proof can be advanced to justify it.

But let us kneel beneath the Cross, and there pray: 'Lord I do believe, help thou my unbelief!' At least for the space of one moment let us command all else to silence, the anguish of our own heart and the poignant question of our spirit. Let us be silent in order that we can *listen*, and so hear just this one word issuing from the lethal darkness of this man in the moment of his death: 'Father into thy hands I commend my spirit'. And then – O miracle of grace! – we are able to believe that everything has been accepted by God and redeemed. For let us look more closely into this death of his, and hearken more attentively!

There is one here who is in mortal straits. He has been spared nothing. He has no illusions. This is death. He has no intention whatever of playing the hero in it. There is nothing of the poseur in him. He is not the sort of man who still acts a part even in the moment of death. He has known what is in man. Those about him, therefore, have not made his death any easier, neither those whom we call his enemies, and who feel themselves to be so, yet for whom he prays, nor those few others who, since he has managed, even in this moment of his death to think lovingly of them, have made the act of dying even harder for him. He has drained the cup of life almost to the last dregs. All is darkness without and within. He is alone with the suffocating malice of the entire world, which is stupid and at the same time diabolically malignant. He knows that the guilt of the world, which clutches ravenously for his heart and life, is not the sort of misunderstanding that turns out on closer examination to be a harmless mistake. It is the incomprehensible guilt which leads to condemnation. He is alone with this. The light of his Father's nearness is transformed, so to say, into the dark fire of judgment. There is only abandonment and feebleness left, burning and at the same time, and in an inexpressible manner, dead. Death in its stark reality has penetrated to his heart, and pierced its way into the innermost depths of his human life; death as absolute. 'My God, my God, why hast thou forsaken me?' And when abandonment and death have pervaded his whole life in this sense, then listen to what he says: 'Father into thy hands I commend my spirit'. It is a fearful thing to fall into the hands of the living God, when in an act of inconceivable love, one has identified one's self in spirit with the sins of the world. And yet when he did thus fall into the hands of the living God what he said was: 'Father, into thy hands I commend my spirit'. If there is one word in all this which is immediately and in itself worthy of our belief it is this one. This word, uttered by him in this moment, *must* be accepted. There is God the Father. One can commit all things to his hands – all things. In such a way that all things are accepted by him.

One is not forced to believe this word, uttered from the Cross to us and extending beyond us into the unfathomable depths of the mystery of existence. But one can believe it. One has only to hearken to him and to keep one's eyes fixed upon him. Then the crucified one, who is the image of our existence, also tells us the answer which God has given in him, the divine Word incarnate, to the question that we ourselves are.

11

THE SCANDAL OF DEATH

EVERY day countless number of people die. Death is the most familiar and everyday of human phenomena. So much is this the case, indeed, that it is possible to hold that we should not make very much fuss about it. Nothing in it can be altered. In the nature of things it is unpleasant for those who have to endure it, provided, of course, that they have some degree of conscious awareness of it, and naturally when the form in which they meet it is too overpowering, too brutally real and vivid, they protest. For the rest one is relieved to assure one's self that to all appearances one is not yet one's self in the toils of death, so that there is no cause for alarm. Only great statesmen, soldiers and doctors are really habituated to death, and, moreover, not over-disturbed by it, since it is others who have to die and – for the time being at any rate – not themselves. How strange all this is! For today the whole of Christendom has a death to celebrate in the most solemn manner. What is the real reason for this? Certainly it was a particularly agonising and unjust death. But death is every bit as terrifying as it occurs in the gas-chambers of Buchenwald or the mud-holes of Vietnam. What then is this celebration of Good Friday meant to signify?

First it is intended simply to serve as a sobering reminder to us of our own deaths. This is not, of course, to deny that Good Friday is first and last the day which commemorates the death of the Lord, and, in the last analysis, his death alone. But one can only truly understand and celebrate this death if one recognises and accepts that one is one's self subject to the power of death. Otherwise one is blind from the outset, and quite incapable of viewing the crucified Lord in a true light. Therefore we must initially think of our own deaths.

This, then, is the situation in which we find ourselves: we are all sitting in the prison-house of our own existence as in the condemned cell, where we are waiting until the time of execution arrives. Until then one can play at cards, enjoy the meal allotted to those under sentence of death, and for the moment forget that the prison door will soon open and we shall be called out for the last journey. But that is precisely what we must *not* forget. Animals are blind to their approaching death, or at most have some dim irrational fear of losing their lives. But we are aware of death, and must not suppress this awareness. We must live with death constantly in view. We know that we shall simply be thrust into the inexorable loneliness of death where no-one can accompany us any further, where the chatter of life ceases, and no-one can hide behind his fellow any longer. No-one can appeal to the opinion of another. The only thing that still counts at this stage is what one can take with one in death: that is I myself as I was in the ultimate depths of my own heart, that heart that was either full of love or full of spite and hidden selfishness, a nuisance to myself and others. We take nothing with us into this state of abandonment except what we ourselves are in the ultimate and radical decision of our own hearts. Already in the here and now we must weigh our life day by day on the scales of death with a view to being able one day to die our own death. We should set the worthlessness of various actions which we perform, on the one hand, against the value of other actions which we should perform on the other. It is necessary to take both into account; to learn the inward serenity of one who can in all calmness go to meet death not because he is in a state of cynical despair about it, but because he is ready to accept the mystery of death as a mystery of unfathomable significance. We should practise, even in this life, how to die, for surely it is clear that while we shall certainly pass out of life in the biological sense, it is not so clear that we have the ability to die a death that is truly human. For whatever freedom is allotted to man, at its heart and centre death lies as a factor which is wholly beyond his control.

On Good Friday we Christians continue to preach the death of that man until all have died, in order that all may learn how to die, since all are destined to die.

But what we preach on Good Friday is also the death of the one man, the Lord. It is in the case of this one man, initially, that we find the courage to believe that he was not only put to death, was not only swallowed up and engulfed by the absurdity of existence, but that he himself died. In other words he has made death into his own act, in which he accepts the inconceivable which is beyond all human control, and himself acts out what has to be endured. This one man, whom we take as the prototype of those who die, and whom we resolve to follow into death, is Jesus. He is dead just as we shall die: in that darkness into which he uttered his groan: 'My God, my God, why hast thou forsaken me?' His death included all that makes death terrifying, and all that death entails was truly endured in his person: the physical anguish, the brutal injustice which was an additional factor in his case, the hatred of his enemies, the mockery of their self-assurance, the collapse of his life's work in ruins, the betrayal of his friends, and, over and above all these terrible factors, precisely the banality of death, which is present wherever it occurs, together with the lamentations of those one leaves behind, who are powerless to help one; the gasping for breath and all the anguish from which no-one returns, the utter and complete loss of power, in which one ceases to be heroic.

Now something still remains to be said concerning the death of Jesus, and it is the most vital point of all. In spite of this, however, it does not entail any alteration to, or revision of the significance which we have already seen in his death and ours. No, the manner of death which he has to undergo is determined by the manner in which he was present then, and the manner in which he will be present among us in the future. So much is this the case that we are really dumbfounded at his words: 'My God, why hast thou forsaken me?' This is what every man will say, whatever he takes as his God in his own personal life. It may be the true God, or it may be money, or success, or science, or social progress, or his children, or carnal lust, or any other of the idols which he sets up upon the altar of his heart. These collapse into ruins, and even the true, the ineffable God seems to have given in and to have disappeared from the temple of the heart, leaving it silent. One seems to be engulfed so that all that one can feel is the sheer numbing physical pain until even that too has spent itself. What still remains to be said concerning Jesus' death and ours is not designed to spare us from death in this sense. Nor do we need in any sense to make special efforts to die in an heroic way or in the manner depicted by Christian tradition. And yet there still is something more to be be said about this death, so brutal and at the same time so banal as it is. It remains to be said not because it is consoling, for perhaps the effect which it will have upon us will be very far from consoling. Perhaps it will fail to console us because at the roots of our being we are already numbered among those who die, and therefore have to die cruelly unconsoled. The point that still remains to be made is necessary, rather, because God has said it to us all at once and all in one in Jesus, in his life, in his understanding of himself, in his death and in his resurrection. What has he said? It is that it is not until we have reached this point, at which our lives and our experience have been reduced absolutely to nil that the true life begins for us. This should not be understood in the sense that this true life is a further continuation of our present lives, stretching out beyond our deaths in a temporal prolongation. Rather it is because that quality which constitutes the distinguishing characteristic of our lives achieves in this true life its final transcendence over the whole of time. And this quality is the freedom and faithfulness of the love which comes from God, which bears him in itself, and which must be freely accepted and put into practice in the act of living. It is not as though this were inherent in the very nature of death, with all its absurdity. In itself death simply poses the most radical question of all. It calls everything into question and thereby forces us to decide whether we shall opt, even against our own consciences, for those factors in our lives which are consoling and at the same time controllable, so long as it is in our power to do so, or whether we shall give our ultimate loyalty to our consciences, even though they appear to do nothing for us. But in this question which death poses there is another answer, a blessed answer, which is already included in the question itself. This is because Jesus has died, or, to put it in a more prudent and exact form, because that which death, for all its absurdity, contains within itself in the way of mystery and blessing, has been given in him and in him made worthy of belief; because, to put it still more accurately, God has redeemed our death by decreeing that the death which he imposes upon us is a death in Jesus Christ the crucified one, in him in whom God himself took our death upon himself and made it his own. It must be reiterated that death in all its stark reality is not thereby removed from us. But we can die *this* death, in which the assurance offered us by the Son can become ours, and in which the element of incomprehensibility and of anguish which death contains can actually be a sharing in that which Jesus endured in his death. In this sense the death of Jesus is died by many who do not explicitly believe in him at all, or know him by name, yet who, by remaining faithful to the end, let themselves be received by death without thereby pronouncing a curse upon life. The death of Jesus is died by many because in one's brethren too one can encounter the death of the Son of Man, who lets himself be discovered in his brethren even by those who believe that they do not know him. For to accept one's death is in itself a way of knowing him and entering into communion with him. The life of man is indeed full of doubts. But the worst doubt of all is that involved in refusing to accept the truth of life itself.

There is no consolation which can render us immune to such doubts. But there is the incomprehensible mystery that the doubt *itself* can be consoling if it is patiently and willingly endured, and not itself erected into the last of the idols of our human lives. *This* consolation in death is called by the true name of Jesus of Nazareth. Today we, who are dying, stand at the point where he died and preach his death and our own until he comes in our death.

12

'HE DESCENDED INTO HELL'

WHEN we come to consider Holy Saturday we can notice something strange about it. In our religious life we miss it out. We celebrate Good Friday and Easter, the death and resurrection of the Son of Man, who is our salvation. But the day which falls between these two, namely Holy Saturday, is overlooked by us. It carries no significance in our religious life, in the catechism of our heart. And yet there is a significance in this day that goes beyond what the printed catechism has to tell us about it. It is a significance that we ourselves acknowledge every time we say the Apostles' Creed, the earliest and most hallowed formula of our faith. 'He descended into hell'. This is the clause devoted to Holy Saturday and giving expression to the inward significance of it. Now we might say that although this credal formula is so short, consisting as it does of only a couple of short lines, it does mean that not only God and eternal life, not only the Lord and his Church, not only Good Friday and Easter, but Holy Saturday too has a special article of the creed devoted to it. And surely it follows from this that in our religious life Holy Saturday needs to be marked by something more than merely a kind of pause between the two great days on which we commemorate the event of our redemption. In this sense Holy Saturday could be said to have a content of its own and a value of its own in our lives. In view of this it ought to be celebrated as the *anamnesis*, the sacred commemoration of the reality which we acknowledge when we utter the words 'He descended into hell'.

But in that case what do we mean by this credal formula? And why should not the words we utter in it refer simply to a past event as such, something precisely which we continue to remember as having taken place long ago? Why should these words in the credal formula refer rather to something that still continues to have a vital effect upon our lives in the present? It is because this particular aspect also of the life and death of the Lord is something that we have to live out in our own lives until all is consummated.

Let us examine the faith of the early Church upon this point from the period of the New Testament itself up to the fifth century, in which this declaration that Christ descended into the realm of the dead was accorded a place in the Western form of the Apostles' Creed. For it is precisely the faith of the Church on this point that has been expressed in a fixed and crystallised form in this article of the creed concerning Christ's descent into hell. From such an investigation it can be established unmistakably that two ideas at any rate, distinct though mutually interpenetrating, are being expressed in this formula: First, Jesus truly did die and, moreover, the death that he died is the only one that can avail to redeem our death; second, this death brought redemption and release to all those members of the human race who had died before Christ and who, even though at their deaths they were just and in principle saved, had to wait for the salvation laid up for them until the fulness of salvation as such had been achieved in Christ. Both of these two real factors, therefore, are covered by the single credal formula. But of the two it is only to the first that we propose to devote some measure of consideration here, since it has a more decisive effect upon our lives.

'He descended into hell'. Or, to give a clearer and more precise rendering, he descended into the realm of the dead. This assertion, therefore, declares initially that Jesus truly did die. When we read Peter's great Pentecost sermon in the Acts of the Apostles (2:22–36) we can see that the underlying intention here is to state who Jesus was and what befell him in his life. Thus when Peter wants to tell us that Jesus was the one who was put to death and rose from the dead then, in order to express the fact that this was in very truth a real death, he says that death held Jesus as it were in fetters, that he was swallowed up by Hades, Luke's rendering of the Hebrew word Sheol, which in Jewish theology signifies the realm of the dead. The Jews believed in some sort of survival after death, and so according to their anthropology the dead man entered the realm of the dead, a 'place', that is to say, if we may express this unimaginable state of survival after death in such terms at all. The devotional theology of Jesus' own time had developed these ideas and had (rightly) conceived of a wide variation in terms of happiness or woe in the states of life open to man in his survival after death. These were determined, it was held, according to the sort of life which the dead man had lived while still on this earth. An instance in which this is clearly brought out is Jesus' own parable of Lazarus the poor man and Dives the rich reveller. Nevertheless all the dead were included in a *single* sphere, a single basic state. And this is designated precisely as Sheol, the realm of the dead. When, therefore, Peter wanted to bring out the fact that Jesus had truly died, then no other way of doing this was open to him than by explicitly declaring, 'Jesus descended into the realm of the dead, Sheol or Hades'. Probably Paul too is thinking of this when in Rom 10:7: he speaks of one who has to descend into the 'abyss', 'that is to bring Christ up from the dead', and this one has indeed 'descended into the lower parts of the earth' (Eph 4:9 f.). In just the same way Jesus himself had said that he would be 'in the heart of the earth' for three days and three nights (Mt 12:40).

There is no doubt that these ways of expressing the truth with which we are here concerned do include a certain figurative element. The dead are certainly not in a place which lies at the innermost point of our physical earth. Indeed in terms of our conceptions of the spatial dimension of the cosmos they are not 'in place' at all. Sheol plays no part in the frame of reference provided by our physical sciences. This is not because there is not, and never could be, any such reality as this realm of the dead, but because the very nature of this state is such that it belongs to a totally different dimension from that of our finite conceptual world, and is wholly incommensurable with it. But we would fail to do justice to the full depths of meaning contained in the words we have quoted if we were to take them as signifying nothing more concerning the death of Jesus than the actual fact that he died. Over and above this they have also something to tell us about the state of being dead as this applies to him. In fact it is quite clear that these words look beyond the actual process of dying to the fact of *being in a state of death*. They therefore oblige us to ask ourselves what we mean when we say that the experience of Jesus consisted not merely in the act of dying but in the state of being dead as well. He was not simply the man who died but, over and above this, the man who was in the state of death.

What, then, are the special implications of this state of having died and of being dead which project us into some further dimension in the meaning of death itself? Since death and the state of being dead are so closely connected it is impossible to regard the two terms as wholly distinct from each other. The one throws light upon the other. The man who has died is no longer there. He has been withdrawn from us into a sphere which is remote and from which no echo returns, into darkness and silence. He has departed from us. This does not carry with it in any immediate or primary sense the connotation of having 'passed over' into 'another world'. Let us examine somewhat more closely this idea of what it means to be a dead man. The dead man has departed from this life. This world of ours, so familiar to him, so much his own as it was, the physical mode of existence in all its dimensions, all the fulness and colour of concrete reality. From all this the dead man has indeed been withdrawn, never more to return to this world in its unglorified state. Yet the form of existence which he does lead is not of the phantom- or ghost-like kind, one which has absolutely nothing to do with the worldly mode of existence. The simplicity of the spirit's mode of existence does indeed imply a certain perfection. But this is not to say that already at this stage it amounts to an absolute and definitive perfection in every possible respect. When we make this assertion we mean neither to deny nor to call in question the fact that with regard to the finitude of human nature there is an intrinsic distinction to be drawn, corresponding to the true and justifiable distinction between 'soul' and 'body'. Precisely in virtue of its openness to reality as such the spirit is not wholly removed from the world at death; indeed the underlying unity of reality as a whole actually opens up to it, so to say, at a new and deeper level. All things become present to it immediately and without distortion. For this reason the dead man is more closely and intimately united to the inward meaning of all that is real. But this totality of the real is still present to it in a peculiarly dim and remote manner. For the dead man this experience of the world in depth, as it were, is painful rather than joyful. He cannot really entertain it or express to himself that in it which is the object of desire to world and finite spirit alike, namely to come to themselves. Everything has become less real, has receded into remoteness, has become more alien and more lonely.

We recognise that this account does not cover everything that there is to say about the dead. Moreover it is quite evident that the state of death as applied to Jesus had further and quite different aspects in virtue of the fact that in death he was the one who was infinitely close to God and the one who, as dead, conquered death itself. But for all this he was precisely the *man* who died. Not only for us but also, and primarily, for him the significance of the resurrection is that it was an event that gave him something new, something which, so long as he was dead, he had had to do without. And however important it is for us on Holy Saturday not to think of him *merely* as dead, nevertheless he was in fact and in truth the man who had died. His own death was the price which he paid in order to ensure that the state of being dead should have a new significance for us. He descended into this state of death. He endured the nadir of human existence, the ultimate fall into immeasurable depths to which it is subject. And because he submitted to this fate, yielding himself up into the hands of his Father, his entry into this eternal love was initially experienced by him as a collapse into the darkness and anonymity of death, into the real and genuine state of being dead. It is precisely because he was, in an ineffable sense, the one who was alive, that he necessarily felt the disembodied state in which he continued to exist after death so intensely as something to be overcome, something unnatural. He more than any other must have felt himself, in this disembodied state, excluded from that which was his due, that which he willed to be: the one who is alive in the most intensely real sense. He who is the source of light for the entire world, and that too in the created life-principle of his own human existence in all its fulness and breadth (we call this life-principle of bodily existence the soul), was thrust by death into death – in other words to that region where there is no light and no clear bodily mode of being, so that the 'soul' is deprived of that state in which it wills to be. He was in the state of death. In deed and in truth between his dying on Good Friday and the life which he takes up on Easter Day he has his Holy Saturday. We declare our belief in the fact that he descended into the realm of the dead.

Death and life are not simply two events which follow one upon another and are distinct one from the other in human existence. They interpenetrate one another. We are in process of dying all through our lives, and what we call death is the culminating point of an act of dying that extends over the whole span of life. This is why we are constantly undergoing a foretaste of that descent into death which the Lord took upon himself. Do we not sometimes feel as though an immeasurable distance lay silently between us and the things of this world, dividing us from them? Are we not slowly in process of becoming those who depart? Are we not constantly and ever anew saying goodbye? Is not that which is familiar to us changing to an ever-increasing extent into that which is alien and almost hostile and repellant? Long before the hour in which we close our eyes for the last time we are already being drawn back into the depths of the world. This descent into the poverty of our own being has already commenced, and has been in progress ever since we received our human natures, even though only in an invisible and hidden manner, at the roots of our being. This basic condition to which our nature is subject, and which, for all our activity, we can do nothing to evade, is at the same time the factor which makes it possible for us already in the here and now really to participate with Jesus, our brother and the sharer in our human nature, in the celebration of Holy Saturday. Since we are hewn from the same block and since we too are already dying our own deaths in the midst of our lives, we are in a position to understand his fate not merely as outsiders and bystanders, but by actually sharing in it. By faith we experience that his descent into the utter feebleness of our human existence has consecrated all the 'Holy Saturday' hours in our lives. Left to ourselves all that we are would simply be solitary, defenceless and exposed in the midst of the darkness and emptiness of death. But since he has shared our fate and has redeemed us in it this Holy Saturday, in the midst of all its darkness, brings us the light of life. Since he has descended into the unfathomable and bottomless depths of the world there is no longer any abyss in human experience in which man is abandoned and alone. There is one who has gone before him and has endured all such abysses, so that we might conquer. Henceforward whatever disasters may befall, at the bottom of them all is to be found eternal life. 'He who descended is he who also ascended far above all the heavens, that he might fill all things' (Eph 4:10).

13

HIDDEN VICTORY

On Good Friday and Easter we celebrate the death and resurrection of the Son of Man, who is our salvation. But generally speaking the day which falls between these two, namely 'Holy Saturday' does not carry much weight in our religious lives. Now perhaps by failing to travel every step of the journey between Good Friday and Easter morning we are depriving the terms 'death' and 'resurrection' of something of their inner significance.

I

Manifestly Holy Saturday ought to have its due place in our life of faith, since we do in fact acknowledge the meaning of it in the Apostles' Creed every time we say 'He descended into hell' or, to give a better rendering, 'into the realm of the dead'. But what is the real message conveyed by this formula, so familiar as it is to us? For the meaning of it forms the content of this particular day.

First and foremost it declares that Jesus has truly died, because in the language of the bible 'truly to die' and 'to descend into the realm of the dead' are synonymous phrases. Let us not suppose that the underlying meaning of this clause is something which is immediately self-evident and devoid of further implications. The Son of God has truly died. He, the Son of God, the sinless, the free, he who alone, in a certain sense, is self-authenticating, he who, unlike the rest of us, is not already called in question and questionable right from the very roots of his being – he it is who, in very truth, has shared in this incomprehensible absurdity which we call death, in which it is made brutally apparent what we are: the ones who are divided against themselves, radically contingent in their being, those who take refuge from a thousand unsolved questions in the ultimate all-embracing riddle of death. He has made himself one with us in death. He has shared our ultimate fate.

There is a further message contained in these words, 'He descended into the realm of the dead'. Jesus is he who is truly in a state of death, and not merely one who dies. But what, then, does it imply, this 'being in a state of death', this being dead, over and above the actual fact of dying? While we are attempting to draw a certain distinction at this point, it does not in fact make any difference whether one particular formulation applies more especially and primarily to the act of dying while another applies rather to the state of being dead. For an assertion that the former is the case is also an assertion, at least indirectly, of the latter. The dead man is the one who has departed, the one who is silent, the one who is remote. The reason he has gone is not that he wanted, in some sense, to change to a different mode of being. Certainly this also is true. But thereby he has also, in very truth, become one who has been withdrawn from that dimension in which alone he can be wholly himself with all the fulness that his nature demands, a dimension constituted by the world, by his own body, by the concrete mode of his existence. Certainly he no longer wishes to possess all this in the form in which he possessed it before his death, unglorified and subject to corruption. But neither does he on that account wish to live the life of a phantom, a disembodied spirit. In this state of disembodiment and spirituality he may have achieved a very advanced state of perfection (This was at least the case with Jesus, who in the depths of his spirit lived in a state of absolute proximity to God in his infinity). But a disembodied spirit of this kind, remote from this world and its physical mode of existence, is still not absolutely perfect in all respects. It is like a seed which has an innate inclination to develop and grow into its due fulness of flowering and fruitfulness, like the idea of an artist which demands to be expressed in that visual form in which alone it can really achieve its due mode of existence. He who is dead and not yet risen is alive indeed, but the dimension in which he now exists is one in which, while he retains his essential identity, his nature has, so to say, been resolved into its basic constituents, and his existence has become featureless and remote from that mode which is natural to it. He has all things – indeed all things are more closely and immediately present to him than ever. He exists at the 'heart' of the world, nearer than ever before to the innermost kernel of all reality. In fact it is only now that he becomes truly near to all this. Yet in spite of this, this reality in its wholeness and stripped of all deception is present to him, as as it were, at one remove from himself. It is, so to say, separated from him as by an invisible barrier. He cannot communicate with it. Thus the dead man is open to the suffering that all this entails, but is somehow excluded from the possibility of taking action in order to make this reality his own and to express himself physically in it. What we, on our side of the dividing line, experience of the dead has its exact counterpart in what they experience from their side (though they do have other experiences as well): everything is, as it were, encompassed by an infinite remoteness. Everything is there, but how unreal it has all become, how distant and how dead! One is, as it were, engulfed in an infinite loneliness, left utterly to one's self, and at the same time alien to one's self, left exposed and defenceless in that state of being dead which is intrinsic in human nature itself.

II

Our life is hidden with Christ in God, St Paul tells us. Here is a saying that is especially appropriate to Holy Saturday. God's life is in us; the immeasurable value of Christ's humanity and the infinite future are already present to us. But the mode in which they are present is a 'hidden' one. They are, in a mysterious manner, withheld from us. They are present in that mysterious hope in which we think not of that which is to survive and to continue into later times in order to hold fast to the reality that is already present to us, but in which we are, in a certain sense, taken out of ourselves, so that the inconceivable future becomes the centre of our existence, and so becomes present to us as a mystery which we do not yet understand. This situation of hope becomes manifest on Holy Saturday. It is the situation of one who stands between a present that is already vanishing, and a future which is so far present only in hope.

Now death and life are not simply two distinct phases in human existence, the one following upon the other and quite distinct from it. They interpenetrate one another. We are dying throughout our entire life, and what we call death is the end of a process of dying that is life-long, and therefore we are constantly undergoing a foretaste of that final descent into death which the Lord has taken upon himself.

Do we not sometimes feel that between us and the things of this world lies an infinite distance and silence, separating us from them? Are we not slowly becoming those who have to say goodbye? Ah yes! It is not only in that moment which we call death, in order to conceal from ourselves that we are already, even now, in process of dying, that we descend into the underworld. It is not only in that moment that we are withdrawn into the 'heart' of the world, which at first seems to us to be a shadowy abyss. This descent, this journey to the underworld has already begun long since. At least there is a subtle orientation in that direction which affects the course of our lives at their very roots. And it is for this reason that we can truly celebrate Holy Saturday with the Lord – can already, in the here and now, share in his fate and recognise in faith that his Holy Saturday redeems and consecrates our own. Our Holy Saturday, taken in isolation from his, would simply be a state of living death. Since he has endured it and redeemed it it is the day which carries eternal life concealed within its expectant silence. For since he has descended into the underworld human life no longer culminates in an abyss into which man is cast headlong, and at the bottom of which he cannot find eternal life. Hence that saying of scripture: 'He who descends, he it is also who ascends above all the heavens in order to fulfil all things'.

The life of the present recedes from us, and it is this that we then call our life. But that fuller life which is to endure for ever is still concealed – in that silent future which we are going to meet, the future which we call by the name of 'God', and are able so to call it because our demand for the future as it should be is unconditional and infinite. For only by demanding this kind of future shall we do justice to God who comes to meet us and to be our own future. And it is in this sense that our life is hidden in God. That is at once the pain and the blessing of our life as we live it, our pain, our anguish and – let us say it in all calmness – our disappointment, so constantly renewed. Life is not as we would have it in the innermost depths and in the very centre of our hearts.

The factors of goodness, beauty and vitality in life constantly bloom afresh like an endless promise, only to die once more without having fulfilled that promise. And the promise of an eternal future, however appealing and attractive it may be, is constantly veiled under the appearance of mere illusion in the trials to which our faith is exposed, in the cares of every day. Holy Saturday lasts all our life long. Can we hold out to the end of it in sincerity, in faithfulness, in calmness and in patience, precisely as a time during which we must endure, as a time which has no festivals in the true sense, which is 'non-liturgical', just as the real Holy Saturday is said to be?

If we do this, if we supplicate for and obtain the grace of that firmness and patience which is achieved in a life that can do without any powerful or compelling movements of the senses (few of which are wholly devoid of some element of sinfulness), then this 'Holy Saturday' life of ours will suddenly be filled (though we may not try to force it to this conclusion) with the joy and sureness of its approaching Easter. One notices that precisely the final moment is sustained and lasts on into a blessed and unfathomable future, an Easter day that lasts for ever, and that is on the point of breaking out upon us, or better from within the very midst of our own lives, and becoming our true life. Perhaps too it is only in a certain freedom from tension, anxiety and care, not to be accounted for in merely rational terms, that we first become aware of the presence of this hidden life within us. At any rate it is there. It is still Holy Saturday. Our life is still hidden. But even if hidden it is already present. Its hiddenness implies that this is the moment of faith and of hope, and besides these of that love which is already with us and which will endure.

III

At Easter we are led all too easily to celebrate the resurrection with noisy jubilation, with the blaring of trumpets, with words and music. And certainly no-one can be blamed or suspected of unworthy motives if he indulges in such Easter jubilation, seeing that it is the joy of the eternal victory of life that suddenly breaks out with all its holiness and power from the heart of the believer. But to those who are still pilgrims and, moreover, who still have the path of faith to travel, to those who are more keenly aware of the death and the futility which is present in their human lives than of the glory of the life that is indestructible and eternal a gentler and more modest Easter joy is also permissible. Joy in this particular sense is also possible for those who have become tired to death under the burden of everyday toils and disappointments.

If we wish to understand Easter we must first understand ourselves, that is accept ourselves as we really are. Now we are children of the earth, and as such subject to death. This much is certain. And when we put the question to ourselves of what is to become of us, destined as we are to die, then, as both our own experience and the scriptures testify, we have no reason to assert that we are, in any ultimate sense, divided into two component parts and to ascribe two different destinies to the soul and body respectively. We are children of the earth, and precisely as such we are also spirit and freedom. And we claim a final and definitive state of freedom, responsibility and love corresponding to what we are. We must make this claim if we have really understood what these words mean. Now it clearly follows from this that we wish this final and definitive state to apply to us in our complete natures as concrete physical beings. Again in the last analysis the question of what is meant by spirit in this claim that we make and what the grace of divine life means in this context is a secondary one. What must be recognised is that this insistent and inalienable demand to arrive finally at the definitive state of the freedom and wholeness of eternal life, to apply to us as one and undivided, is alive in us. And if this is the case, then we know at the same time, and need not disguise it from ourselves, that we are quite unable to 'picture' this final and definitive state to ourselves. Such a thing would be still more absurd than to suppose that the caterpillar could imagine what it would be like to be a butterfly. For it is clear that the 'transformation' which our whole earthly life must undergo, as the scripture also tells us, and which pervades it right to its very roots, implies a final and definitive state in a mode of existence that is lifted right out of the temporal order. Any attempt at predicting such a thing would be doomed to failure from the outset. We know nothing more of it than that we shall exist as those who have been perfected and have entered into the unfathomable mystery of love which we call God. And that is enough.

When we think of our own consummation in this way does it lead us away from the resurrection of Jesus? No. So far from this, we have prepared ourselves to understand it, although admittedly this preparation for our understanding of the resurrection derives, once more, from the resurrection itself. In him, the inconceivable – inconceivable in itself – hope of our final perfection becomes faith. We know in fact that in that act which we call his resurrection he has not returned into our earthly state of existence, but that his life has been transformed into the fulness of the presence of God so that he has been withdrawn from our earthly state. Even such experiences as the disciples had of their risen Lord, and which were granted to console and strengthen them, were, in a certain sense, the necessary translation of his own unique and inconceivable perfection into terms which we, in our mortality, can understand here, confined as we are to space and time. The knowledge of these experiences does not justify us in depicting, in terms of our own human ideas, the state of perfection as it applies to the risen Lord who, as man, is uniquely one and whole. But if we obey the innermost longing of our humanity for the final and definitive state that is his, and so with pure hearts direct our gaze wholly and exclusively upon him, his understanding of himself, his death and his disciples' Easter experience of him, then indeed we are not forced, but rather empowered and emboldened to say: 'He is risen'. We can say it quite soberly and calmly because we are only asserting what we are at basis awaiting for ourselves, if we take our humanity in earnest, and do not suppose that it can evade responsibility for the eternal in it by escaping into nothingness. And conversely when we look upon him we can believe that at death life does not, in any ultimate sense, sink into the empty void of absurdity, but rather falls into the unfathomable depths of God. He is the first of those who are born through death into a final and definitive state that is predestined for all humanity, because he, being truly man, is also the Word in which God utters himself, and utters himself to us. And so when we too believe this Word and take it to our hearts, the statement, 'He is risen' becomes the essential content of our faith and hope as a whole. For what we mean when we say 'He is risen' is that in death he has overcome and redeemed for ever the very heart and centre of all earthly being. In his resurrection he has held fast to this victory, and he has remained victor ever since. When in the creed we acknowledge that he has ascended into heaven this is only another way of saying that for a while he has withdrawn his glorified humanity from our view, and chiefly in order that the world may no longer be cut off from God as by an intervening chasm.

Christ is already at the heart and centre of all the poor things of this earth, which we cannot do without because the earth is our mother. He is present in the blind hope of all creatures who, without knowing it, are striving to participate in the glorification of his body. He is present in the history of the earth, whose blind course he steers with unearthly accuracy through all victories and all defeats onwards to the day predestined for it, to the day on which his glory will break out of its own depths to transform all things. He is present in all tears and in every death as the hidden joy and life which conquers by seeming to die. He is in the beggar to whom we give alms as the secret riches in which the almsgiver is allowed to share. He is in the wretchedness, the defeats and failures of his servants as the victory which belongs to God alone. He is in our feebleness as the power which may allow itself to appear weak because it is invincible. Even in the midst of sins he is still present as the compassion of the eternal love, ready to be patient even to the end. He is there as the innermost essence of all things, and the most secret law which still triumphs and imposes its authority even when every kind of order seems to be breaking up. He is with us as the light of day and the air are with us, which we do not notice; as the secret law of a movement that we do not comprehend because that part of the movement which we ourselves experience is too brief for us to infer from it the pattern of the movement as a whole. But he is there, the heart of this earthly world and the secret seal of its eternal validity. He is risen. He who hopes utters these words in his heart: He is risen.

14

EXPERIENCING EASTER

THE way of the Cross – *our* way of the Cross – is something with which we are all familiar. Today it means, generally speaking, something different. The street-plan has been altered. This is, in fact, often brought home to us today in the politics of these changing times. Today the way of the Cross means calamity, cancer, divorce, atomic war, being thrown on the scrap-heap and very much more of the same kind. The road to be travelled has grown longer, and new street-names appear beside the old at its intersections. But for all this it is still the old way of the Cross, which leads by way of much tribulation and pain to final death. Furthermore, in the hospitals of today this death is no different from what it was in earlier times. The eyes wander, seeking round in vain to find some fixed point on which to focus. The words of the doctors, kindly meant though they may be, have a decidedly hollow and distant ring. And so on. Finally a man is laid in a grave. But this is 'of no further concern to the man himself'.

The question, therefore, is simply this: whether the individual concerned is still there to take an interest in his own life and his own death. In so far as anything can be established 'empirically' at all it can be said that those who remain behind are no longer concerned. That much is certain. The dead man is cut off, removed from the activities in which we are engaged. All that is left behind is something strange and rather ludicrous, something that we make to disappear quickly in the process called burial because we cannot really put it to any practical use (unless the Nazis and their later disciples make soap out of it). But what is the situation of one who has disappeared in this way? 'I' may permit myself not to trouble others with this question as it applies to me. But for my own part I cannot ignore it, for I know that *I* must die. And when I neglect something which so truly concerns *me*, then *ipso facto* I have precisely made up my mind in one particular direction. In this case, with the best will in the world, it is quite impossible to be so indifferent to the fact of death as 'not even deliberately to ignore it'.

But surely we should not regard it as so completely clear that with death 'everything is over'. Surely it has not been convincingly established that the rest of the tragedy called human life which we have mentioned above is nothing more than a fulfilment of the 'law of the conservation of energy'. For even before death the matter which we are considering, and which now with death begins to assume quite different forms, was already undergoing changes, though it is true that in the case of a human body the direction in which these changes tended was a little less constant and unambiguous than is the case with other units of matter. But even allowing for all this, there was at that earlier stage something different there as well: precisely a man, with the love, faithfulness, pain, responsibility, freedom and much more besides which being human entails. In view of this what right have we, properly speaking, to assert that everything in man has simply disappeared from reality and turned into pure nothingness – evaporated, dissolved? (Even this way of putting it would turn out to be untenable, because even when something is 'dissolved' all the basic elements of which it was formerly composed still remain, whereas *ex hypothesi* the human being who was there would have simply to cease to exist. Formerly 'I' was there, but after my death there would have to be absolutely nothing there any longer at all). But what real reason have we for asserting that everything is absolutely 'finished' in this way? Is it that we no longer observe anything of what was formerly there? This argument seems somewhat weak. Logically speaking the only conclusion we could draw from this is that 'for me who remain behind the dead man is no longer there'. But does this mean that *in himself* he is no longer there? Must he be there *for me* in order to be there at all? Is it conceivable that his 'basic constituents' were such that they were capable of being transformed in such a manner that the new creature which emerged from the change no longer played any further part in our world? (It should be noticed that on this hypothesis it would be no more necessary for the individual to be 'aware' of these basic constituents in his nature than that he should be conscious of the chemical processes involved in the material changes which in fact he does undergo).

When we look closely at this life of ours it is of its very nature not the sort of life in which man wants to go on indefinitely taking part in activities on *this* plane. Of its very nature it strives to reach a conclusion to its present mode of existence. Time becomes an illusion if it involves self-consciousness as with us and is incapable of attaining its fulfilment. If it were capable of being extended indefinitely it would become hell in the sense that it would be a meaningless void. No moment would have any value because it would always be possible to postpone and put off everything endlessly to a future that was infinite and so never made actual. Nothing would ever be too late for us (there would always be enough), and on this hypothesis everything would fall into the void of absolute indifference, where it would have no value. When, therefore, someone departs this life nothing could be easier to understand (If he did not do so one would have to put him to death by force). But when the dying man departs, cannot that element which is absolutely proper to him as person survive unchanged and elevated above the 'space-time' dimension of the merely physical precisely because it was all along something more than the mere interplay of the 'elements' of physics and biochemistry, because it was capable of love, faithfulness, and perhaps too sheer baseness and similar qualities; because while it *come to be* in this dimension of space and time, nevertheless it does not achieve its final fulfilment *in* this dimension. (In other words it no longer remains behind on that plane on which those who do actually remain behind do continue to exist). We should not understand the existence upon which we enter at death as a mere 'lasting on' of temporal existence in that peculiarly indefinite and limitless state in which it is always open to fresh content, and is therefore, strictly speaking, a mere empty void. If this is the sense in which we think of human existence, then death puts an end to it for the *whole* man. Anyone who thinks that the immortality of the soul means simply that it 'lasts on' in time beyond death, so that after death a new period of time open up before it, will admittedly involve himself in difficulties which are insuperable both in the realm of ideas and in accounting for the real and objective achievement of man's true final state which does take place in death. But let us consider the case of one who supposes that 'with death everything is over'. The arguments by which he justifies this position are that since the period allotted to an indvidual man began at a specific point in time it must also end at a specific point, so that the total extent of the individual's existence really does not extend beyond his death. A further and final argument in justification of such a position might be as follows:— Let us imagine time as evolving endlessly in its own course into an indefinite future, while its content undergoes as infinite series of permutations. This would imply that the idea of anything old lasting throughout its extent is ruled out. Now properly speaking this is quite unrealisable in fact, and would be more terrible than any hell. Anyone who takes up this position is being led astray by the limitations of his own imagination as it bears upon our human experience of time every bit as much as he who conceives of the human soul 'lasting on'.

In reality 'eternity' is present *in* time and emerges from it as it were as a ripened fruit growing out of it. Eternity does not really emerge 'after' the allotted span of human life; rather it completely removes the individual concerned from time, in that it itself becomes disengaged from *that* time, a limited span of which was allotted to the individual concerned in order that he might exercise freedom in working his way towards his final and definitive state. Eternity is not a way of expressing pure time which lasts inconceivably long. Rather it is the mode appropriate to that spirituality and freedom which is brought to its fulness in time, and for this reason eternity can only be understood on the basis of a right understanding of time. A time which does not, as it were, act as a starting-point for the spirit and for freedom does not in any sense give birth to eternity. (Such, for instance, is the time proper to animals). The final and definitive state of man, therefore, is something that pertains to the dimension of spirituality and freedom in his mode of being, something that is achieved by the exercise of these attributes. As such it transcends time, and must be detached from it in our minds. Yet because, almost in spite of ourselves, we do find ourselves envisaging it as an infinite prolongation of time, we do fall into intellectual embarrassments. Just as with modern physics, we must learn to think in terms that are abstract and non-imaginative, and in this sense 'de-mythologised'. Then we shall be able to say: 'Through death (not *after* it) the definitive fulness of human existence, achieved by the exercise of freedom in time, *is present* (not 'begins to take place')'. What has come to be, what was formerly subject to temporal conditions, now *is*. It exists as something that has been freed from its former temporal limitations. And this state of liberation came about in virtue of the fact that man is spiritual and free, and in order that the elements of freedom and spirituality in man might have final and definitive validity. Is it not possible, therefore, that what we call our life is in fact simply the brief flash of a process by which something comes to be (in freedom and responsibility), which *is* – is in a definitive sense because it belongs to the dimension of things which 'are' in this special sense (and which are not merely in a constant process of becoming)? And does it not follow from this that the process of becoming ceases when the state of being begins, and that the only reason why we do not notice this is that we ourselves are still involved in this process of becoming?

It is really quite impossible to confine reality to the level of those things the existence of which even the most stupid and superficial of men are neither able nor anxious to contest. It is quite certain that reality extends beyond this level. Just as scientific systems have been evolved in order to establish that even in the sphere of the material world the objectively real extends beyond the immediately observable to the human senses, so too there are experiences for the achievement of which, while no systems have been evolved, still a more highly developed spirituality is required. And these experiences put us in touch with eternity in that dimension in which it is no longer conceived of as a further prolongation of time stretching away 'on the other side of' our present lives, but is rooted rather in the time of freedom and responsibility as in the sphere proper to its own development, and from there emerges into life in its fulness, in which time is totally abolished. Anyone who has had to take a morally right decision in a matter of life and death (involving love, faithfulness, sacrifice and so forth), and has taken it radically and without any ulterior inducements, so that he gains absolutely no advantage whatever from it except the intrinsic goodness which he has recognised as involved in the actual decision itself, has already experienced in this decision that dimension of eternity of which we are speaking here. And when he goes on from this retrospectively to reflect upon the decision he has taken, and tries to translate this experience into theory, he may arrive at a false interpretation, even to the point of doubting or denying the reality of 'eternal life', and in that case it is regrettable because it is false and above all because it entails the danger of enfeebling or calling in question totally moral decisions of this kind. But it does not for one moment alter the actual experience itself.

It is not necessary here to draw speculative distinctions among the factors involved in this experience between those factors which belong to the spiritual and immortal nature of man, which even as a sinner he cannot evade, and what is to be ascribed to that grace or support which is bestowed by God in his eternity, and which for the Christian interpretation of existence attains its climax, its absolute validity and its manifestation in Jesus Christ, in his criminal's death on the Cross and in the victory which he won there.

But what are we to say of the individual who of his own resources chooses to doubt the validity of his own experience on the grounds that to him, so petty and abject as he is, it is not sufficiently clear, or on the grounds that in that deep sense of mistrust concerning the very meaning of existence from which we sinners all suffer painfully because we are cowards it seems to him 'too good to be true'? Such an one as this must hold firm to human experience itself as found in the experience of him who has risen. There is such a thing as Easter faith. Those possessing it are beyond all reckoning. It is present first in the disciples of Jesus, and the witness which they bear to their Easter experience and their Easter faith is to acknowledge him who was crucified and who saw his designs collapse in total failure on the Cross as one who was victorious with every fibre of his being, and was definitively and finally received and accepted by God.

One must not attempt to resolve this Easter experience into its constituent elements in order subsequently to reassemble them. Here too the whole is greater than the sum of its parts. Our encounter with Jesus who was conscious of being the Son of God as incomprehensible mystery, and who, in his own incomprehensible understanding of himself dared to call that mystery his Father, even in the moment of his death when he felt himself abandoned by God – this encounter itself belongs intrinsically to the experience of Easter taken in its uniqueness and totality. It is an encounter with the love and faithfulness of Jesus, with his flawless obedience, with the darkness of his death, with his total and unreserved acceptance of death, and with the Easter event itself. It may be that we of today cannot draw any clear distinction within the Easter event as understood here between Easter itself (precisely the fact of the risen Christ) and the Easter experience of the disciples. In other words it may be that as far as we are concerned that Easter experience of the disciples can never be merely an external transmission of information (as though they acted as a telephone wire or a telescope) which is, as it were, discarded the moment we have made contact with the event itself. In the case of Jesus' disciples their Easter faith and their Easter experience (their belief and the grounds for that belief) are already blended into each other indissolubly. And the basis for their belief (the risen Christ) is only experienced powerfully and compellingly as providing grounds for faith when the act of faith itself has already been posited. In other cases too there are objects of experience which, while they are objectively real and valid, are still only accessible *in* the experience of someone else. And the more significant and the more central to existential reality something is, the more likely this is to be so. Certainly the case here is quite different from that in which a reliable and trustworthy witness brings us news of something – for instance that he has seen someone jump into the water. In such a case the *possibility* of such an experience is already recognised and understood as a matter of our own experience independently of the information we receive about the actual event. And therefore this information on the part of the eye-witness puts us directly in contact with the actual event which he informs us about in such a way that the reliability and trustworthiness of the witness becomes superfluous in the sense that we already have reasons of our own for realising that such an event is possible, and we do not need to be able to recognise this reliability of his. In a certain sense we have already been put directly in touch with the event itself. In the case of Easter, however, it is quite otherwise. This experience is, in the nature of things, *sui generis*. For the experience of something 'other-worldly' that needs to be 'made manifest' no longer belongs to our 'space-time' dimension, and is not *ipso facto* available to 'this-worldly' minds to grasp. Certainly it is not in any sense an experience which we can 'understand' on the basis of the experiences which we already have. We have not already acquired knowledge of the possibilities of, and necessary conditions for such an experience taking place such that we could rely on our own resources and apply the everyday criteria of our own pre-existing knowledge to judge of the question of whether we could accept such an event as actually taking place and being experienced in the here and now. The appeal to the empty grave as an occurrence which belongs to the world of our normal experience, and which is accessible to everyone, is no real help at all, in attempting to solve this question. An empty grave cannot provide evidence for a resurrection leading to the final perfection of the individual concerned, because there are so many ways of accounting for such a phenomenon. We have no similar experience, no experience on the same plane with which to compare the Easter experience of the first disciples (that is not counting the 'experience of the Spirit' [Gal 3:1 ff.]), and we are therefore forced to rely upon the evidence of the disciples in a manner that is essentially more radical than when we are asked to accept the evidence of eye-witnesses in other circumstances. This is not to deny that this experience in itself and as such has an intrinsic structure of its own; in other words that in their experience the disciples are able to distinguish between the objective basis of their experience as such, and the actual psychological process of the experience. They are able to say '*He* reveals himself to us and our experience is not simply a substitute for him.' Nor is it denied that we too can in some sense establish the same distinction between the initial cause of the experience and the actual psychological process of it. We can point to the number of the witnesses, to the fact that in their dispositions they were in no sense attuned to or pre-conditioned to the actual experience which they underwent. We can point to the effects of this experience in the real world etc. But all this does not for one moment alter the fact that this Easter experience bears no comparison with other human experiences, and is unique, and that therefore our relationship to this experience cannot be regarded as on the same plane as our relationship to the accounts of natural events brought to us by eye-witnesses. Without the experience of the Spirit, i.e., in this case, without the experience of the meaningfulness of existence which we receive from faith (existence, that is to say, as it is, as a whole), we cannot achieve the necessary trustful self-commitment to the Easter witness of the disciples. And this remains true in spite of the fact that in many cases one acquires the strength to accept the meaningfulness of existence in faith precisely by committing one's self in trust to the Easter experiences of the disciples, and in spite of the fact that in all cases it is only in this Easter faith that one's realisation of this meaningfulness can become fully and properly what it ought to be. Only he who hopes can perceive the fulfilment of hope, and it is when that fulfilment is in view that hope can acquire its full and due actuality, and so rest content. It is neither possible nor needful to break out of this 'circle', but he who is called to hope in the 'resurrection' of his own flesh (the flesh that he *is*, and not merely 'has') can, by God's grace, break into this 'circle'.

Here too how could it be otherwise, seeing that the total self-commitment of the person has to be achieved not in relation to this or that objective among many others on the same level, but in relation to the ultimate meaning of existence as a whole, which is manifested in history. This being the object of one's self-commitment, it cannot be authenticated on any other grounds except those of itself, however many factors may be included in it which *mutually* condition one another. (Thus too even the reality of the risen Christ as experienced itself supplies the basis for the experience, and conversely the event only 'manifests itself' to the eye of faith). The one fact which we must never overlook is that the consummation of a human existence, achieved in virtue of the fact that it has been drawn into the immediate presence of God, can never be of itself a piece of evidence capable of being inserted into the sphere of space and time proper to 'this-worldly' experiences, and available as such in that sphere. At most it can 'make itself felt' in a human life, and precisely demand the response of total decision in that life (admittedly in all its dimensions). Nor have we any need to 'picture to ourselves' how a man 'appears' in the genuine totality of his being ('with body and soul', as we say). We can admit without disquiet that we are incapable of 'imagining' what a 'physical' resurrection will be, because (unlike the restoring of a dead man to life, for instance), it is, and is intended to be, utterly different from any restoration to a former state. Rather it signifies that radical kind of transformation (of which we already find mention in Paul as a condition for perfection) which the person must undergo as a free earthly being, bringing his own existence to its fulness in order to achieve that ultimate perfection in which he rises above time and reaches beyond it to the timelessness of eternity. When we speak of a 'physical' resurrection we are merely saying that we think of the whole man as perfected, and, in accordance with our own experience of human reality, cannot regard him as divided into an ever-enduring 'spirit' and a merely transient 'physical nature'.

In view of this, on what grounds should we be *forbidden* by our moral conscience with regard to truth to rely on the Easter experience of the first disciples? Nothing *compels* us to believe them if we decide not to do so and to remain sceptical. But there is much to give us strength to believe in them. What is demanded of us in this is both the boldest course and at the same time the clearest: to hazard our whole existence on the fact that, taken as a whole, it is orientated towards God; that it has a final and definitive meaning, that it is capable of salvation and redemption; that this meaning has actually been realised in Jesus, who is in this an effective prototype for us all; and that as we look upon him it becomes possible for us to believe it of ourselves as the first disciples have done. We are always in the position of 'wanting to' do something (namely to believe), and to this end we explore the depths of our own natures with a view to summoning up that historical objectivity which will enable us to attain to such belief. But they, the first disciples, actually have believed in very deed and in very truth – believed absolutely and totally, and to the point of death.

Have we a better solution to offer to the basic question of the meaning of our own existence? Is it really more honest, or simply, in the last analysis, more cowardly, when confronted with this basic question, to shrug one's shoulders in scepticism and yet to continue on (to the extent that we do live and strive to live decently) as though everything did in fact have a meaning after all? There is no need to maintain that everyone who supposes that he is unable to believe in the resurrection of Jesus is not able to remain ultimately and unreservedly true to his own conscience in his life. But it certainly will be maintained here that he who really does this whether he realises it explicitly or not does in fact believe in the risen Lord even though for him he is nameless. And it makes no difference to this whether the personal interpretations of his existence which he has worked out for himself agree with, or contradict faith in the resurrection. For such a one, even though he does not explicitly recognize the truth of the resurrection, is, in the basic decision by which the whole of his existence is orientated, tending towards the fulness of existence ('with body and soul') in salvation and redemption. He tends towards this fulness of existence as that which transforms this temporal state itself – tends, therefore, towards the meaning of history itself, and is at most not yet aware of whether history has already arrived at that point which even such faith acknowledges. But then *this* faith, which is also our own, need not shrink (in view of Jesus and the faith of his disciples) to acknowledge: 'It has already taken place'.

In *his* history at least the prison-house of this age has already been thrown open. And then we too can say explicitly: 'I believe in the resurrection of the body, that is the transformation and ultimate consummation of my own existence'. The Way of the Cross has a fifteenth station, at which we take leave of the march of time to be received into the inconceivable wonder of the love of God.

15

ENCOUNTERS WITH THE RISEN CHRIST

Hope of the Despairing

AMONG the mysteries of the gospel, so human and at the same time so altogether divine, and because of this so consoling also, is to be numbered the story of the two disciples who were journeying to Emmaus. If we read this story aright we recognise with amazement that it is a story about ourselves. We need only to tell this story to realise that it is a part of our own lives that is recorded in it, and at the same time the whole of our lives; a part, because the same thing happens again and again in our lives, the whole because our entire life is summed up in this one story of the disciples of Emmaus. As we read we notice that we are actually passing through our own Emmaus story. And as we read we hope and pray that our story too may have the same ending as that recorded in the twenty-fourth chapter of Luke's gospel.

They had been so full of hope; but now they believe that they can hope no longer. For the way matters have turned out is far from being in conformity with their hopes, or – to put it more precisely – with the interpretations which they themselves had placed on those hopes. They supposed that what they were hoping for was deliverance and freedom. We do not know whether they had fastened their hopes upon something that was not really capable of being an object of hope at all, or whether it was merely that their hopes were true and right, yet that they were simply disappointed by what they actually experienced. We do not know which of these two alternatives is correct. Nor did they themselves know this, for our understanding of our hopes, and because of this the hopes themselves, are always still in process of development. The point at which they finally arrive, and what becomes of them on the uncharted ways of this life does not depend merely upon ourselves. For we too are not the sovereign masters of our own course. But in any case when the death sentence was pronounced, and he in whom their hopes were centred was nailed to the Cross, and later when he was buried, then, so they believed, everything was over indeed. The only thing left to do was to give up and take to flight. There are situations in which there really is nothing more to hope for, in which there is nothing more to be said except 'We did hope'. Thus these disciples feel that they have been brought face to face with reality, that they are realists, and they do not let themselves be delayed in their flight by the pious fantasies of well-meaning women. No, they say, we are not falling into that mistake a second time. It is not virtue but cowardice and stupidity, so they imagine, to refuse to recognise the facts. And now, once and for all, it is a sheer matter of fact, which no amount of theorising in the world can interpret away that their hope has been hung on the gallows, and then buried in the grave. They are going away – either going home or going somewhere else, but in any case going.

How strange this is. Each of them is wholly alone, cast into the grave of his own hopeless loneliness. Why, then, are they walking together? Why are they actually still talking to one another, these two modern existentialists? Why are they seeking consolation from one another when in very truth there is no hope that it could be worth their while to discuss? They are running away and – talking. Just like ourselves. They are talking even though in reality it is meaningless to do so, and by the very fact of doing so they are bearing unconscious witness against their own convictions. That they should still be able to talk together like this – that is the beginning of grace. They want to blunt the edge of their own inconsolable loneliness by talk; to cover the void of their own hearts with chatter. And in doing so they give God the opportunity of joining in in their discussion. How often it happens that grace is actually present in our very flight from it! Sometimes God is already speaking with us when we imagine that we are quite alone, and only talking about him, the God that is dead. A stranger meets us on the way. It is the Lord. Our eyes, as they look round joylessly, are held by him. But they fail to recognise him. He who is taken up with himself and has a heart that is devoid of hope has strangely little place in his spirit and heart for others. But while it is salvation even to recognise him, still this remains true first and last, that even clear vision cannot bring it about that he, the Lord, is present and accompanies us; that he himself is actually accompanying us on the journey as we flee from him. This is something that he bestows, and he alone. Though admittedly he does accost many on the way who never notice it.

He is there on the way to Emmaus like one who knows even less than we ourselves, like a stranger, as though he were passing us by. We do not know when he comes or when he will go if we do not say: 'Stay with us Lord for it is toward evening'. Despair and grief had not yet pierced so deeply and lethally into the hearts of the disciples that these hearts refused an answer to the question of the traveller; that in the bitterness that kills they cynically refused to pay any heed to the word of light and consolation. Their heart is not yet so proud that it has taken refuge in a narcissism of pain and death, shamefully hugging its despair to itself. They let the stranger speak, though he knows less than they do. They really listen to him. What he says to them is that mystery which alone is self-explanatory. He speaks to them of the predestined death that ransoms and sets free. He shows them quietly how everything in the world and in scripture alike contains this single message, that the one fulfilment of all hope is to be found there, precisely where they believed that they had been deceived and that they were forced to despair. As for the so-called facts of the case, he only tells them precisely what these disillusioned realists have already seen for themselves, seen all too clearly: that Jesus is the crucified one. But consider the way he presents this fact to them, not as something which he shrinks from or denies, but as something which he accepts, something precious and enduring, something with an intrinsic meaning of its own. And in this way, when they look steadfastly at these facts, with a gaze that no longer flinches away from them, when they accept them calmly for what they are, then the facts themselves are illuminated from within, and disclose their own intrinsic truth: precisely that this descent of Jesus into failure and death is the way by which he enters upon the blessed destiny which is his by right, and attains to his own glory. He shows them this not as a general law in the logic of human existence, as though it followed as a matter of basic necessity that any death should be followed by a new becoming. When he speaks of this descent into darkness as the way of entering into supreme glory he applies it as a law of absolute necessity to *Jesus* and to Jesus alone; to Jesus as believed in, and to all others only to the extent that they do believe in him.

Scripture does not record that the disciples made any answer to what the unknown traveller said to them. They are silent. Because what is in question here, so far from being some theoretical question, some improved scientific theory, is that on which one dares to wager one's whole heart and spirit right to the last: to discover life itself in the very abyss of death, in the very depths of its despair, and to snatch light as it were from the dragon's jaws. That is why silence is appropriate here, for it is here that the heart is re-born. But before this is achieved amid that silence and expectancy that makes it possible, the disciples can say one word, a word of courteous solicitude such as befits simple hearts that are full of kindness: 'Stay with us for it is toward evening and the day is now far spent'. They are anxious about the night that confronts the stranger, he who so fills the night of their own hearts with light. Even as they seek to stay their brother pilgrim they invite him who is their Lord and the goal of their own journey to be their guest. They offer the pilgrim a roof, and thereby arrive home themselves. They break bread with him, and it is then, not while they are discussing the theology of human existence on the way, but in the celebration of fellowship and communion, that they recognise their Lord. It is he. The words which the stranger has spoken to them are the words of the Lord. By breaking bread with them he roots himself in their hearts. And they recognise the truth. Truly he is risen; out of the grave of the world, and out of the chasm of gloom of their own hearts.

How often we ourselves have experienced the same thing, even though, perhaps, only faintly and in small degree, and always lasting only for part of our lives. It may be that he who could survey our entire life-span too in his future will see that we are still on the way to Emmaus, that our eyes are still veiled, waiting for that countenance in which their whole destiny can be read, and however eager we may already have been to speak of the Lord, however much our hearts may have been quietly kindled by his word, yet in the last analysis he still continues to walk among us unrecognised.

In fact it may be that the greatness of life has still to come. We are actually bound to journey on on our pilgrimage, to travel and never to believe that we have reached our goal. For we are still on the way to the Last Supper of eternal life, where the Lord will rise and gird himself in order to give us the wine of inexpressible joy. Because we are still on the way we need not wonder at the fact that our heart constantly becomes weary, or angry, and weeps and complains at the disappointment of its hopes; that again and again we have the impression that we are fleeing from the death of our hope into a sterile void. Even on such a journey the Lord can go with us as the divine compassion present in a hidden manner in our midst, to disclose to hearts that are willing to receive it the meaning of scripture and of life. Even a way such as this can lead to the Emmaus of our own lives, where we shall know the Lord in the breaking of bread.

The Good Shepherd

The second Sunday after Easter is called 'Good Shepherd Sunday'. Obviously the name is derived from the section of the gospel appointed to be read on this Sunday. This consists of three verses from the tenth chapter of John, the chapter which contains three 'shepherd' parables. Our text comprises the third of these, and this arrangement of the sections of scripture included in this gospel is something which we have in common with Evangelical Christians also. In this gospel Christ calls himself the good or the true shepherd. In explaining this appellation which he applies to himself he points out that as the owner of the flock he, unlike the hireling, lays down his life for his sheep; that he knows them and they him, and he goes on to predict that one day he will be the one shepherd over all who will lead all the scattered sheep, Jews and Gentiles alike, into the unity of one shelter in his fold, so that there shall be one shepherd and one flock.

It is an age-old picture which Jesus makes use of here in one of his designations of himself in the Johannine gospel, all of which begin with that phrase of unfathomable meaning, 'I am'. The image itself derives from the nomadic culture of patriarchal times, when the supreme authority was vested in the father. In this image the true shepherd, as the owner of the flock, is simply to be identified with the Lord, the upholder of all things in existence. Among the Greeks king and generals are considered to be the shepherds of the peoples under them. In the Old Testament Yahweh is the shepherd and king of his people. In Ezek. 34 we find a prophetic threat of judgment and condemnation of the shepherds of the people, who have forgotten their duty and become self-seeking. Here the living God of history promises that he will take up and gather his people anew as their shepherd. And then we find the following oracular promise concerning the son of David: 'I will set up over them one shepherd, my servant David, and he shall feed them. He shall be their shepherd' (Ezek 34:23).

In this tradition Jesus clothes himself in an archetypal image: 'I am the true, the real shepherd'. Again in the synoptics he applies 'shepherd' images to himself (Mk 14:27; Mt 25:32; 26-31), even though in these passages attention is focused rather on the salvation to which the sheep themselves are destined to attain (Mt 18:12–14; Lk 15:3–7; Mk 6:34; Mt 9:36). Since then this image has become a part of the language of Christendom. For the author of the Epistle to the Hebrews Jesus is the great shepherd of the sheep (13:20). For Peter Jesus, considered as the example and reward of his apostles, is said to be the chief shepherd (1 Pet 5:4), the shepherd and protector of our souls (1 Pet 2:25), while for Revelation he is the shepherd who pastures the peoples with an iron rod (2:27). This is why the early Christians depicted the Lord as the Good Shepherd carrying the sheep. This is the most ancient and the most frequent motif in the art of the catacombs, which was thereby designed to present the Lord as the leader gathering souls into Paradise. And when Abercius of Hieropolis in Phrygia (2nd c.) wanted to tell later generations that he had become a Christian he had the following inscription set on his tombstone: 'I am a disciple of a holy shepherd who feeds the flocks of his sheep on mountains and pastures, and has great eyes that see all things'.

Now let us consider that saying of the Lord's in the Johannine gospel, 'I am the good shepherd'. If we want to understand this saying aright we must take it the opposite way round to what everyday linguistic usage might lead us to expect. This sentence does not consist of a determination or specification of the phrase 'I am', which, in itself, might be thought to be empty and vague. If we took it in this sense we would only know what 'I' was from the clear information supplied by the predicate. Here, on the contrary, Jesus is uttering the words 'I am' in an absolute sense that is self-subsistent and all-comprehending. And the reference to the 'shepherd' only derives its true meaning from these preceding words, 'I am'. Thus one can only realise what is meant by the reference to the good shepherd when one has first understood what 'I am' means. In this case the subject determines the predicate, and not the other way round. This appears from the very fact that Jesus utters a whole series of such 'I am' sayings. He says: 'I am – the messiah (4:26), the bread of life (6:35), the living bread from heaven (6:42, 51), the true vine (15:1, 5), the light of the world (8:12; 12:46), the door (10:7), the shepherd (10:11, 14), the resurrection and the life (11:25), the way, the truth and the life (14:6), the first and the last (Rev 1:17; 22:13), the beginning and the end (Rev 22:13), the root and the bright morning star (Rev 22:16).

In virtue of its authority, which extends over the whole of existence, and makes itself present to man in this way, the 'I am' of Jesus is in itself, and without any further addition, the object of faith which pronounces judgment upon the sins of unbelief. Jesus speaks of those who 'do not believe that I am' (8:24). He also declares: 'I tell you this now before it takes place, that when it does take place you may believe that "I am"' (13:19). Just as God is, in the deepest and most ultimate sense, not to be portrayed by any being other than himself – indeed not to be conceived of from any point outside his own being. just as he cannot be included in any system of reference pertaining to our own existence, such as we can understand or apply, and just as he cannot be fitted into any such system, just as he is the one who specifies and determines rather than the one who is specified – a subject in the absolute, and not one which is susceptible of predicates, just as he reveals himself in this guise to Moses as 'I am who am', so too Jesus is the 'I am' in an absolute sense: God whose existence is absolutely sovereign, absolutely independent, and prior to the existence of any other being, and it is as such that he proclaims himself in the words 'I am'. 'I am all, the beginning and the end, the way and the light, the truth and the life, the slain one and the victory over death, root and flower: I am'. And therefore in him, the presence of God for us in a guise which we can apprehend, all things are gathered up as in their origin. That is why all things belong to him. That is why he gathers all things to himself, of which he is author and maker, as into the unity of the end towards which all are tending, just as he constitutes the unity of their common beginning too. Because he is the 'I am', therefore he is the true shepherd, he who alone makes comprehensible what this means: to be the true shepherd.

It is not, therefore, by making use of an already familiar image that Christ makes himself comprehensible to us, even though the image itself is one which we cannot fail to recognise. Rather it is on the basis of his 'I am' that he makes it clear to us who the shepherd really is. Because he is, therefore there is one to whom all the scattered and lost ones belong, one who knows all things, however scattered and confused they may be in a dark and meaningless void; one whom the ultimate instinct of reality, still cohering even in its confusion, yet recognises; one who, by entering into this confusion and offering himself up in sacrifice there, ventures into the desolation of death and so achieves the gathering of the scattered; one, in short, who can unite all things. And because there is this 'I am', therefore there is the shepherd.

The great thinker of our times has called man 'the shepherd of being', and summed up in this phrase the whole destiny and value of man, which, by our own resources, we recognise in ourselves. But the truth which Jesus is uttering to us here is still more basic and primary, and when we let it speak to us in a spirit of faith this truth reveals itself to us as an experience of ours that is more basic and more primary: the fact that we are those over whom the shepherd of men watches, and whom he gathers and guides. He, this shepherd of ours, is no abstract idea which we foster and shepherd as man 'shepherds the winds', but rather he who is *there*, acting upon us, the crucified and risen Lord, he who is invoked at baptism. We do not speak of him. Rather he says his word to us. He is present in the celebration of the Lord's supper, in which he gives us his flesh and blood. Where he is present and active by his grace, there the beginning of that unity has already been achieved which abolishes all conceivable divisions. Where he is the living God is, God as present and close to us. 'Come', run the words of Ps 94:6, 'Let us worship and bow down; let us kneel before the Lord, our maker. For he is our God and we are the people of his pasture and the sheep of his hand'. And Thomas Aquinas writes in his poem: 'Merciful *shepherd*, thou true bread, show thyself compassionate towards us. Do thou protect us and shepherd us. Do thou prepare for us the eternal blessing that will be ours in the land without death'.

Here we must break off, yet holding firm to the truth that is ours, the truth that we, the scattered ones, are those whose very existence is divided and remote from the rest; those who wander about, those who are disunited, those who are cut off from one another as by barriers, those who are hunted by wolves, those who do not know who they belong to (apart from that one whom they are unwilling to belong to, and who seems to come after them in the guise of the wolf of death). If we held fast to him, and then the word came to us, came to us *there* where we really are the lost ones, the word 'I am' – then we would know indeed that *he* is the true shepherd.

16

HE WILL COME AGAIN

'THIS Jesus who was taken up from you into heaven will come in the same way as you saw him go into heaven' (Acts 1:11). This quotation from the Acts of the Apostles may serve to introduce the considerations which follow on the festival of Christ's Ascension.

The first thing which we must recognise is that what the two angels are saying here has the force of a refusal or a dismissal. It informs the apostles that their master will not show himself again in visible form, in that unambiguously human and apprehensible form in which they have hitherto been privileged to know him, until he returns in glory at the end of time. The intimacy which they have hitherto enjoyed is over – over until the end of time. The axiom that is now in force is 'Blessed are those who have not seen and yet believed', those who hope utterly against hope, who are willing to let their whole existence depend upon something which is not humanly apprehensible. We have only the message of preaching to rely upon for what belongs to the apostles directly: to have seen with their own eyes what they have seen and have actually touched with their hands. It is not given to us to share this privilege of theirs. It is the unrepeatable privilege that belongs to the origins. At the same time it is the blessing that is promised for the end. The idea that in the intervening period too this privilege might be enjoyed – that is what the angels refuse to allow. Even though mystical apparitions of the Lord have occurred in subsequent times, this does not invalidate the denial that they are uttering here. The Lord does not appear in his real bodily form. He is remote. He is in a state in which he is sought by faith, he for whom we must wait until he comes again, the one for whose return we keep watch, but who has still to come. Christian life, therefore, is essentially a life of the provisional and transitory. Implicitly it involves the recognition of the fact that nothing definitive and enduring can be attained here; the courage to face the fact that we have here no abiding city. It means that we are forbidden to make any attempt at constructing our ultimate goal in this present dimension of space and time. We shall be able to perceive the reconciliation of the finite and the infinite only when everything is at an end – not in the present. He has gone away. Even as the realisation had dawned – at long last – of who he was, even then he had already gone away. He is no longer there as he was *then*. We can no longer see him as he was *before*.

But the angels' word is also a word of consolation and of promise. 'Just as' Jesus has gone, 'even so' will he return. Properly speaking he has now no further destiny to fulfil. There is no need for us to fear that because he has gone away he may return as someone else who, in the meantime, has undergone a transformation, so that he is no longer the person whom we knew, and of whom we have experience. He is the same who was among us, and it is 'so' that he will return. 'So' he remains to all eternity; 'so' and not otherwise. He has not gone in order to destroy his identity, in order to escape from the state which was his when he was here among us, and which he experienced and endured here among us. He is, and he remains, the same as he was here, in order that he may 'so' return as he was then. He has 'gone away' from our human history precisely that the ultimate significance of this human history may endure; in order that it may not be dissipated in the void of the past, but may be able to return, i.e. may manifest itself at that point at which we shall have attained to our own final and definitive state as that which has endured throughout. Nothing in him and in his life has been lost. All has been retained, and therefore 'it will come again'. It will manifest the fact that it has endured in its entirety. We imagine that what departs also ceases to exist, that what is taken away from us cannot also return. But it is not so. The Lord has gone away as man. He has taken with him his human life, not merely a human nature in the abstract, still open to all the possibilities and indifferent as to which of them is made actual in it. No, it is a human life that he has taken with him into the glory of his Father. Certainly the particular concrete events of this life really have disappeared. Indeed there was an inherent tendency in them really to disappear because, precisely, by doing so they bear witness to what is final and definitive. He is no longer a child. He is no longer a youth, no longer the man, no longer the crucified one, the one who dies and sinks into the darkness of death. He has left all that behind him. But precisely because of this all that which he did undergo and subsequently left behind has entered into life in his own personhood, has become a part of himself as he was when he went away from us in order that when he returns he may be just the same. Because he was that which we experienced therefore he will return as he was then: as the man who was a child, and for whom this fact remains eternally present, as the man who walked upon this earth, as the man who bore with us, who addressed words of sincerity and love, grace and forgiveness to us, as the man who went to his death, as the man who has already experienced everything that we have to bear in the way of joy and pain, life and death, victory and defeat. If we rightly understood the significance of the preterite in these statements of ours concerning his 'past life', then we would understand that the only factor which really has disappeared in them is that of 'anxiety' (*Angst*). The events referred to in these statements could disappear, and what has happened once and for all in history could not remain eternally in force. But the true time which has been won by his redemptive work is not inaugurated in order that that which is initiated may disappear, but is rather the beginning of that which endures. And eternity does not come 'after' time, but is the sheer validity of that which has taken place in time, but endures for ever. And therefore he comes 'so', just as he has gone. In the 'interval' nothing will happen, for in his temporal life itself that eternity which endures has been worked out and suffered for. When this enduring eternity appears to us in the future, it will be the validity of his own history that comes to meet us. This history has now been filled with the glory of God (that is why he has returned home); but likewise this history has become the finally valid and enduring factor which can be restored.

But this means that the word of the angel is a word of promise addressed to us, a word that promises us our eternal and enduring validity. Why has he really gone when, by this entry into the glory of his Father, he is still, nevertheless, the one who remains? It is because he wants to give us an opportunity to live *his* life; in order that when he returns he may find in us that which he brings with him to us of himself: a human life which belongs to God. In his Spirit, in his Church, in his word, in his sacraments he has indeed remained with us in order that we may continue his life. On the basis of this objective existence with us he must penetrate into all departments of our life in order to conform our life to his – penetrate what we do and what we suffer, our joy and our pain, our strength and our feebleness, our life and our death. It is his will to live on in all this. And if he will so return as he has gone, then the word which we are here considering is a promise that he will give us the grace to live his life, for otherwise he could not come as he has gone.

Lord, when you return even as you have departed from us, as a true man, then may you find yourself in us as the one who bears all, is patient, is faithful, is kind, is selfless; as the one who cleaves to the Father even in the darkness of death, the one who loves, the one who is joyful. Lord, may you find yourself in us, being what we would so much wish to be yet are not. But your grace has not only endured. In reality, it has come to us simply in virtue of the fact that you, having ascended and been enthroned at the right hand of God, have poured out your Spirit into our hearts. And so we truly believe that against all experience you do continue your life in us even though it seems to be only ourselves – Ah! almost always only ourselves and not you – that we find within ourselves. You have ascended into heaven and are seated at the right hand of God with our life. You are coming back with that life in order to find your life in ours. And the fact that you will find it there – that will be our eternity even when we, together with all that we are and have lived and have possessed and have borne, shall have entered into the glory of your Father through your second coming.

17

THE FESTIVAL OF THE FUTURE OF THE WORLD

We are celebrating the festival of Christ's ascension. We know that properly speaking we are thereby celebrating the conclusion of the festival of Easter, Easter once again, because by his resurrection the Lord has already entered into his full and final consummation. Thus what Christendom is celebrating in this festival, and what it is thereby making explicit, is something which, even though it was already implicitly contained in our Easter faith, is nevertheless new, something which goes beyond what we celebrated at Easter. This is the recognition of the fact that in the fulness of glory upon which he has entered the Lord has been withdrawn from his followers; that the full unveiling of the Easter glory which is to embrace all things is something for which we are still waiting; that the 'little while' is still continuing, in which the fulness of our life in Christ is still withheld from us and from the world itself. Thus the festival of the ascension is, in a very true and proper sense, the festival of faith as such; the festival, therefore, not so much of the real facts in which we believe, but of faith itself. For faith does in fact imply holding fast to that which we have not experienced for ourselves. It implies a building on invisible foundations, a committing of one's self to that which only seems to be there because of the actual act of trust and self-commitment in itself. But when we let the Lord go, and do not cling on to him, so that he is hidden until the end and is only present among his own in a mysterious manner in his Spirit, then we are saying that we are ready to perform precisely that act which we call faith. This is an eschatological entity. It cannot be reduced to the formal acceptance of any kind of truth such as is always possible and can be viewed wholly in abstraction from the content of belief. To believe is to live by the future, to exist in the power of that which, even though it is the centre of our own existence, has, nevertheless, been withdrawn into the future that awaits us. It is a living by anticipation, a being true to a reality that lies in the future. In a single word it is eschatological existence. Ascension is the festival of faith as such.

In this sense the ascension becomes the festival of holy pain. He has departed from us. It is frightening that we feel so little pain about this. He himself thought that he had to console us. But our hearts, so withered and shallow as they are, respond to his consolation merely with amazement. We have to spend a long time in recollecting ourselves before we can realise – perhaps – even to some little extent, the fact that we should be inconsolable at the fact of his remoteness from us. For this we would have really to be holding fast to him. We would have to be overwhelmed with terror and anxiety at the void which his departure leaves for us. Now at last someone was there who is not superfluous; someone who does not become a burden but bears burdens because he is good – good in so unobtrusive a manner that we were already at the stage almost of taking his goodness for granted; someone who called the impenetrable riddle that lies behind all apprehensible things his Father, and in doing so gave the impression of being neither incredibly naïve nor tastelessly presumptuous, one indeed who almost led the world into the temptation of taking it for granted when he allowed us too to utter the words 'Our Father' into this divine darkness. It was the compassion of God and his wisdom that were with us in him. At last we were able to think of God in a manner somewhat different from the abstractions of the philosophers. At last one was there who really knew something, and yet did not have to be abstruse in speaking of it; one whom one only had to make contact with, whom one dared to kiss, whom one struck on the shoulder in friendliness; someone who sought nothing for himself – and in these trivialities we had everything, *everything* made physically present to us: God, his pity, his grace, his nearness. Now he has gone. He wanted to console us by saying that precisely by so doing his Spirit, and in this living Spirit of his, himself would come to us. That is a consolation. Oh yes. For if he were only physically present to us without his Spirit taking possession of us his presence to us would be of as little avail to us as to a Judas who sits at his side or kisses him. But when his Spirit is in us, then we are his, the Lord's, and he is ours. But the fact that we have him only in order to seek him, to be able to seek him and to have to seek him, that he should be among us only in order that it may still be revealed to us what we are in virtue of this fact – this makes the joy and blessedness of possessing him in his Spirit a pain as well. It is the pain of waiting, the pain of the birth-pangs of eternal life, the pain of hope, the pain of pilgrimage. Yet if only we could feel this blessed pain, this grace of the festival of the Ascension more ardently and more keenly! But we are content with this life. Today we are often proud that our loyalties are to the earth (though naturally this can have a good sense). We do not look above or into the future like the men of Galilee. We keep our gaze fixed on the foreground of our lives and on the present. We are not those who wait, those who look, those who are unsatisfied; not those who hunger and thirst for that justice which is to be found only in the future, that future which will bring us the return of the Lord if we keep watch for it. May God give us the grace to celebrate this festival as a festival of blessed pain!

The Ascension is a festival of the future of the world. The flesh is redeemed and glorified, for the Lord has risen for ever. We Christians are, therefore, the most sublime of materialists. We neither can nor should conceive of any ultimate fulness of the spirit and of reality without thinking too of matter enduring as well in a state of final perfection. It is true that we cannot picture to ourselves in the concrete how matter would have to appear in this state of final endurance and glorification for all eternity. But we have so to love our own physicality and the worldly environment appropriate to it that we cannot reconcile ourselves to conceiving of ourselves as existing to all eternity otherwise than with the material side of our natures enduring too in a state of final perfection. And – one shudders at the 'blasphemy' which such an idea must represent for the Greek mentality – we could not conceive of the divine Logos either in the eternal perfection which belongs to it for ever otherwise than as existing for ever in the state of material incarnation which it has assumed. As materialists we are more crassly materialist than those who call themselves so. For among these it would still be possible to imagine that matter as a whole and in its entirety could, so to say, be raised at one blow onto a new plane and undergo a radical qualitative change such that, for purposes of definition, it could no longer be called matter because this future state would be so utterly different from the former one in which it originated. We can entertain no such theory. We recognise and believe that this matter will last for ever, and be glorified for ever. It must be glorified. It must undergo a transformation the depths of which we can only sense with fear and trembling in that process which we experience as our death. But it remains. It continues to perform its function for ever.

It celebrates a festival that lasts for ever. Already even now it is such that its ultimate nature can survive permanently; and such too that God has assumed it as his own body. *Non horruisti virginis uterum. Non horruisti materiae beatam aeternitatem.* And already for this world as a whole the process of fermentation has already commenced which will bring it to this momentous conclusion. It is already filled with the forces of this indescribable transformation. And this inner dynamism in it is called, as Paul boldly confirms for us in speaking of the resurrection of the flesh, the holy Pneuma of God. It is a free grace. It is not the sort of entity which the world could lay claim to as something proper to itself, something belonging to it autonomously and as of right. But it is the true, the ultimate perfection of the world in all its power, which brooded and hovered over the primordial chaos, and which will preserve all things and perfect all things which were and are. And this power of all powers, this meaning which is the ultimate meaning of all meanings, is now present at the very heart and centre of all reality including material reality, and has already, in the glorified flesh of the Son, brought the beginning of the world triumphantly to its final goal of perfection. The Ascension is the festival of the true future of the world. The festival we are celebrating is an eschatological one. In this celebration we anticipate the festival of the universal and glorious transfiguration of the world which has already commenced, and which, since the ascension, has been ripening and developing towards the point where it will become manifest.

And there is a truth which we must repeat yet again, even though it is one which we have already seen from the obverse side of the same single reality, and have already stated. Considered as an event the ascension does not only have the connotation of departure and distance. On the contrary it is a festival of the nearness of God. The Lord had to die in order really to come close to us. For the physical nearness of those who are still imprisoned in the flesh, and who have not yet passed through death, is precisely remoteness; though it is a nearness, the sweetness of it is, nevertheless, only the pledge of the true nearness that can only be achieved in the future. And if the death, resurrection and ascension of the Lord constitute one single event, the particular aspects and phases of which cannot be separated one from another, then the separation implicit in this festival is simply another way of expressing the nearness of the Lord in his Spirit, which has been imparted to us through his death and resurrection. Thus he is closer to us than he ever was; closer than he was during the time when he was still in the flesh, closer so long as his Spirit is in us, so long as his life and his death have taken possession of us, so long as his Spirit in faith hope and love has loosened the fetters of our finite state and turned it into the infinitude of his Father, so long as we have abandoned the merely finite and, by his Spirit, have become strong enough boldly and lovingly to sustain the most intimate and at the same time the most 'otherworldly' reality of the incomprehensible mystery of God. In his death the Lord has broken the old vessel of the Spirit and has left it unrepaired. Properly speaking the infinitude with which the world has been endowed is the one new vessel into which his Spirit is poured out, for his body, even though it is truly glorified, no longer separates him from us. Rather it has itself become a sheer openness to the world. The Ascension is the festival of the true nearness of the Lord in his holy Spirit.

And it is in this sense that the Ascension is the festival which celebrates our preparation for Pentecost. This festival is simply a transition from the Easter of Christ to the beginning of our Easter, which we call Pentecost. For our sharing in the Easter of Christ is achieved through the Spirit of Christ bestowed at Pentecost. And thus we celebrate the Ascension of Christ by watching and praying for his Spirit: Come and be near to us as Spirit, since you have withdrawn from us your nearness in the flesh. In all these great festivals of Christian living let us beware of intoxicating ourselves with great words. It is not the majesty of the words of theological speculation that constitute the realities in the communication of which the true celebration of such festivals consists. Rather it is the reality of the Spirit of grace himself which both celebrates and is celebrated in us. But this reality, as the living and life-giving, the victorious and the transforming, can also be experienced in microcosm; best of all perhaps in keeping faith with him in a spirit of joy and thanksgiving to God for the life of spring, in the courage and joyfulness which we show in our everyday life, in the calmness, tolerance and love which we show to our neighbour, and many other small miracles of grace of this kind in the ordinary course of life. And all liturgical celebration achieves its meaning only if it finds a true and sustained projection of itself in the ordinary course of life in this way. For where the Spirit performs the miracle of faithfulness and courage in our poor lives from day to day, there is the Spirit of Christ. And where the Spirit of Christ is present the true festival of the Ascension of the Lord is celebrated.

18

THE CHURCH AS THE SUBJECT OF THE SENDING OF THE SPIRIT

EASTER and Pentecost are the two festivals in our ecclesiastical year which go back to apostolic times. This is because they were already included in the synagogal calendar, in which they fall at the same time of year, although admittedly their content there is different. In the time of the early Church Easter and Pentecost were not, properly speaking, two distinct festivals, or even two distinct 'festal cycles' existing independently side by side. Rather Pentecost is the culmination of Easter. Easter is the 'glorification' (*doxa*) of the Redeemer Christ, a glorification which includes his exaltation upon the Cross and his exaltation at the right hand of the Father in a single festival. Pentecost is the manifestation of that phenomenon which the Lord speaks of in John, 'If anyone thirst, let him come to me and drink. He who believes in me, as the scripture has said, "Out of his (the messiah's) heart shall flow rivers of living water"'. And John adds to this: 'As yet the Spirit had not been given because Jesus was not yet glorified', and further, 'It is to your advantage that I go away, for if I do not go away the Counsellor will not come to you'. Out of the death and resurrection by which the Lord is taken away from the world, therefore, springs up the Spirit. If Jesus is not glorified it is not given. It will only be poured out if Jesus, by his death, has overcome the world and its prince. On the Cross water and blood flow down from his pierced side as a sign of the fact that the living water of the Spirit, which springs up to eternal life, and which is to flow as a stream from the heart of the messiah, can only come from the Lord 'glorified' in his crucifixion. The Spirit only comes in water and blood. *Because* Easter, that is death and resurrection, has come, *therefore* Pentecost has come. And Pentecost is only the event to which all the events of Easter are orientated with an intrinsic teleology of their own in order to find their fulfilment in Pentecost.

But we must ask ourselves what Pentecost really is. It is the festival of the descent of the Holy Spirit, the festival in the baptism of the Spirit, the festival of the 'pouring out of the Spirit of God upon all flesh', the beginning of that dwelling of the Spirit permanently and enduringly 'in the vessel of the flesh and in the Church', to quote Irenaeus' words. Truly Pentecost is not a mere transitory visitation by the Spirit, a mystical ecstasy lasting for a moment. It is not even, in the first instance, a charismatic gift bestowed personally upon the apostles, as it were as private mystics or charismatics. Rather Pentecost, in all its external expressions which seem so strange, is at basis only the outward manifestation of the much more vital fact that henceforward the Spirit will never more be wholly withdrawn from the world until the end of time. For this permanent dwelling of the Spirit in the world is only the outcome of that overshadowing of the Spirit which took place in the incarnation of the Son of the Father. And because the Church is nothing else than the visible manifestation of the Spirit in the world, therefore the Church, which was born of the water and blood flowing from the dead body of Jesus, from the 'second Adam' asleep on the Cross, only becomes visible and manifest for the first time at Pentecost.

Let us develop these ideas a little further. 'The Spirit was not yet given', John declares, referring to the time when Jesus was not yet glorified. And yet we pray: '*Qui locutus est per prophetas*', 'thou who hast spoken through the prophets'. Even in this short declaration of faith, therefore, we acknowledge that the Spirit was at work in the world even before Christ, because we know that many times over and in many ways God spoke of old to our fathers. There was no Spirit and yet there was a Spirit. How can these two statements be reconciled? Is it merely that before the Redeemer came the Spirit was present in a lesser degree, so that now he is poured out in abundant measure upon men? No, though certainly this is also true. But taken in isolation this answer would not suffice, and would not meet the crucial difficulty. Formerly the Spirit was never in the world in the way that it is in it now, now that the fulness and the end of the ages has arrived. The Spirit of whom we speak is the Lord, for the Lord is Spirit, God is Spirit. But how is God in the world? Can he manifest himself within the confines of this finite state? He himself as he is, can he impart himself – not his gifts, his finite works but *himself* – to man? It might be said that he reveals himself in the creation. Well, but this is only the hem of his garment, the curtain that veils him. For the creation, nature as the theologians call it, tells us of God only as one who is remote, since the process of nature is cyclic, and it turns back upon itself. Of itself nature does not open up any way to man which can lead him into the inaccessible light of the depths of the Godhead, into the inner life of God himself, into his presence and before his countenance. God himself, therefore, had to come in order to lift us out of the cycle of birth and death, and in order to build a way for us by which we could be led out of the bondage of our humanity, confined as it is to the finitude of its own nature and of the world, into the life of God himself. And *this* God who comes into *this* world for *this* purpose we call the Holy Spirit. The Spirit of God in the Christian sense, the holy Pneuma, is present where the deliverance of man from the world and from sin and from finitude is achieved, and where the way is opened for him to enter into the presence of God himself.

But how is the Spirit to come upon us? How can we possess him, or – to put it better – how can we allow ourselves to be possessed by him? At what point in this finite state of ours does he decide that we shall be allowed to break into the life of the infinite? Does he not move where he wills? Is his work not so mysterious and incalculable that man never knows whence he comes or whither he is going, or where he will allow himself to be found? Are not the ways by which the Lord, the Spirit, comes not untraceable, so that we only know where he is to be found when he has already taken possession of us? Is there anything visible, apprehensible, to which we can point and say: 'Behold, here and now lay hold of this. Then you can be sure that the Spirit who moves where he will has taken possession of you'?

Yes, there is such a thing, because we believe in the incarnation of the eternal Logos, because God himself has entered into the dimension of history, into the confines of space and time; because of his free grace he has assumed for ever a part of this finitude of ours which belongs to space and time: that part which we call the humanity of Jesus. He has assumed this and made it his own life in such a way as to keep it evermore as belonging to his own being. Therefore there is a 'here and now' in the world into which God has come in order to deliver us and to lead us into his own life, in which there is no 'here and now'. In Jesus of Nazareth we have the living God of the living Spirit and of grace. The Church is nothing else than the further projection of the historicity and of the visibility of Jesus through space and time, and every word of its message, every one of its sacramental signs, is, once more, nothing else than a part of the world in its earthiness, with which the Spirit has united itself indissolubly since the day on which the Logos became flesh.

At Pentecost this Spirit has become manifest. Not merely the Spirit who moves intermittently and mysteriously here and there, who takes a prophet and uses him as his 'instrument' so long as he wills to do so, but who never remains lastingly among men, and who provides no lasting sign of his presence and power, but the Spirit of the Son who has become man. That is why – something which seems so contradictory – Peter's sermon, delivered on the very day on which the Spirit descends straight from above into the hearts of the apostles, does not invite the penitents to look upwards too, to see whether the Spirit coming from the realm which is beyond time and beyond history is not descending upon them as well. No, he has only one message for them: Be baptized! It is in the 'here and now' of the sacramental sign that the Spirit of Pentecost is present. And he is in this sign evermore and always. It is at that point, therefore, at which the visible sign is effected by the visible messenger, that Pentecost takes place. It is at that point that the Holy Spirit becomes present. Prior to the death and glorification of Jesus this was not the case, and it is for this reason that at that time the Holy Spirit had not yet been given. Previously there was indeed a Spirit of God, but not a Spirit of God made man. Before the incarnation of the Logos the invisible was not present in a mode that was visible and *lasting*. There was a juridical order which God had instituted for the people of Israel. But this juridical order did not constitute a Church. It was binding upon the men of that time, but it did not bring about any grace, any Holy Spirit. There was a Spirit, but it merely hovered and did not actually descend at any point. It never became 'visible'. Now, on the other hand, in the fulness of time, a visible mode of this kind has actually been achieved, in the incarnate Logos and in his Body, the Church. *Ubi est ecclesia ibi et Spiritus Dei; et ubi Spiritus Dei illic et ecclesia et omnis gratia.* These are the words of Irenaeus: 'Where the Church is, there is the Spirit of God; and where the Spirit of God is there is the Church and every grace'. *In ecclesia posuit Deus ... universam operationem Spiritus.* 'God ordained that the entire work of the Spirit should take place in the Church'. And where the Spirit is active, there, at any rate remotely, a stage is achieved in the construction of the visible Body of the Church.

Thus for Catholics the life of the Spirit, wherever it occurs, is always included within the fold of the Church. And everything else is not the life of the Holy Spirit but rather mere religious excitement. There is no Holy Spirit apart from the holy Body that is the Church. For this reason we are only 'spiritualised', i.e. taken possession of and permeated by the Holy Spirit, we only act in and by the Holy Spirit if we are incorporated in the Body of the Church. For Pentecost is the festival of that Spirit *cujus non sunt participes omnes qui non currunt ad ecclesiam*, 'in whom only those who hasten to the Church have a share'. Once more we are quoting the words of Irenaeus. And when Paul tells us that the Spirit quickens while the letter kills, the letter here refers to the Old Covenant. But the Spirit which quickens is that which rested upon Jesus of Nazareth and which lives on in the visible historical Church. We must not let the Church begin only at that point at which it no longer gives us unease.

Because the Church is there, therefore there is also a continual Pentecost. Therefore the outpouring of the Spirit upon all flesh is still continually taking place. Therefore we ourselves can still pray continually: *Veni Sancte Spiritus*, 'Come, Holy Spirit'. And because we say this prayer in the Church, therefore we know that we are heard. For the Spirit of the Lord is not far from us.

But for all this may we not sometimes ask: Where, then, is the Spirit in us? Where are his mighty works, his fire and his rushing wind? Do we not all too often seek in vain for the Spirit in the visible Church? Are not many true indeed to the letter without possessing the Spirit, orthodox without being moved by the Spirit of God? And does it not sometimes seem as though there were, after all, more of the Holy Spirit in many movements of religious enthusiasm than there, where the Holy Spirit has built his temple for ever?

Certainly the Holy Spirit remains always in his Church. This Church will always be the place in which he dwells in order to descend upon all who await him there with hearts ready to receive him. But for us as individuals all this is far from being a comfortable guarantee that he is able to work in us as he would wish to, and as the times demand that he should be at work. We cannot have a comfortable guarantee of this merely on the grounds that we go in and out of the house of the Lord. He is not to be found apart from the letter of the New Covenant, but not everyone who recognises this letter as sacred and says 'Lord, Lord' is *ipso facto* a Christian filled with the Spirit, spiritual in the sense that God, our own responsibility and our own age demand that we should be spiritual. Only he who is a member of the Church *and* independent, humble *and* daring, obedient *and* conscious of his own personal responsibility, a pray-er *and* a doer, adhering to the Church in her past *and* in her future – only such a one as this makes room for the Spirit of God at Pentecost, who appears in the form of a mighty rushing wind, the Spirit who is always ancient and always young – for this Spirit to do its work in him, to renew the face of his own soul, to use those who are his own in order to transform the earth as well.

And yet ... Is this the ultimate answer, the solution to every riddle? Where is the Spirit in us, even though we offer him a willing heart in spite of all denials, though we wait for him, though we do not say that we are children of Abraham, knowing very well that God is able to raise up such children even from stones, and to fit them as living stones into the temple of the Spirit? The Spirit comes in tongues of fire and signs and wonders when it pleases *him* to do so. But for ourselves, he has commanded *us* to believe in him, in his power and in his presence, even when we do not feel them. The Lord has commanded us not to think out beforehand how we should bear witness to him, because in the moment when we do have to bear such witness – not necessarily before that moment – the Spirit will come to our aid. But in doing this he has also warned us against obstinately seeking to have a tangible and perceptible assurance of his advent to us. Our task is to regard our feebleness as a sign of his complete power; to live in hope against all hope. He who gives the honour to God in this way, and does not seek to possess it for himself, he who commits himself to God in faith without vision, in him the Spirit lives and works. In so far as externals are concerned in such a case everything seems drab and everyday, a mere fulfilment of one's duty, patient expectation, wearisome struggles against manifold temptations. But viewed from within, Christian life consists of a *sobria ebrietas spiritus*, a clear-sighted and sober intoxication by the Spirit. The Spirit lives within us. There his light shines quietly and, as it were, with an inner life of its own. There his power is growing, though still hidden, as seed grows even though the husbandman sleeps. But when the hour of testing arrives, then – perhaps when we least expect it – the Spirit of wisdom and power will be with us. In this time, then, we will pray for the Holy Spirit, for the good Spirit whom the Father gives to all his children who ask him for it. We will seek him in his Church. With Mary, who was overshadowed by the Spirit, and with Peter, as once in the room of the Last Supper, we will 'be of one mind, constant in prayer'. We will ask God for a humble, and at the same time a bold heart, one which is ready to receive the Spirit of freedom and love, for a believing heart that does not demand signs and wonders, but rather for faith to believe that it is not in the context of pageantry, but in a spirit of quiet and recollection that the living God fills the hearts of his believers with the Holy Spirit who is eternal life.

19

THE SPIRIT THAT IS OVER ALL LIFE

ONLY by a process of sober and realistic questioning can we reach back beyond the religious practices to which we have become habituated to the origin of all our festivals, customs and observances. We are celebrating Pentecost. What is it, then, that we are really celebrating on this day? What is the special significance of this festival for ourselves in particular? It is with these two questions that the following meditations are concerned.

I

The answer to this question is not easy. Certainly it is not as one of the three Persons of the holy Trinity that we are celebrating the Holy Ghost. For the great festivals of the ecclesiastical year constitute a sacred *anamnesis*. That is to say, they celebrate *events* in saving history. But by commemorating them we make sure that they shall continue to exercise their influence as enduring forces in our Christian lives. But when we say that we are celebrating the descent of the Holy Spirit upon the Church at the first Pentecost after the exaltation of the Lord, then we are brought up short with the question: How is it, then, that in the credo at Mass we actually acknowledge the Spirit who has spoken through the prophets? Does not the power of the Spirit make its impact upon humanity throughout all the ages? Must he not have been present all along and from the very outset if without him there can be no salvation, no forgiveness of sins, no faith, no love of God, no consolation in view of eternity? Must he not have been descending continuously and right from the first if God does indeed will the salvation of all men from the beginning of human history right to the end, in all ages and among all nations? And if our only reply to this question were to be: 'The Spirit who presides always and throughout all history, and who is powerful to forgive, to deliver and to justify, has on this festival of Pentecost descended precisely upon the *Church*, then the further question immediately arises: 'In that case what can truly be said to have been altered in the history of mankind and its salvation if this humanity of ours has actually been all along – in spite of all sins and all abomination of desolation – the primordial ocean over which the Spirit of God broods? If mankind has always and right from the first included among its members the community of those who, as consecrated and chosen children of grace, have journeyed towards the goal of the eternal life which God bestows?' And then we might seek to say in rejoinder: 'But now, since Pentecost has come, this community of those endowed with the Spirit in the world has been made manifest. Now the people of God, scattered throughout the world of sin as in a diaspora, has become a visible institution, a concrete reality of history'. And then once more it may be asked: 'Even if the people of God has acquired the status of a concrete body in this way, and as such has become visible in history as the Church, does this really have much to do with the Holy Spirit, or is it not precisely the outcome of the work of Jesus in founding the Church, when he gathered the believers about his apostles and gave them this status of an historical institution which we call the Church by causing them to believe in the word which he had addressed to them in history, and to accept his sacraments? And with regard to the Spirit itself, is not the situation that just as he was poured out formerly, so too he is now, and so he will be to the end of time, and that he is poured out also into that other world of those who do not belong to this historical institution of the people of God called the Church? Thus is the birth of the Church not something which has little to do with the Spirit and its outpourings, seeing that the Spirit was given *before* the Church, and is given to those *not included in* the Church? Furthermore, if we consider what belongs to the Church independently of this outpouring of the Spirit, namely its institutional status, its constitution, its system of law, its official organisation, then is not all this, if not actually contrary to the Spirit, at least different from the Spirit?' And if the only reply we could make to all this was that now the Spirit has been poured out in greater fulness, that since Pentecost it is more powerfully and more abundantly at work, then certainly we Christians would not care to deny this. But we would still have to ask: 'Was the Spirit really bestowed in lesser measure and less freely upon the men of former ages? Were they really less beloved by God?' And we will feel embarrassed and disconcerted (if we possess any of that courageous realism which is also a gift of the Spirit) as we secretly torment ourselves with the question: 'Is then the outpouring of the Spirit upon the Church really so powerful, so overwhelmingly convincing, so authoritative that everything that has gone before in the history of the Holy Spirit seems petty and obscure by comparison?' And then if all we can say is that at Pentecost the Spirit is poured out over the institutional element in the Church as founded by Jesus, over its lawful authorities, the sacramental signs and the word of preaching in it, then, once more, this might prompt another question: 'Why is that so significant, seeing that already even without this institutional factor, this Spirit of the Father was at work, manifesting itself, judging and sanctifying, beginning with the prophets and extending right up to the time of those who dwelt quietly in the land, already looking for that eternal kingdom of God which we ourselves are still awaiting?' If we sought to rely *only* upon the words of Jesus in scripture, and upon those of the apostles, according to which, precisely: 'The Spirit was not yet given because Jesus had not yet been glorified', so that the disciples had to wait for the Spirit which the Lord promised to them at his departure, then we should still be faced with the unsolved question of how, in that case, this statement that 'the Spirit was not yet given' can be reconciled with that other truth that this Spirit has, nevertheless, spoken through the prophets, and worked, dwelt and brought to maturity eternal life in all men of all ages who believe, hope and love, by the grace of God, *that* grace which denies God's mercy to no-one who is ready to receive it.

If we wish to understand what Pentecost really is, we must first recognise one point: Christmas, Good Friday, Easter and Pentecost (in other words all those 'once and for all' events which we celebrate in the great festivals of Christendom) are so closely interconnected that they merely represent the temporal development of one and the same salvific event, the time structure of a single deed of God performed in history and upon mankind. This deed of God, one and indivisible, yet taking place in a historical process that is phased, is the definitive and irrevocable acceptance of humanity in the incarnation of the Logos. In that the Logos assumed a human 'nature', he necessarily assumed also a human historicity, so that this assumption of the reality of human nature was only complete when he had brought the history of this reality to its consummation by his death. What is unique, new and 'once and for all' in this single historical **event of assuming human nature and human history is its definitive** finality. Always and everywhere where human history has been wrought out the dialogue between God and man, issuing in salvation or perdition, has taken place. Always and everywhere, therefore, the Spirit has been present to judge and to endow with grace. But this single dialogue, which runs continuously through the whole history of humanity, was *open*. Before the incarnation of the Logos no word of God had entered into world history as an event, no word which God imposed finally and definitively, no word in which God addressed himself definitively and irrevocably to the world, no word which expressed him definitively and exhaustively, no word which disclosed the ultimate and all-comprehending plan of God, no word which brought out the meaning of the real climax in the drama of world history, no word which drew this drama to its ultimate issue and brought out its ultimate meaning. And still less was it revealed before Christ what the import of this ultimate and all-embracing word would be, whether it would import judgment or grace, remoteness or nearness, Lordship or Fatherhood, the relationship of servant or of child, law or grace, the order of created nature or the freedom of the Spirit of God imparting itself and thereby bestowing the infinitude of God upon men. The dialogue lasted throughout the whole history of mankind from the beginning up to Christ. But the last word was not yet spoken. The whole of it still remained open. History was able to develop in either an upward or a downward direction. All was still ultimately in the balance. Every commitment was provisional and subject to revision. Every dispensation was subject to change and decay. One age might be followed by another which abolished the provisions of the first, and did not really so much as allow what was unique and proper to it to be brought to its fulness. But since the Word has taken flesh and submitted to death and to the other conditions of our history, and has subjected itself to these conditions in a final and irrevocable manner because it assumed our human nature as a factor most intimately inherent in itself, now everything is different, everything has become final. However much the individual has to experience his own private destiny as still open and undecided, since the incarnation, death and resurrection of Christ human history as a whole has already arrived at its goal. It has been assumed by God for ever. It has been endowed with grace to all eternity. It can never more be abandoned. The factor of sinfulness in it has already been included in this gesture of acceptance on God's part, and has been outweighed by the power of the grace which has conquered it. The world is predestined to **salvation and** not to perdition, to life and not to death. God no longer waits for the decision of the world as though it had to say the last word. On the contrary he has spoken the ultimate word as his own Word, and *at the same time* as that of the world itself. And this word is reconciliation, life, light, victory and the glory of God himself, which he himself has implanted in the innermost depths of the world itself to become its glory. And all this is now no longer hidden in the eternal decrees of God, (though it has, of course, been present in these right from the beginning, albeit in a manner which was not available to creatures to recognise and to examine), but has rather become manifest, has been brought into being and given objective reality in the world itself, rooted in the very heart of the world to become the active principle that directs it to its goal. The result is that this active force inherent in the world already bears within itself all the fulness of perfection, and has already imparted this fulness to the world. When, therefore, we say that at Pentecost the Spirit has descended upon all flesh, then we no longer say this only of that Spirit which has always presided in the world, for we are speaking of the eschatological Spirit, the Spirit as the irrevocable gift. This is the Spirit of the eternal predestination of the world as a whole to life and to victory, the invincible Spirit which has been implanted in the world and in its history, and indissolubly wedded to it. This Spirit was not there before Christ, and since Pentecost it has been revealed that *this* Spirit is the Spirit of *Christ*, that in its outpouring and its work in the world it shares in the finality of Christ himself; that it is the Spirit of the crucified and risen Christ, and therefore the Spirit who will no longer disappear from the world and from the community of Christ. It has been revealed that the Spirit is the Spirit of the risen Christ, and that it has been promised as such irrevocably and invincibly to the world – it is this that was revealed at Pentecost and was accepted in an attitude of faith by those upon whom the Spirit descended.

II

What is it which brings this event of the Spirit home to us personally? How does it make its message penetrate into our existence in order to prepare us ever anew for the tasks of our lives? Here we may mention only two basic attitudes which derive from this Spirit of Pentecost: responsibility and trust.

1. *Responsibility*

At first sight one might suppose that if this is the situation, if the Spirit is now irrevocably and triumphantly present, if it can never more by any means be removed from the world, if, in a certain sense, it is present as *opus operatum*, as of formal pre-definition, as that which is eschatologically final and definitive, then surely, one might say, everything has been made quite simple and quite secure. Then one can depend upon the fact of the Spirit's presence, and the burden of responsibility and of care has been removed from man, as also has the anguish and struggle involved in not knowing what the final issue of events will be. But this only seems to be the case. In reality the situation in which man finds himself has been rendered more acute. The hour of victory in the grace of the Spirit is also the hour of decision and judgment, and that too in a more radical sense than ever before. Such is the situation of man in the age inaugurated by Christ, always viewed from the point of view of scripture. What has been offered to men here is indeed the highest and most all-conquering gift of all. But it is also the last; the one which compels man to an ultimate decision, which can never more be revised. This decision is no merely provisional one. Once taken the negotiations leading up to it can never more be re-opened. Certainly we are all now living in the age of the Spirit of God now come among us finally and definitively; the age of the eschatologically victorious Church; the age of Christ, which is also the eternal *future*. At the same time it is certainly true that the decision which the *individual* has to take still always remains open. But now because the *situation* in which the decision is taken can no longer be changed, precisely the same principle applies to this final and 'once and for all' decision. Only in Christ is there any '*topos metanoias*', any place for repentance and conversion. The sins against the Spirit cannot be forgiven. There can be no other sacrifice for all eternity outside the dispensation of Christ. One cannot pray for one who, in a spirit of unbelief, absolutely denies Christ. These and similar formulations, the underlying purport of which is to bring out the radical character of the decision involved in the existential situation after Christ, recur again and again in scripture. And what is true as a general and universal principle has an urgent and ever more insistent application to the life of the individual Christian too. Here too, in the genesis of his spiritual being, he reproduces the philogenesis which runs through salvific history up to the time of Christ. Precisely because God has spoken his ultimate word to mankind as a whole, it has the same force for the individual as such. Life is compressed into a single decisive moment. The discussion between God and man is drawn more and more to a single point of intensity and crisis. Life is more and more compressed into a single all-embracing decision. And it is precisely in the nature of this as radical decision that the power of grace, which in itself is victorious, is made manifest. For what applies to other relationships between God and his creatures applies in this case too. The fact that God's power is effective in all that is does not diminish the autonomous power of the creature. On the contrary, both powers increase in the same, and not in inverse proportion. And for this reason the eschatological triumph of the grace of the Spirit of Pentecost 'is manifested' precisely in the creature's acceptance of the responsibility of creaturely freedom at its most radical, and where the issue is literally one of life and death. If there were any individual case in which this triumph of Pentecostal grace did not appear, this would also be a sign that this grace of God, in its own sovereign freedom, had 'omitted' the individual concerned from its operation and had rejected him. The hour of victory for the grace of Pentecost is also the hour of responsibility in its most intense form. Those who acknowledge this grace truly, and not merely in words, are also at the same time the men who so act as though everything depended upon them. But in this they recognise calmly that while they play their part in this manner nothing else is achieved except the victory of grace. And once more it must be reiterated that all that has been said applies most of all to those who, as ministers of the Church, must be first and foremost the bearers of this victorious grace of the Spirit.

2. *Trust*

We have seen that if we understand it rightly the triumphant grace of the Spirit in the Church, both as a whole and, in derivation from this, in its application to the individual too, should spur us on to accept responsibility in its most radical form. But however true this may be, it is also true that in the last analysis this Spirit of Pentecost provides grounds for absolute trust. Let us consider the case of one who believes in it, waits for it and is ready to make it manifest in his own life for what it is in itself, in other words as that which, even as it is bestowed, brings with it the power to accept it as well. Such a one as this can trust and hope indeed. He does not know in what *form* or *manner* it will be victorious, but he knows the *fact that* it will be so. He knows that he may not try to prevent it from making failure, death and defeat the form in which its victory is made manifest. He knows that the Spirit of grace, precisely because it is the Spirit of the freedom and infinitude of God, does not exclude anything (except his sins, all of which, so far as he knows, have been forgiven and pardoned), but can rather draw *anything at all* into the pattern of his coming, his victory and his final and permanent presence if it pleases him to do so: distance and nearness, exultation and tears, life and death, the heights and the depths, honour and dishonour. But precisely because of this it is also true that nothing is in a position to prevent his victory. Everything can remain to all appearances as it was before. But everything can also have been thrust, by these means, into the glory of God. Everything can be permeated with God and with his love. The hidden dynamism which is in everything and which drives everything onwards can be elevated and transformed into eternal life. The Spirit which is God's absolute and triumphant nearness needs no victories such as the world needs, no confirmation of the kind without which the world cannot be sure of its victories. One who has submitted himself to this Spirit and is aware of being one with it in an attitude of Pentecostal trust – such a one as this knows that all the depths to which he can sink have been enveloped in the depths of the infinite love of God. He knows, even without testing, that all his own downfalls have already been swallowed up in that victory which belongs to the Spirit alone. All his own weakness has already been healed at its roots, and only still survives as a pain which proclaims the greatness of the healing. He who believes in and loves the Spirit of Pentecost, who lets that Spirit be the Spirit of loving faith in himself, and make it his own act in him, such a one as this can say with all confidence: 'Everything has already been decided and the history of the world and of my personal life has already been accomplished in the life and death of him who, in obedience and love, died on behalf of his Church. And because of his attitude to his Church, he let his heart be pierced so that the water of the Spirit of Pentecost might gush forth over all who believe in him, and who, by this faith of theirs, become sharers in the victory accomplished in the life of this one man'. And as we listen to this declaration we should not take it merely in the abstract as having a general application. We must face up to the needs of our own existence, unique and unrepeatable as it is, which we are so eager to run away from, which we suppress and are unwilling to acknowledge. We must be willing to face up to this need of ours, and the dire peril in which we stand, and then, in an act of faith inspired by the

Spirit of God dwelling in our innermost hearts, make bold to say: 'The victory of the grace which has been given me is the answer to all this. Let me be confident. Let me have trust. For it is Pentecost, the day on which it has been revealed that God himself, in Christ Jesus the crucified and risen Lord, has said his last and irrevocable word to you, and has made it the gift of the Holy Spirit to you, bestowed upon you without regret on God's part and in such a way that no-one can take it from you, in such a way that it has a permanent and inalienable place in your life.'

PART THREE

The Sacrament of the Lord

20

SUNDAY, THE DAY OF THE LORD

WE come together to celebrate the Last Supper of the Lord. We commemorate the death which has redeemed us. In the liturgical ceremonies we say our 'yes' of faith to *that* sacrifice as our sacrifice, which he has offered on our behalf to God in his eternity once and for all. It is a sacrifice of himself, and of us in him. We receive the crucified and risen Lord as the forgiveness of our sins, as the Lord of our life, as the love that unites us, and as the presence, in a mysterious and hidden manner, of the future glory that will be ours. We celebrate the Last Supper of the Lord in festal splendour in order that we may be able to do it more perfectly within the simple rhythm of the average and the everyday factors in our lives. The day which is set apart for every Catholic Christian by the celebration of this sacrifice is Sunday, the day of the Lord, on which Christ the Lord himself celebrates it with those who believe in him.

What is Sunday? First of all it is certain, even from the point of view of its historical background in the sabbath of the Old Testament, that it is simply a day of rest. When we look closely at this Old Testament background we are actually compelled to conclude that the decree of rest from work on the sabbath was ordained by God as an end in itself, and not to enable his people to engage in an act of formal worship. For in the original sabbath commandment and the manner in which this was observed no provision whatever was made for the performance of such cultic duties. It really was for the sake of men and not for himself that God interposed this commandment of his. From the point of view of its origin, therefore, Sunday too is primarily a day on which man must do no work, a day on which he must not attempt to support his physical life by toil in the struggle with nature and in the process of adapting himself to the laws of nature. It is a day which serves to remind us that man has not only to fit in obediently with the rhythm of nature, consisting of day and night, waking and sleeping, vigour and weariness, as though he were merely a part of the natural order and subject to its laws. What this day reminds us of rather is that man is the lord of nature and not its slave, that he directs and controls the rhythms of nature by his own power, adapts and transforms nature by his own designs, makes it serve his interests and contribute to his life. The whole of the natural order is included within a single dimension of space, and a single dimension of time. But man makes nature his servant in such a way that from the space and time that belong to it he carves out, so to say, a space-time dimension for himself, where he can exercise his own freedom and his own autonomy in order to shape nature according to his own designs and, at the same time, to keep himself free and to be his own master. Sunday is the tangible expression, which takes the form of a communal celebration, of the fact that within this space-time dimension which he has made for himself man is autonomous and free — not subject, therefore, to nature's behests. Sunday is the celebration of a partial victory in the history of mankind, a celebration which is still relatively recent in origin. It is a victory won in a struggle which has lasted right from the origins, and which is still incessantly waged. Right at the beginning of man's history God himself has commanded him to engage in this struggle. It is a struggle in which he seeks more and more to bring nature into subjection. Sunday is set apart from the rhythm of nature. As a day it is characterised not by the fact that for sheer weariness we cannot continue any longer, nor yet by mere negative inactivity. On the contrary, this day is an event, a celebration, regularly recurring, of the fact that man liberates himself to a real though limited extent, from the compulsion of nature. And the commmandment of God at the creation which empowers and emboldens man, and lays it upon him as a duty (Gen 1:28) to engage in this struggle for his own liberation, is followed by a further commandment, namely to celebrate his victory in this struggle. Viewed from this point of view the efforts of humanity to enlarge this space-time dimension of its own personal freedom still further are in principle wholly legitimate. Those, however, who set this goal before them must bear in mind that they are only continuing a struggle which the Old Testament and Christendom have already long regarded as ordained by God's commandment, a struggle which they have already begun and have already celebrated by a day of rest.

Sunday, then, is the expression in tangible and liturgical terms, of the power actively to dispose of things instead of being disposed of, of the creative exercise of freedom on the part of spiritual beings instead of the passivity of merely natural ones. And this is manifested by the fact that *in the last analysis* it is the person as spiritual who constitutes the law of nature and not *vice versa*. And in consequence of this everything points to the fact that Sunday is the day on which man truly recognises *himself* as one who is more than a mere member of the natural order. To view Sunday in a merely materialist way or actually to spend it like this is to deny its true nature. If it is so regarded it can only be one factor in a rhythmic physiological process, a mere answering of one's biological needs. On this view enjoyment as one of the factors appropriate to Sunday would represent a mere pleasurable reaction on the part of one's physiological make-up. Now let us imagine a man who celebrates Sunday in *this* spirit. He is in process of emancipating himself from nature, yet he uses his dominion over nature merely in order to realise the purely natural side of his own being, to answer his biological needs, and to find pleasure on the purely physiological plane. In other words he is actually lowering himself in subjection to nature, instead of asserting his dominion over it and recognising that Sunday is at once an expression of the fact that he himself is above nature and of the demand that he shall be so. Now if this were to be our attitude Sunday would not be a day of holiness dedicated to mankind, but a pagan day dedicated to nature, on which man voluntarily turned back to adore that from which he has been liberated. For this reason Sunday can only be rightly observed if man realises himself *as man*. Now man is spirit, freedom, a being of absolute truth and love, capable of reflecting upon himself; and he realises himself when, confronted by the absolute mystery which we call God, he believes and so dares to commit himself to the incomprehensible. But this means that man is also the being to which this mystery imparts itself in absolute freedom, in grace therefore, as radical nearness, as forgiveness and as that which fills man with this life of God himself. This absolute self-bestowal of God is made apprehensible, revealed and imparted through a historical medium, one which can, in the power of God's all-embracing will to save, extend its influence universally to all ages, peoples and cultural environments. This is Jesus Christ who as God-man is unique. He is the salvation of those who know that they believe in him, and also of those who do actually believe even though they suppose that they do not do so. For in him, the Lord, unification and reconciliation have been achieved in one supreme respect: the question which calls everything in life, right up to the point of death itself, in question has been answered with the only answer possible, the infinitude of the blessed mystery of God. The fact that reconciliation has been achieved for us in this way is celebrated in the Church's sacrifice, in which the God-man continues to abide in the midst of his community, making the final and definitive state to which he attained in his death and subsequent glorification eternally effective among his followers. Man does not truly celebrate Sunday until he regards it as a means of maintaining his conquest of nature. He can only take this attitude to it if he is willing to lose himself in faith and love in the mystery of God. But the only way in which he will be received into this mystery is to be possessed by the Word of God. When he is possessed in this way it means that he is slain and brought to life again. Certainly this may occur wherever man accepts the fact that his existence is doomed to death, and in so doing, upheld by the grace of God, accepts the life of God in a spirit of patient faith and love. And he does this even though he is not able so much as to express to himself what is taking place in the depths of his own spiritual being. By faith, then, we can accept our own existence, doomed to death as it is, as life. And this in itself constitutes a celebration of the death of the Lord, albeit a dumb and uncomprehending one. But once our life has been imbued with grace *this* sort of celebration emerges from our inward depths and acquires an existence of its own. It becomes an objective factor for us, and acquires a central place in the 'space-time' environment of our existence. The death of the Lord generates life, and this 'celebration' of that death in us is alive with that life. Through grace the fact of its one-ness with that life-generating death becomes explicit. The life-generating death itself becomes real and effective once more *in virtue of the fact* that it thereby becomes apprehensible in the dimension of space and time and is made manifest in sign and symbol. And when it has attained this status this 'celebration' of the death of the Lord is called the eucharistic sacrifice, the Mass of the holy Church, the Sunday liturgy. Sunday comes to be celebrated in this liturgy. In it the true meaning of the freedom and grace which Sunday represents is revealed and made effective. It is the discovery of the infinitude of God as our eternal life.

Once this has been understood it becomes immediately clear what Sunday demands of us. It must not be wholly taken up with leisure activities in a process of enslavement to the enjoyment industries, whereby man is false to himself and to the mystery of his own existence. Sunday must not be threatened by the 'shift-system' as applied to the working week. Where this is erected into a principle in its own right, instead of merely making provision for exceptions in particular cases, it may, it is true, cater for men's biological needs for rest and refreshment, but it cannot provide them with any opportunity for the *celebration* of the community of God as a whole. Sunday must not be merely one of the free days, but must be a holy day, and provision must be made for it in the allotment of the other free periods. It is a day on which work and recreation alike are summed up and put in order, and both are incorporated in the prelude to that final consummation in which eternal rest becomes eternal life. This day has a character which we Christians can and must defend in the juridical dispositions of public life as well. For we are not doing violence to anyone if we demand that the free time allotted to everyone, to be used each according to his own conscience, shall fall on the same day, a day which we Christians for our part fill with the celebration of the advent of that eternal freedom which comes from the living God.

Man as he develops struggles free from the foreordained dispositions of the natural order, and to the extent that he does so new possibilities of exercising his freedom open up before him. He has a broader range of possibilities to choose from in arranging and filling his personal and intellectual life, but also new opportunities for arbitrary behaviour without reference to his obligations. And for this reason it now becomes the task of the believer and the spiritual man to take personal responsibility for ensuring that Sunday shall be Sunday; to preserve a cheerful and relaxed asceticism with regard to the addictions and the hedonistic escapism of the present age, and to exercise a religious creativity himself in shaping the pattern of Sunday. He can no longer expect that Sunday as it should really be will impose itself and define its own character by sheer force of social custom. We have to create it for ourselves, each one for himself. And we have constantly to renew this process. Nor do we have any very readily available prescriptions for this. For such prescriptions, even when they derive from Christian circles, are too often simply romantic in outlook, representing glorified versions of the Sunday observances of former times. We cannot be excused from constantly bending ourselves to the task of making Sunday itself constantly new. We cannot evade this task even upon the pretext that it is no longer possible to adopt the bourgeois pattern of thought of the nineteenth century. We must still understand and hold firm to the meaning and the function of Sunday on the basis of the gospel. Only then have we truly understood what it means for us to be and to live as Christians. This is God's day, the day of the Lord, which knows no evening, the day of that freedom and that rest which is life itself, a day of God, the mystery of whom we have been favoured to receive, and which alone can avail to bring all else to its final goal. But in the sacred work of celebrating the sacrifice of the Church that is done which we have to do every Sunday and which, when stripped of its veils and made manifest, proves to be eternal life.

21

THE EUCHARIST AND OUR DAILY LIVES

By way of revising what we learnt from the catechism let us begin by saying something about the actual nature of the Eucharist. In this sacrament saving history as a whole, and at the same time our own personal saving history attains its highest point. In this sacrament the enduring basis for our own Christian thought is constantly re-asserted and made tangibly present in symbol. This climax to the history of salvation as a whole, and to our own personal saving history, is God incarnate. But the fact that he is there where we are, the fact that the eternal Word of the Father, containing within itself all wisdom and glory, has taken to itself our flesh, our life, our destiny, our everyday activities, our death – it is in virtue of this fact that our life is redeemed and hallowed, in virtue of this fact that it is encompassed by the eternal pardon of God, in virtue of this fact that it has been inwardly healed, in virtue of this fact that it is united with God and his eternity and his own eternal and glorious life. It is because of this that his deed of compassion, the sentence of death to which he submitted, was not in vain. The incarnate Word of the eternal Father, which in the incarnation has assumed our life, is the salvation of the world and is our salvation, the salvation wrought out in the personal history of our own lives. This incarnate Word of the Father has penetrated into both of these, the life of the world as a whole, and the entirely personal life which we lead as individuals at this particular point in space and time, and at this particular point in history. He has come into the world at Christmas. He is present among us, has laid hold of our lives in the most absolute and most ultimate manner possible. He could not have made himself more intimately present in our lives than by allowing us to receive his divine Body in holy Communion. In this sacrament it is he who is the salvation of the world who comes to us with his light, with his grace, with his forgiveness, with his power. He himself accepts us who accept him by the act of receiving him, and it really is an episode in saving history that is enacted in this personal history of our own lives. In this sacrament of the altar the universal deed of salvation wrought by God upon the whole world in the incarnation of his eternal Son lays hold of us and of our whole concrete personal lives. In this sacrament we are touched by God's forgiveness, the grace of Jesus Christ, and we are united with God as our eternal life. The Eucharist, the Last Supper, holy Communion, the Mass or, as we like to express it, the eternal celebration of our own salvation bestowed upon us by God himself, is the definitive religious act of our lives, in other words the act that unites us to God. Before we go any further we must momentarily leave this point in order to take up a further one, likewise concerned with this glory which exists at the centre of our lives. We must look into the factor of the everyday in our lives. Let us put forward certain ideas concerning the nature of this factor of the everyday.

We are all familiar with it, this 'everyday'. The first point to be recognised about it is simply that it belongs to the realm of the profane. When we return from the communion rail we like to join our hands and maintain an attitude of recollection. Very soon, so it seems, we find ourselves leaving the sphere of the sacred constituted by the presence of God to go out into the world, the sphere of the earthly, the sphere of the everyday, the profane, the unhallowed, into the realm of business, the world of multitudinous affairs, cares, struggles, in which general confusion prevails throughout and all words are lost and drowned in the universal clamour; where everyone pursues his own desires and aims, where the struggle for life is waged, where there is no common understanding, where factions are the order of the day, where the most divergent views are maintained, where there is hunger and care and inward loneliness. The moment we leave the sphere of the sacred we enter upon the sphere of the everyday, the world which is so full of profanity, and in this world God seems to be remote. We speak of a thousand matters, the newspapers and the general talk are full of anything and everything. And perhaps in the midst of this chorus we come across a small shabby religious pamphlet, or a sermon comes stammering down to us from the pulpit telling of matters which the world does not take seriously. Truly the world of the everyday is a world that is remote from God, and yet it is this world that we must constantly enter. Outside it is, as it were, dark and it is cold, and wherever we are we feel isolated. It is precisely the world of the everyday, and for those who come out of the sphere of God's sacred presence into everyday life this element of the everyday, so profane, so remote from God, will in fact be even more harshly oppressive.

Those who have finally and permanently confined themselves to this sphere of profane and everyday life, or who attempt to do so, no longer feel how profane and how remote from God the everyday life of this world is in which they live. They are, indeed, themselves simply an element in this world. They have standards of their own adapted to the conditions of this world, and for this reason they do not feel – at any rate on the surface of their lives – the contradiction between their true purpose and destiny and their everyday lives. But we recognise that we have to answer to God for our lives. And even though we cannot regard this world in its profanity and remoteness from God as self-authenticating, nevertheless we must go out into this world. We must commit ourselves to it, share in its cares, its struggles, its discussions, its ideas etc., and so we shall constantly feel this world in its profanity, its remoteness from God, its godlessness as something that is oppressive. Inevitably, to some extent, it divides us against ourselves, because we bear God and our responsibility to him in our hearts, and yet at the same time must constantly go out – indeed are sent out – into the world anew, even though it is quite alien to this state of ours of being interiorly filled with God, and to this sense of having to answer to the divine and eternal Master of our own hearts for our lives, which we carry within us. The result is that again and again we must anxiously be putting the question to ourselves, as in fact we do, of how in that case this process of dividing our lives between the everyday on the one hand and God in our hearts on the other can be sustained. And ever anew it will actually be borne in upon us that we, who go out into the world, are ourselves in constant danger of becoming merely worldly. We feel how real the danger is, that our own standards will be altered, that we shall gradually begin to adopt the standards of the world that is merely profane, everyday, and remote from God, that to us too the only things that are near and familiar are precisely these things of everyday life, that they are taking possession of our hearts to the exclusion of all else. We notice then how God, his will, his love, his accustomed nearness, his grace, his forgiveness, somehow seem to be turning into mere ideological tenets. How the call of God to us penetrates only very faintly to the ear of our hearts. How we, who have to live in a world that is profane, remote from God and everyday in character, are threatening to become everyday more profane and more remote from God ourselves.

And over and above this is the fact that this element of the everyday in what we do is now truly dark and ambiguous. For what part does it play in our lives? We try to do our duty, and when we have done our best we still do not know in the end whether we have done it aright. In what we do the motifs of heaven and earth are intermingled in such a manner that it is ultimately beyond our powers of reflection to analyse or distinguish between them. They constitute such a mixture of light and darkness that all we are left with is a strange obscurity and ambiguity, a sort of twilight when we seek to examine and reflect upon them. In the end we have done all sorts of things, and do not know whether what we have done really is what we should have done. We grope onwards, questing, questioning, anxiously probing throughout our daily lives, and at the end we do not know whom we have been servant to, whether it really was God, really was our neighbour, or whether we, having become everyday in our attitude, have by our actions only paid tribute to necessity and simply go on because we have no longer the strength to take some other course of action. How dark, how ambiguous everyday life is after all, even with respect to the value of what we do in it in God's eyes, from the moral aspect. And over and above these factors which are inherent in the very nature of the everyday there is also its toilsomeness, the attitudes characteristic of it of indifference, lovelessness, unvarying routine, the stresses which it imposes on us, the unrewardingness of it, the monotony of our voices, the weariness of our nerves, our hearts, our spirits, the experience of being overworked, the experience that the inner resources of our hearts are exhausted. And all this toilsomeness amounts to one thing: nothing else than a slow death (we shall be returning to this point at a later stage).

The factor of the everyday in our lives, therefore, is characterised as profane, remote from God, ambiguous, dark, toilsome and advancing towards death. But a further factor in addition to this is that this general mediocrity, this sense of monotony in the everyday, can actually make our hearts themselves so filled with mediocrity, so weary, so depressed, so ambiguous and dark that we can no longer have any true awareness of these characteristics of the everyday. When an eye full of light looks into the darkness it does see the darkness to some extent, and when a heart that is bold and filled with inward vitality looks at the everyday then it is sensitive enough to feel the monotony, the profanity of the everyday. But when the eye of the spirit itself is dark and dimmed, when the heart itself is also bowed down with the everyday then it is as though we no longer possessed the faculty we need to evaluate the everyday really as everyday, and to impose great and generous demands upon ourselves in regard to it, measuring it by the standard of high ideals and recognising it for what it really is.

It might be said that the everyday so devours us — this at least is the danger — so absorbs us into itself that we believe that it is quite impossible for there to be anything else except this everyday, and everything else is quite ruled out. And then we ourselves — this is the danger — become a still more mediocre 'everyday', which no longer recognises itself as such at all, but is, as it were, inwardly closed in upon itself to such an extent that it never looks up to the true and infinite life which we call God. Instead it constantly turns back upon itself.

Our considerations of the nature of the Eucharist and the nature of the everyday up to this point might even lead one to suppose at first that no two factors could be more contradictory, more set at opposite poles, more mutually opposed and mutually repellant. For the former factor consists in the sacred celebration of the nearness of God, the high point of atonement in our saving history, in which we encounter the eternal word of God become flesh; and the second factor is this one of the everyday, of which we have been speaking. There is the ambience of the holy. There is the nearness of God. There is the light of eternal life. There is eternal power. There is eternal glory, the eternal transcendence over death and, instead of that element of the average and the mediocre which is no longer capable of insight into itself, there is the infinitude of God. There is the boundlessness of eternal life. And here, in the everyday, profanity, remoteness from God, darkness and toilsomeness, the doom of death, the mediocre and the average. What an immense gulf seems to open up between these two factors in our lives! What an abyss seems to divide these two elements in our lives from one another, even though both are present in those lives! And we ourselves do in fact feel this. And if we no longer felt it, if we no longer felt this encounter with the incarnate Word of God in the Eucharist as supremely the immense, the exalted, the holy, the eternal and the divine in our lives, if what the Eucharist brings about in our hearts were actually to be so withered up into a minor but burdensome religious duty, then it would be precisely the factor of the everyday itself, and our own 'everyday' hearts that would have, as it were, swallowed up and devoured this, the supreme event in the celebration of the divine in our lives, that would have reduced even this to an element in the everyday. But we who believe, who seek, who love, know what this celebration of the Last Supper of the Lord means, and on the basis of this we realise how great the difference between these two factors in our lives must seem to be.

It is only here that we arrive at the real point of our argument. Our thesis must now be stated as follows: This sacrament of the eternal encounter with God, this climax in our personal saving history, in the history of our individual lives, which is the Eucharist, is in fact the sacrament of the everyday.

Why should this be so? To begin with, this becomes clear in the Church's tradition concerning this sacrament and in her official teaching. In the second chapter of the thirteenth session of the Council of Trent the nature of the holy Eucharist, its meaning, its function and its significance, are more exactly described. This chapter contains a statement about the Eucharist such as is not to be found either before or after the Council of Trent. It consists of a solemn declaration of the Church's teaching on the point. It is laid down that this sacrament is *'animarum cibus quo alantur et confortentur'*, that the Eucharist is the food of souls, by means of which they are nourished and strengthened. The Eucharist, therefore, is here regarded as our daily bread.

What can be more everyday than one's daily bread? Every day the same thing happens: we eat and drink. We feed ourselves, to adopt the mode of expression customary in profane spheres. It is only rarely that a meal taken in the purely human sphere can be counted as an elevated, fine and fully human event, celebrated in a manner that edifies the spirit. For the most part eating and drinking for the sustenance of our own life is precisely something which belongs to the context of the everyday. And so in the same way, the Church tells us, the Eucharist is the daily bread of poor Christians, by means of which they must nourish themselves ever anew, and strengthen themselves ever anew.

This alone is enough to show that the Eucharist is regarded as the food of a man who becomes hungry again and again, who becomes weak again and again – in other words one who, so far as his spiritual life is concerned, is a man of the everyday.

The same chapter of this Council goes on to say that the Eucharist has a remedial function too in that by means of it we are freed from our daily sins and preserved from mortal sin. Again in this description of the sacrament we find a real echo of the everyday and the wearisome as it exists throughout our lives – lives in which the wretchedness, feebleness, moral weakness, moral weariness and moral instability which are in man manifest themselves every day. For in this chapter the Eucharist is called the *antidotum*, the remedy by means of which we are freed from daily sins – painfully evident as these are in the constantly renewed onslaughts and constantly renewed struggles – and by means of which we must be guarded against the death of the soul. Here too, in this characterisation of the Eucharist, therefore, man is depicted as we experience him for ourselves in our everyday lives. And the Eucharist itself is viewed in its effects precisely upon man in this guise, in the toilsomeness and weakness of his everyday life. It is viewed as the antidote to this enduring condition of ours. And the same passage goes on to say that through this sacrament we must be united to one another by bonds of faith, hope and love in order that we may all be of one accord, and that there may be no divisions among us. Again it is the factor of the everyday in the life of men, who live and have to live with one another, that is envisaged, and again in this portrayal of the Eucharist in the official teaching of the Church this supreme sacrament of sacred fellowship with God is shown in the central impact which it has upon our everyday lives. Let us recognise in all calmness that it is in order that we may to some extent live in harmony one with another, at least in the context of the everyday, tolerate one another, bear one another's burdens in peace, in patience, in hope and in some little degree of love, that this Bread of life is imparted to us. This definitive description, put forward by the solemn and official teaching of the Church, is itself enough to enable us to recognise suddenly and surprisingly that this supreme mystery of Christendom, the holy and most holy sacrament of the altar, is manifestly the sacrament of our everyday lives.

And let us examine this truth somewhat more closely still.

Who is bestowed upon us in this sacrament? What does this sacrament stand for? What is the message of this most holy celebration in the holiest hour of our lives? It is the crucified Lord and his death. His fate is the redeeming factor in our lives. He, the incarnate Word, is our salvation through his life and through his death.

His fate is certainly more than merely everyday. His fate is the mystery of the Cross. His fate which redeems us is the mystery of Good Friday. But while it is true that he whom we receive as our Redeemer through his life and death is also more than one who has taken a mere everyday lot upon himself, it also remains true at the same time that this fate of death which redeems us is, basically speaking, nothing more than the everyday which, as we may express it, manifests itself here in its purest and most concentrated form. This death represents the ultimate in what we mean by the everyday. We cannot find a more precise way of expressing it than that which we have just given. But at the same time it was frustration, it was pain, it was the negation of its Victim's intentions and designs, it was the betrayal of friends. This Good Friday was loneliness itself. This Good Friday was that mysterious cry, the real meaning of which man cannot so much as guess at, 'My God, my God, why hast thou forsaken me?' This Good Friday was the futility of life, the hatred of enemies, betrayal of friends, loneliness, remoteness from God, an exposure of the stupidity of human aims and designs, and death. What is all this? Precisely, as we may express it, the concentrated, the pure essence of what is apportioned to us again and again gradually and piecemeal in our everyday lives. Seneca the sage said long ago that when we start to live we begin to die, and Gregory the Great, in a sermon which we read repeatedly in our breviaries, explains that life is, properly speaking, nothing else than the 'prolixitas mortis', a thread of death that runs right through life. It is, as it were, a slow, long-drawn-out death, one that is, so to say, administered and received a drop at a time. And that is precisely how it is! We should not condemn life. We should recognise its joys, its glory, its greatness, its loyalties, its beauties. And we should praise them in a spirit of thankfulness. But we Christians have neither a right nor a duty to act in a spirit of false optimism, as though life consisted simply in joy and glory for their own sake. For it is sickness, it is loneliness, it is remoteness from God, it is anxiety about the future of one's plans, it is pain, it is toil, it is hardship, in one word it is – the everyday. And even if we take the burden of the everyday upon ourselves – God give us the grace to do so – in a spirit of genuine, wholesome and indefatigable vitality, with the feeling of being well-equipped to take it, with lively hearts and with the optimism of one who is precisely bold and healthy, not woebegone, not over-sensitive – even if we do all this, I say, and even if we recognise that it is precisely our Christian duty not to indulge in self-pity, not to shoot at the little sparrows of our everyday burdens with the artillery of the sacred and the supernatural in a spirit of false idealism – still it nevertheless remains true that a man who really faces up to his life as it is must feel the factor of the everyday as a heavy burden upon him. Indeed he will feel it to be so more and more, and thereby will gradually be initiated into the hard and unwelcome truth that the everyday, that is that which precisely provides the content of our lives as a whole, is the 'prolixitas mortis', the act of dying long drawn out.

Now if Jesus' redeeming deed, his life and death, is received by us in him whom we receive as our crucified Lord, then precisely what is at basis the pure essence of the everyday in the Body of Christ is also received. When we receive the Lord in the Eucharist as him who died on the Cross, then we receive the innermost governing factor of the everyday, because the crucified Lord in his Cross and in his death only expresses in visible terms the lot that is imparted to us in the 'prolixitas mortis' of everyday, as it were piecemeal and drop by drop, or as though we were gradually habituating ourselves to death by practising it again and again. When we receive the crucified Lord we are receiving daily, as the innermost law of our life, the precise counterpart of this slow death in the person of him who, precisely because he is the crucified Lord, sends us into our everyday with the words: 'Go, you are sent forth' with which Mass concludes. Now the everyday in our life is properly speaking not something which has nothing to do with what takes place in the celebration of this sacred mystery. On the contrary, it is through the inner dynamism of what is celebrated here and what is received here, through the power and directive force which it contains within itself, that we are sent out into this 'everyday'. For we have received the crucified Lord and have thereby received his death and his Cross as well. But what is set before our eyes in the holy *sign* of the Body and Blood of Christ, what has been brought home to us in this way, that same reality is what we encounter as the *truth* of what is signified in our everyday lives as well. How can we be surprised that the everyday is as it is if we have understood that in every communion we receive we submit ourselves to the Cross of the Lord because it is in his crucifixion and death that we receive him, because we take into ourselves and into our hearts that glorified Lord who has only achieved his glorification by enduring a life which led through the sheer and absolute ruin of death. No, the law of life to which Christ submitted himself in his life and death is what we receive in the sacrament of his life because we receive him as crucified and, as Paul puts it, proclaim the death of the Lord until he comes again. This is why we must realise that the first and *primary* significance of the Eucharist is not that it provides us with *strength* for our everyday lives, that it is nourishment to help us by constantly renewing our strength and so enabling us to endure the 'everyday', though of course it does have this function also. But the Eucharist as first and foremost the holy deed wrought by God upon us itself assigns the everyday to us as our task. Viewed in its ultimate perspective the position is not that the everyday is simply something which is assigned to us by chance, by the laws of the earth and of our own lives to be our lot, and then God intervenes, so to say, from outside the situation and helps us to endure this alien and godless situation in which we are placed. This is not the state of affairs at all. At basis it is rather that this 'everyday' *itself* is something that is given to us by God in Jesus Christ *through* the bond which we have with him in the grace of baptism, and the giving of it is constantly renewed in the sacrament of the altar. The fact that when we receive Jesus we receive his life as the innermost law of our own lives, and thereby the life that consists in crucifixion and death veiled in the obscurity of faith – it is this that is summed up in a single phrase drawn from the context of the secular, namely '*Our everyday*'. For it is in this that we live, to this that we are, as it were, constantly nailed and crucified, in this that we die, and in this that our dying is hidden with Christ, hidden in the drabness of the routine and the humdrum, in the blankness of the everyday. Each day and daily we receive the actual everyday of Christ himself and of his life, his life as it drains away into death – it is this that we receive in the Eucharist. And this everyday life which we receive from God in this form is our daily life as something that is given to us by Christ himself together with the strength, the interior illumination, the interior grace which enables us to endure this everyday. He and his strength, he and his meaning, he and his interior light, he and his daily forgiveness and interior sanctification – the person of Jesus, and these attributes of his together with him, are bestowed upon us by God in the sacrament of the Eucharist.

Finally let us consider now how we can make this truth which we have been examining in some measure a part of our practical lives as well. It is not enough to recognise a truth of religion, to understand it in the abstract with one's mind. We must also take steps to show that we acknowledge it and value it in our lives. It must be put into practice. It must gradually be assimilated. It must permeate our whole interior man (though this can only be a slow process), so that the awareness of it becomes a spontaneous part of ourselves. It must to some extent strike its roots into the deepest levels of our life, our heart, our whole existence, those from which our true life takes its rise. And in view of this it is, of course, of little or no use simply to listen to such considerations on the theological and purely speculative level, and with minds more or less willing to accept what we hear. We have to say to ourselves: 'Merely because we have understood these points with our minds, this is far from meaning that we have taken them into our hearts or made them, in any effective sense, an intrinsic factor, part of the basic pattern of our lives, an element in the inward law which governs them in all their dimensions and at all levels. This we must do, but it is only a gradual process. We must first consciously exercise ourselves in putting this truth into practice. Only so can it be accorded its true place in our lives. For instance it is possible to express in fine words what truthfulness or love etc. mean, and everyone who then hears these words can understand them. But to the mature man one thing is absolutely clear from the experience of his life. It is that when one has practised truthfulness in one's life, when one really has remained faithful through tests and trials, then, even though one cannot say anything more or anything finer about truthfulness, love, faithfulness etc., still one has understood what they really are in a quite different way from when one has simply achieved a speculative understanding of these statements at the purely conceptual level. Thus the truth which has been lived, experienced, suffered involves an insight into what truth means which is quite different in kind from that which can be achieved merely in terms of abstract ideas. Now applying this to the sheer truth as such that the Eucharist is the sacrament of the everyday, we have really to commit ourselves to practising, experiencing, living and suffering this truth, until, from being merely a truth at the theological and conceptual level, it has become a truth of the interior man, a truth of the heart.

In order for one to exercise one's self in such a truth there is much that is needful. First and foremost in order to exercise ourselves in this truth we must, if we may so express it, *withdraw into ourselves*. We must be recollected. It is difficult to express what this really means. But first it is important simply to bear with one's self, not, as it were, constantly to be seeking to escape from one's self into outside occupations; to manage to live – in the contemporary scene it is necessary to say this – without having a radio constantly in the background, to bear with one's self and not to give one's self up to empty talk and gossip, and to a reading of the illustrated papers that is a mere waste of time and a dissipation; to draw one's self back, when circumstances demand, from that more subtle form of distraction and of wasting one's own life which consists in an over-busy and all-devouring fulfilment of one's duty, or rather of what we sometimes like to regard as our duty in order to find an excuse for avoiding our real duty. No we must contain ourselves and, as it were, allow our own life-force, the basic resources of our own being, to be withdrawn and gathered into the depths of our hearts. For when we do achieve this state of withdrawal, in which we, so to say, contain ourselves, we still have a further state to achieve: to *stand fast*. It is by no means the case that in order rightly to achieve this state of recollection and rightly to carry out this process of containing ourselves, rightly to arrive at the attitude of meditation which is necessary, we have actually to withdraw ourselves from the everyday as though the act of containing ourselves in this manner entailed a flight from the everyday. No, what has to be achieved in this state of recollection is that we face up to ourselves as we really are; that we stand firm and confront ourselves; that we do not run away from this. But this in turn implies that we face up to the everyday in our lives. Despite all his efforts the abiding loneliness of man is constantly being brought home to him. He feels himself somehow naked and defenceless. At some level in his being he is a prey to anxiety (*Angst*), feels pain, is in some sense disappointed with his life. But when they become conscious of these experiences men take fright. They run away from them. They seek, as it were, to bury them beneath the surface of their lives, and for this purpose they grasp at palliatives of the most varied kinds – I am not speaking here of medicines – which life has to offer, precisely chatter, conversation, mere external dissipations. They do not stand firm in face of the real truth of the everyday, and this is precisely what we ought to achieve courageously, honourably and without illusions.

This does not, of course, change the everyday in any way at first. Its impact upon us is not less burdensome than before. It confronts us just as it really is, bringing home to us how drably average our lives are, how mediocre our achievements, and the disappointments of our life in this or that respect. Obviously we must not fall into an attitude of pessimism. God has endowed man directly with strength to bear much, to put up with much, even to disregard much that takes place in his life. And this strength that God has given us must be preserved and used. Obviously we must not indulge in self-pity. But even the experienced man, the brave man, he who has a cheerful heart, constantly arrives in the end, by way of that grey fog of the everyday, in a situation in which he either runs away from it, avoids it, suppresses it, refuses to admit the truth of it, grasps at the palliative drugs of the everyday, or alternatively finds himself faced with the question of how he can put up with this everyday at all. And in the last analysis it is precisely the believer – and only he – who can put up with it. Now in saying this we may, and indeed must, be fully ready to recognise that there may be many who face up to life bravely, calmly, cheerfully and in a spirit of selfless love, yet who do not regard themselves as believers at all. But by the way they live their lives such men avoid falling into an attitude of cynical resignation. On the contrary, in their calm acceptance of their lives they actually achieve, implicitly and in principle, what the conscious and professed believer does explicitly and in the full knowledge of what he is doing and how he does it.

But in any case the process of living the truth and practising it, as we have conceived of this in the present context, necessarily involves this attitude of containing one's self, standing firm, bearing and enduring the everyday within the context of the everyday itself by living it in a spirit of faith, hope and love – in other words in the surrender of our whole being to God through these three theological virtues. And in fact the situation is such that these divine virtues have to be practised in the concrete circumstances of our everyday. They must not for one moment be reduced to mere Sunday attitudes, but must be genuinely exercised in our hearts. And they can only be so when they are practised in the down-to-earth, factual, hard, drab realities of the everyday. And this is what we do when we accept our disappointments without being shattered by them because we know that they are, as it were, the medicaments by which our humanity is really healed in its innermost depths. For this humanity of ours is healthy only when it allows God to be God, when it genuinely hopes for eternal life and when on the basis of this hope it genuinely endures the hopelessness of the everyday. It is precisely then, in this acceptance of the futility, the drabness, the mediocrity, the disappointments of the everyday that faith, hope and love are really exercised in very truth. Indeed there is no other way whatever of truly practising these virtues. When we confine ourselves merely to praying for 'the divine virtues to be awakened in us', to employ the terminology of the relevant forms of prayer, then we do indeed give evidence of the fact that our will is good, that we want to have what is signified by this formula, namely faith, hope and love. But the actual process of putting these virtues into practice and exercising them takes place in the context of the everyday, and the everyday provides material for the exercise of these virtues. It is in the situation in which we feel anxiety (*Angst*), pain and need, and nevertheless still commit ourselves to God – it is in that situation that we really put into practice what is meant by the acceptance of the everyday, and in this the exercise of the holy and God-given virtues of our lives.

And it is only when we are prepared in this way that we can understand the fact that when we receive holy Communion we are accepting the everyday. For then we can say: 'Come Lord, enter my heart, you who are crucified, who have died, who love, who are faithful, truthful, patient and humble, you who have taken upon yourself a slow and toilsome life in a single corner of the world, denied by those who are your own, too little loved by your friends, betrayed by them, subjected to the law, made the plaything of politics right from the very first, a refugee child, a carpenter's son, a creature who found only barrenness and futility as a result of his labours, a man who loved and who found no love in response, you who were too exalted for those about you to understand, you who were left desolate, who were brought to the point of feeling yourself forsaken by God, you who sacrificed all, who commend yourself into the hands of your Father, you who cry: "My God, my Father, why have you forsaken me?", I will receive you as you are, make you the innermost law of my life, take you as at once the burden and the strength of my life. When I receive you I accept my everyday just as it is. I do not need to have any lofty feelings in my heart to recount to you. I can lay my everyday before you just as it is, for I receive it from you yourself, the everyday and its inward light, the everyday and its meaning, the everyday and the power to endure it, the sheer familiarity of it which becomes the hiddenness of your eternal life'.

If the everyday is itself received in the act of receiving holy Communion, if in this act of receiving holy Communion we practise how to accept our everyday, then the everyday will be a further projection of the Communion we receive into the reality of our lives. If we receive the Lord and his grace only in the sacrament, if we do not make the everyday itself a means of receiving the grace of God by accepting it in the guise in which it is mercifully presented to us of the toilsome, the drab and the everyday, then, basically speaking, our Communion will not have been brought to its full and true significance. For there is one point that we must never forget: Simply stated as an abstract proposition of theology it is a truth of faith that the Christian, by every good work, by every act of faithfulness performed in the context of the everyday, by every deed done in the grace of God in the everyday, grows in this same grace of God. By such acts performed in the everyday his eternal life itself develops, is advanced, is intensified and plunges deeper roots into the ultimate basis of his own being. The communion with God in his grace can itself truly grow in the context of the everyday.

Where the everyday is truly and effectively endured an abiding communion with Jesus Christ and his eternal life is achieved, not indeed in the sacramental sign but in the reality of what is signified by that sign, namely in the grace of God. In other words it may be asserted as an absolute truth of faith that the everyday is a continuation and further projection of Communion, provided only that in the power of the Eucharist we manage to endure and to sustain our everyday.

But let us not deceive ourselves. The process of enduring the everyday has itself a very everyday aspect. Enduring the everyday does not consist merely in so filling our hearts with enthusiasm that we render ourselves quite immune to the 'everyday-ness', the monotony, the routine, the mediocrity, the mere toilsomeness and the creeping death that is in the everyday. Nor does it consist in making something exalted and glorious of our everyday. No, this is not the everyday into which we are sent by Jesus Christ in holy Communion itself. We are truly sent into the everyday, and this means into the everyday in all its pettiness and triviality. When we receive holy Communion, and when we pray to Jesus Christ: 'Help me to endure my everyday from an innermost source of strength', then we cannot pray, 'Turn my everyday into a festival day'. Rather we must say: 'Let my everyday be an everyday. My feet hurt me, my nerves are overstrained, my everyday is drab and boring, I always have the same things to do' etc., 'Lord, remain in my everyday. I know that enduring this everyday, accepting this everyday, itself in its turn also remains an everyday act. But that is as you have willed it to be, and therefore my everyday is, in fact, nothing else than the enduring projection of what has been initiated in Communion. It is itself communion, for in this everyday, when it is endured in this everyday manner, when we 'carry on', when we are disappointed, when we rise and when we fall, when we still manage to be kind even though our nerves are worn out, when we begin to pray even though we have no inclination to do so, when we still bend ourselves to our tasks even though they are hateful – in all this communion is achieved, because in this way we grow in the grace of Christ. In other words we attain to an ever-closer union with Jesus Christ and his eternal life. What takes place in holy Communion itself has its exact counterpart in what is achieved here in the everyday, although always with the reservation that

that other Communion takes place through the explicit sacramental sign, and is is endowed with that unique power which can only be achieved precisely in the sphere of God's sacraments.

The everyday is the continuation and growth of Communion and its projection into the drabness of reality, and therefore our own everyday in all its monotonous and unvarying familiarity, becomes a preparation, constantly renewed, for Communion. The everyday as endured – endured in spite of being merely burdensome, is the finest preparation for Communion. By Communion we are sent forth into the everyday and the everyday needs only to be viewed and interpreted in a truly Christian perspective in order that *ipso facto* and in itself it may send us to Jesus Christ, into the everyday-ness of his own life, into the death of his own life.

There is a final question with regard to this need to practise living the truth, one which we should constantly be putting to ourselves: Where in our lives does the point of convergence and correlation lie between these two factors, Communion and the everyday, and how can such a correlation be achieved? Our life and the Communion we receive constitute an enduring encounter with the hidden Lord, with deliverance from need and distress, and with the need and distress of others too which, when we help them in bearing it, delivers us ourselves. In Communion, as in the everyday activities appropriate to our various callings, we encounter the Lord only in a hidden manner, in the first case under the appearance of bread and wine, in the second in the guise in which he reveals himself to us in the neighbour whom we serve.

Thus the everyday and Communion are two factors which constitute an everyday encounter with the veiled and hidden Lord, who is visible only to the eye of faith. Now this eye of faith must see somewhat more deeply into the significance of our everyday, and must perceive in the midst of our everyday lives in their everyday-ness Jesus Christ present in his brothers and sisters. The same eye of faith must also perceive the Lord in his sacramental presence, and seek him there. Finally these two factors, the experience of the everyday as seen through the eye of faith on the one hand, and the celebration of the Eucharist on the other, must be correlated and made complementary. Each must be interpreted in the light of the other. Only when we do all this do we achieve a real and effective encounter with Jesus Christ, our Lord, our life, our judgment, our eternity.

PART FOUR

Christian Virtues

22

ON TRUTHFULNESS

THE question of truthfulness is far deeper and more penetrating than one might suppose from a reading of the relevant treatise in moral theology, that on the eighth commandment, concerning truthfulness and lies. Now since this is the position, in other words since an attempt must be made to include these deeper levels of the theme, which usually go unexplored, in our present investigation of the subject, therefore (this must be emphasised right at the outset for the considerations which follow) we must be permitted in this treatment to leave on one side those aspects of the question which are concerned directly with religious pedagogy. We shall do this in the confident belief that this task is far better left to those who are engaged *ex professo* in the pastoral field.

I

The first point to be recognised is simply that truthfulness has something to do with truth. It is the will to truth, a mentality, an attitude of mind, in which one reverences truth first as something of intrinsic value in itself, and second as something that is due to one's fellow man, with whom one must always strive to communicate in such a way that truth too can be an intrinsic part of what one has in common with him. It is an attitude and disposition which must constantly permeate one's every thought and utterance, one's whole demeanour, everything that one does, to the point at which it proves itself to be the definitive characteristic of one's whole activity, making itself felt in all that one does. *Only* on this basis, and with these predispositions can truthfulness become a fixed and enduring attitude freely adopted, in which one speaks the truth to one's neighbour and avoids lying to or deceiving one's fellow man.

Even at this early point we discover a noteworthy and perilous shortcoming in the ethos of our own age. The man of today suffers to no small extent from an incapacity to realise the meaning and value of truth in itself. At any rate he finds it extremely difficult to do so. It should be noted that what we are immediately concerned with here is not truthfulness but truth. For we shall only acquire a real and effective understanding of what truthfulness means when we have renewed our understanding of the meaning and value of truth itself. Today, however, this understanding is threatened. It is not possible here to point out the historical causes and origins of this state of affairs, in which our understanding of truth is imperilled. This would take us too far back in history. The religious dissensions and conflicts, the breaking up of society into many self-contained units, the anti-metaphysical positions which are characteristic of the new age, the purely descriptive positivism of modern natural science, the recognition that the knowledge of the individual is conditioned by far-reaching sociological factors, the deliberate manipulation on the part of political forces of the conclusions of the sciences and of public opinion, the fact that today the individual has a direct and vivid realisation of how manifold opinions, religious and moral outlooks are in the world, the experience of sudden and world-wide revolutions in thought taking place almost overnight – these and similar manifestations are in part causes and in part symptoms of what we are speaking of here: modern man labours under the false impression that only in those cases in which empirical reality is quite directly subject to diagnosis and control on man's part is there much chance of gaining any accurate knowledge of such reality. Modern man regards his own thoughts as unverifiable, as mere opinion, as a view which can neither command reality in all its aspects nor offer any very strong grounds for confidence in the reliability of his own cognitive processes. This attitude of relativism and scepticism on the part of modern man with regard to his own cognitive processes leads to a further phenomenon, still more important than the first. Modern man (and this extends very largely into the sphere of faith itself) is really very far from feeling that truth is important in itself; that it has a value either in itself or even, considered as knowledge, that it has any significance in itself for salvation. In other words modern man is by no means convinced that a deficiency in truth, quite regardless of whether it is culpable or not, could imperil his own life either in the temporal or the eternal dimension.

We have only to apply the experiment to ourselves to realise the truth of this. Let us ask ourselves, then, whether we are really convinced of the fact that knowledge of divine truth as such constitutes a factor which is essential to salvation itself, such that without it, regardless of the reasons why one may have failed to discover this truth, it is simply impossible to attain to salvation at all. Or again we may ask ourselves whether our position may not fairly be summed up somewhat as follows: We hold that if one does know the truth it is certainly excellent and good, because then one can and must act in conformity with the real facts that one has thereby grasped. But for all that, in the last analysis we do draw a distinction between the sphere of the technical and the practical on the one hand, and the higher spiritual sphere of dispensations and principles on the other. In the former sphere if one fails, no matter how inculpably, to realise and apply the rules, then something unpleasant and injurious may ensue. In the latter sphere, however, if indeed it exists at all, any mistakes we may make cannot possibly result in the same injurious effects. For here one can only be held responsible for *those* mistakes which consist in morally culpable acts (and these only to the extent that they are morally culpable). I believe that it is only by submitting our ideas to this kind of experiment that it is brought home to us how great a danger we all stand in of denying the value of truth *as* truth; how much we all hold, without realising it, that truth is only valuable as providing the prior condition for coping rightly with reality. For we can only adopt a right practical attitude towards reality when we know what properties it has in itself, and what reactions this or that mode of behaviour may be calculated to produce in it. Perhaps this may serve to bring home to us how far we have moved in our inmost convictions from the position that knowledge as such (though admittedly this comes to its full fruition in love) constitutes in itself *the most radical mode of communication with reality*. May we not actually have reached the position of thinking of knowledge as providing merely a *starting-point and prior condition* for such communication with reality, and, indeed, not always even an essential prior condition for it at that?

The successes achieved in the whole interrelated complex of the natural sciences, the developments in technology and other revolutionary changes within the social scene, have all unintentionally contributed to the fact that men have come to prize truth merely as a means of gaining control and mastery over the environment in which they exist (and from this point they have then gone on actually to define the nature of truth in terms corresponding to this essentially functional view). This control over the environmental factors in human life does not consist in knowledge as such; other means are used in the pursuit of it, those namely of technology, medicine, practical genetics etc., and so a basic attitude to life is arrived at in which something is regarded as true only when it can be put to some 'practical use', and all other kinds of knowledge, which cannot be shown to have *this particular* kind of contribution to make are regarded as mere opinions, mere speculative positions which are adopted, secondary side effects to be ascribed to hereditary or racial factors, social conditions etc. In short the concept of truth here is that of a sceptical pragmatism, which each one may seek to justify for himself whether on biological or sociological grounds according as he wishes. In the light of this it is easy to understand why to one who allows these ideas to influence his own thought to any significant extent it really does seem quite right that that ideology is true which is *de facto* effective and powerful. It is true in so far as it claims to shape the future in conformity with the only sort of reality which it will recognise as reality at all: reality on the material and sociological plane with an ideology to correspond to this. Knowledge is reduced to a mere tool, enabling man so to cope with his material and sociological reality that he can gain control over it. This in turn leads to the further conclusion that he is truthful and honourable who assimilates himself to the sociological ideology which has power to shape the future. For it is this, in fact, which constitutes the real and the effective. Anyone, therefore, who succeeded in reawakening his fellow men to a sense of what the nature of truth really is in itself would be performing a vital task indeed. Such a one would also have to enable his fellow men to achieve a renewed grasp of truthfulness as the initial capacity, prior to all presuppositions, to achieve truth in itself, truth in its own unique essence. In saying this we must of course recognise that man is free to use this initial capacity of his or not as he chooses, and he may culpably misuse it and so fall into error. But if we are to attain to the unique essence of truthfulness as defined here the concept of truth on which we must fix our gaze is not one which can be defined in purely neutral and general terms. Certainly it is possible to conceive of truth in a wholly general sense as equivalent to 'correctness or accuracy', the idea that a proposition must correspond to reality quite regardless of what this proposition refers to. To define truth thus would be to do exactly the same in the dimension of knowledge (something which is, in principle perfectly possible) as one does in the dimension of being when one understands 'being' as signifying the being of a 'something or other' completely undefined and in the void, the being of a 'not-not-being'. When we understand being in this way as merely the unique self-identity of the 'something-or-other being' we have obtained no true view of being, We have further to understand that there is *being* as such, being in the absolute. This constitutes the absolutely primary basis (the very root foundation for all truth and all being) for all human knowledge of being, such that even though it is not explicitly adverted to, without it no such knowledge would be possible at all. It is only on the basis of this primary and implicit awareness of being as such, then, that we can really apprehend what is meant by the being of any given existing thing in its reality. What this *properly* means must be based on the ultimate priority of being in the absolute. In the same way too truth in its original and ultimate sense is not the correctness of a proposition which is equally valid in all its possible applications, but truth in the absolute, which man encounters as the horizon, omnipresent and all-encompassing, to every 'concept' in which the individual and the particular are grasped. Man is conscious of this all-encompassing horizon to his ideas not as an explicit object for investigation in itself, but rather as that which constantly impinges upon his awareness. And this is that truth which supports all other particular truths and is not itself supported by any. It is that which is uniquely self-authenticating (in itself) and, precisely in virtue of this fact, that which is to us the incomprehensible mystery.

It is only on the basis of these factors, which we have only been able to indicate in what has been said above, that the ultimate nature of truthfulness as such can be discovered: it is the basic feeling for truth as the initial and absolutely primary communication with reality at its most absolute, and at the same time at its most all-embracing. It is that feeling considered as basic receptivity, submissiveness, readiness not to refuse or to resist that which impinges upon it. It is the openness of man as spirit to being in the absolute (that which provides the basis for the being of all that is). It is that feeling, that initial perception, in which we accept with our minds the mystery of which we are conscious as the foundation and support of all reality, and which we call God, the unique truth of truths which bears its own meaning within itself. It is the basic acceptance of this mystery even though it has no use for us, even though it cannot be exploited by technology and cannot be made to contribute to our biological self-assertion, our physical well-being, our diversion or our enjoyment. It is that feeling for truth which is strict and exacting in its claims upon us, and only bestowed upon us as such; that initial perception which demands a response not merely from the rational faculty of man as refined and developed by technological training, but from his spirit, demands the ultimate decision which is his to make as free, from the whole man. It is at this level that it demands his response, and at the same time makes this response possible.

It must be reiterated that those who define truth as 'the adequation of a statement to the objective state of affairs' are viewing it only as it appears to be, and only in a quite superficial connection, and so as a property which applies with equal validity to every correct proposition. In fact truth, like being, is first and last a property inherent in reality itself (considered as the 'able-to-be-made-manifest' as actually revealed), and simultaneously inherent in knowledge too (considered as openness to the self-manifestation of being). As such it is an analogous entity, and an analogous concept. For this reason it is precisely not applicable in any primary or basic sense in contexts dealing with the practical usefulness of a formula for the technical manipulation of material objects or for predicting the outcome of processes in the natural order. It is not in such contexts of practical living that truth achieves its true applicability, but rather in another context, one in which man as spiritual being realises and possesses his own subjectivity, himself as a whole (a process which ultimately includes the love and freedom pertaining to truth); in which he experiences his own finitude, which he likewise comprehends, accepts and endures as a whole; in which, faced with the question of being as such, being in its totality, he holds firm to the ineffable mystery; in which he does not shrink from the questionability, the radically contingent nature of all individual entities, all of which point him on to the nameless infinite; in which he does not seek to grasp reality by taking possession of it for himself, but rather suffers himself to be grasped by it in its unfathomable depths; in which he does not speak but rather falls dumb with adoration. It is in this context that truth in its proper and ultimate sense comes into its own, and it is here that it enters our lives. And it is the acceptance of this ultimate essence of truth, the truth that so constantly goes unrecognised, that itself constitutes truthfulness in its primary and most basic form; it is this that is presupposed in other contexts, in which truthfulness signifies the assent of the free individual to truth.

II

The second form of truthfulness which we have to explore can be described simply as truthfulness with one's self. At first sight it might seem that this kind of truthfulness is familiar to everyone. Thus we speak of honesty towards one's self. People are warned against 'setting themselves up to be something'; nowadays everyone is familiar with the phenomenon of suppression, masking one's conscience, interior deceitfulness with one's self, dishonesty, 'putting up a façade', sentimentality, affectation and other forms in which a man tries to avoid facing up to his own true nature (that is having that truthfulness which he is empowered to achieve and which the absolute truth requires that he shall achieve). But what we find so often elsewhere occurs here too. One speaks of truthfulness in this sense only because it is no longer able to be taken for granted. One praises something only when it has become lost. One conjures something up only when it is threatening to disappear. One strives to keep something alive only when it is dying. And in fact modern man is sadly deficient in this interior truthfulness.

The reason for this is not immediately to be sought in a moral defect which can then be condemned, branded and campaigned against with exhortations. Not only is this useless but in this case it is also false. For the reason for this deficiency in interior truthfulness is not, in the first instance, a moral defect in the everyday sense of the term. It is to be ascribed rather to the difficulty which modern man feels in really recognising with any clarity which among the forces of his own interior life is the real, the genuine, the truly valid – precisely the 'true'. Modern man too would like not to be dishonest with himself. On the contrary he may, perhaps, even have the impression that he actually is honest with himself in a way that is brutally down-to-earth, harshly realistic, and to a certain extent this is true. He really is genuinely responsive to catchwords, to a certain hollow and anguished idealism. Somewhere and somehow the honest objectivity of natural science and technology really have penetrated into his nature and exercised a formative influence upon him. And we should take grea care that in the forms in which our religion is presented we do not offend against this awareness in the younger generation by an enthusiasm that is less than genuine, by raising anguished theological problems in the wrong place, which then give the impression of being alive to themselves yet failing to correspond to the reality of life. If modern man wants to face the facts in all honesty, if he is willing to hide nothing, if he strives to penetrate beyond the façades of idealism, then he finds himself in an embarrassing position, which can become really lethal in its effects, for it threatens his whole ethos of truthfulness and of sober factuality, and there is a danger that this mood of embarrassment will be exchanged for one of cynicism and total scepticism while still continuing to be taken for truthfulness and valued accordingly. In such a case one has the impression of having penetrated beyond superficial appearances only to find nothing behind them. One imagines that one has had the experience of seeing through everything and of now gazing into an empty and indeterminate void. For the conflict between the realities which one has experienced in this way is forcibly brought home to one. They turn out to be unco-ordinated, contradictory and conflicting. As a result one does not know what really to opt for in one's scale of values, the body or the abstract spirit, instinct or norm, the individual or the collective, brute fact or ideal, what is or what allegedly should be the case. Thus the harsh and onerous impression arises all too easily that man is dishonest because he is unrealistic, because man opts for the spirit, the norm, the ideal in the attempt to bring order out of chaos, in the refusal simply to admit what is, in fact, the case. One believes that it is cowardly or dishonest, a tilting at windmills if one does not 'simply take reality as it is'. And thus a perverted ideal of truth emerges with an equally perverted ideal of truthfulness to correspond to it: a truthfulness which has degenerated into cynicism, which pretends heroically to unmask anything and everything. A man with this attitude supposes his disposition to be realistic and true when he only recognises that as true and real which is endowed with the harsh reality of the physical and the physiological; which is, in its mode of existence, independent of the freedom of the spirit, with its functions as deciding, creating and authenticating. For it is the spirit which recognises and acknowledges that that which is physically and physiologically weaker is in fact superior, and, in the long run, more powerful also. This perverted notion of 'truthfulness' must be resisted and contested, and the true intrinsic nature of truthfulness with one's self must be revealed for what it really is and developed in man. It is the truthfulness of self-criticism, which militates against the prejudices of the superficial, the clamour of the merely instinctive. This is truthfulness considered as courage to recognise what is truer because more real, courage to live by the spirit. Man must realise and patiently and perseveringly live by the fact that an attitude which opts for a hierarchy of values, for form, discipline and order, has in itself and at basis nothing whatever to do with a deceitful and cowardly untruthfulness, that on the contrary it is that attitude of an unbridled yielding to impulses which refuses to be unmasked for what it is, that conceals weakness and decay under the guise of honesty and truthfulness.

Naturally it is not much use to seek to impart this knowledge by means of moral imperatives, when in fact far the best imperative of all consists not in the imperative of exhortation, but in the indicative of insight into a matter. And in this way an appeal must be made to the inner experience of modern man himself, so as to make him understand that it is not those elements in his own make-up which are most conspicuous and most insistently clamorous that *ipso facto* constitute the real in him; that that which he feels most strongly with his emotions is still far from being the real and genuine depths of his being; that the all-devouring obstinacy of the instincts is still far from being irresistible in the true sense; that true happiness can only be attained at the price of toil, discipline, foregoing many things for the sake of one, and can only be attained in the unity of the whole man which is thereby achieved; finally that here, in the finite state of man and of his world, everything tends to immoderation and self-destruction, and hence the will to achieve infinitude which is instilled in man and is legitimate, the will which seeks to rise above the world and is inspired by eschatological hope, must be steadfastly and exclusively orientated towards that promise which is God himself, otherwise this will must itself be perverted and lead to self-destructive immoderation by the fact of being directed towards objects within this world. Everyone has already had such experiences for himself. He only needs to keep them constantly in mind. He only needs to make a more or less systematic evaluation of them.

Thus man can learn that sober interior truthfulness towards one's self is an art acquired by self-discipline, a therapy of the mind enabling us to see through and to deny the pretensions of what is arrogantly put forward as 'truth' itself, autonomous and self-sufficient, but which in fact belongs merely to particular areas within the total scope of human reality; enabling us to learn that real inner truthfulness, so far from contradicting, is actually identical with what good Christian tradition has long been accustomed to call 'self-denial', that truthfulness is that *metanoia* which consists in the courage to face up to one's self, to let that which seems to be self-sufficient stand revealed in its radical contingency in relation to God. In other words truthfulness is that entering into the truth, that freedom, to which only the liberation which Christ has achieved on our behalf can admit us. Once this is realised the sincere individual can then be brought to understand that in order to achieve this process of radical self-questioning which is so necessary, he must find a point outside himself (rather as in the geometry of Archimedes), one which is not subject to the autonomous and uncontrollable ideological vicissitudes of his own subjectivity, in other words authority, community, sound tradition, the Church, the accumulated experience of past ages etc. For even if the individual is rightly inclined to be sceptical with regard to such authorities, still he must also be critical and sceptical with regard to himself (seeing that the representatives of these authorities can at least claim as much for themselves as the sum total of certainty which the individual can offer on his own behalf, namely that he is a man). But the individual must also be brought to realise that he is no longer in a position to be truly critical with regard to himself when, out of arrogance, he absolutely refuses to entertain any such archimedian point outside himself. But when somebody does allow the radical contingency of his own being in regard to God to be revealed in this way in obedience to his word and in truthfulness, refusing therefore to take as the absolute standard of his own attitude and behaviour some impulse within his own nature which, however exalted, is still secondary in comparison to God, then he becomes free because the truth sets him free (Jn 8:32). But admittedly only he who, in the courage of truthfulness with himself, allows the experience of his own interior lack of freedom to come to the fore, can experience this freedom which truth brings. But precisely this courage to be truthful with one's self even when it is hard is itself, once more, a grace of God which is bestowed in the very act in which God makes the individual free in his spirit.

Inevitably in order to do justice to certain aspects of the matter under consideration something ought to be said at this point concerning the grace of this truth and truthfulness that set men free, which is a gift of God. It would have to be pointed out that this bringing out of the individual's own lack of freedom and of the state of bondage into which he had fallen, bondage to the power of sin, of the law, of death, of instinct, to the powers and principalities that are in the world (and these would have to be examined not as presented in earlier times but in their contemporary forms and manifestations, that is as the tyranny of so-called public opinion, the allurements of mass enjoyment, the crazes of modern times etc.) is only possible when God gives his free and liberating Spirit to enable men to achieve it. But this would have to be presented in such a way that it did not strike the hearer as so much religious rhetoric, never allowing him to perceive exactly what it really was intended to convey in the concrete. It is true that what is being treated of here is a genuine experience of *faith*. But however much this may be the case, it would also have to be shown that it is a real experience that is in question here, and not a purely cognitive process confined to the theoretical plane, in which the individual concerned remains detached and uninvolved in relation to some alleged reality existing wholly outside the sphere of his own personal life. Unfortunately, however, it is not possible to enter any further into these questions at this point. We have been treating of truthfulness towards one's self. We have seen that this is a grace of God which comes to men in the word of God, liberating them and giving them the courage to accept themselves as they are. They can do this because one whom God has accepted in his own Son, the Son of Man, can accept himself. On the basis of truthfulness towards one's self as defined here, then, we would have to go on to enlarge upon the concrete forms which such interior truthfulness towards one'self would assume, and the opportunities for exercising it. The nature of these would have to be defined and made recognisable. We would have to treat of truthfulness in expressing one's self in art, in one's presentation of one's self, in the fashions, style of living and enjoyment which one adopted. All these are expressions of interior truthfulness. They have to be regarded as the point of contact between what one is and what one takes one's self for and accepts one's self as. But in treating of all these expressions of one's self one would, admittedly, have to bear constantly in mind that man, even as he truly and genuinely is, is an historical being, one which undergoes changes within its own abiding nature. For this reason it is important not to be too hasty in rejecting what is inappropriate in one's own case as something ungenuine in itself, and, in its application to others, contrary to their true nature. We would be wrong to invoke the concept of interior truthfulness in order to condemn such self-expression in others. But it is impossible here to enter any further into all this.

III

We now come to a third form of truthfulness, the one which is best known, and which is actually called truthfulness almost universally in normal everyday parlance. It is that attitude and outlook which prohibits lying in human intercourse. Here it is human intercourse in its more 'private' forms which we shall primarily be considering. What we shall be speaking of here, then, is truthfulness between men. One who is truthful in this sense is honest, upright, utterly rejects all lying, is reliable and stands by his word.

One might at first sight suppose that it was a moral phenomenon that we had in mind, one which exists more or less independently as a distinct entity in its own right alongside those other forms of truthfulness which we have been discussing hitherto. But this only appears to be the case. In reality truthfulness in human intercourse is merely the outcome and fruit of the forms of truthfulness which have previously been mentioned. In order to see this we have only to ask: What is a liar? or, more precisely: Who finds it necessary to lie? Evidently it is he who feels himself insecure, who imagines that he has to defend himself against an opponent who is too powerful for him, one who believes that he cannot live without the special advantages which can only be obtained by lying, one who is afraid to 'take the blame', who has something to hide which in his opinion would, if it were known, lower him in the esteem of others. The liar attaches value to this esteem as something that is vitally necessary to his existence. In this sense the lie appears as a weapon, presumed to be necessary, in the struggle for self-assertion both interiorly and exteriorly. And considered in this light, as a weapon necessary for one's self-assertion, the lie must seem, in the long run, unavoidable to anyone who has not been interiorly liberated from himself in interior truthfulness, and found the absolute courage he needs in order to discover his true nature in the infinite mystery of truth (moreover on the whole, and in the long run, it does not help in the least to invoke the sort of 'prudence' or practical wisdom involved in such sayings as 'lies will not get you anywhere' or statements that in the long run lies do more harm than good to the liar etc.) Only one who has hidden his own true and ultimate selfhood in God, and delivered it into his protection, only one who has thereby become secure and unassailable in a truly ultimate sense, finds it no longer necessary, in the last analysis, to defend himself. And only one who no longer has to defend himself can in all cases be truthful to his neighbour. Only such a one can really entrust himself to another, because he does not have to fear that he will ever really be lost. Only such a one can take the risk of drawing the short straw in the struggle for existence, because for him all struggle for existence, all earthly self-assertion, is, after all, only secondary and provisional. Admittedly the converse is also true. Only he who renounces all lies and dares, in an act of free and trustful self-surrender, to commit his very existence to the uncontrollable and the incomprehensible can truly experience what it is to be with God, because only in such an experience can it really be understood what is the true meaning of the Word of God. This is something that we fail to apprehend so long as we think of that Word simply as a supreme demiurge of the world. From all this it may be concluded that in the field of human discourse truthfulness means that that inner truthfulness in which man denies 'his own' self is put into practice and put to the test. In this the individual himself achieves an attitude of self criticism in which he renounces himself and thereby finds his true and ultimate essence, together with the protection and unassailability which it needs, by an act of loving self-surrender to that truth which is called the absolute mystery. It appears, therefore, that in this context of human discourse too truthfulness goes down to the ultimate roots of human nature, and must do so if it is to be able to survive at all. And this is the first point to be recognised about this third form of truthfulness. It is truly one of the forms in which the unique essence of truthfulness manifests itself as a state of harmony with truth as such, which is achieved by the individual's own free act.

This analysis should naturally not be taken as implying that this truthfulness between individuals has not other roots as well (at any rate initially): reverence for the other person as a being of truth, justice and love. With regard to a 'virtue' such as this truthfulness between persons precisely is, there is one point which should not be overlooked. The position which it occupies in the moral climate of any particular age is proper to that age and, as practised in other ages, among other nations or in other historical situations, is rightly subject to change. Similarly at specific stages in history it can impose its own characteristics on the whole moral climate of the particular period concerned.

The question that arises at this point, therefore, is whether anything can be said from this point of view concerning truthfulness as applied to our own age in particular. This could then serve in turn as a point of departure for a discussion as to the best strategy and tactics to employ from the educational aspect. In this connection we may perhaps take as our starting-point the consideration that when a particular 'virtue' is singled out in the general moral outlook of a particular age and accorded special preference, so that it is esteemed as a virtue the practice of which will quickly bring one to an understanding of moral values in general, this almost always means that the self-same virtue is especially threatened and assailed in the particular age concerned. The converse is also true. The 'saving grace' arises in response to a need that is felt, and the very fact that special efforts are made to draw down this 'saving grace' upon society is often the first pointer to where the danger really threatens. Virtues which are manifestly in a healthy condition and not particularly threatened are not singled out for special praise precisely because they are being practised. It is rather the virtue which is in danger of disappearing or else which is in process of being introduced into society as a 'saving grace' that is the subject of discussion at least among the wise.

Now on this showing it may legitimately be concluded that truthfulness may be regarded as one of the virtues which is actually exercising a specific and decisive influence in *this* sense and for *these* reasons upon the ethos of our own particular age. The factors which work for good and those which work for evil in the age we live in, as well as those characteristic phenomena which are neither wholly good nor wholly evil, all combine to make it clear that truthfulness is to be numbered among those influences which are particularly lacking in our age, and therefore particularly needful too. It is certain that the father of lies has never had such opportunities to exploit as he has today. All the mass media in the form of the press, films, television, instructional facilities, party propaganda – all these are employed in an educational system which is compulsory and under state control. They are subject to the tyranny of public opinion, exploited in advertising, in the artificial creation of need, brainwashing etc. It is not really that men have become more evil objectively speaking in God's eyes, but rather that the actual possibilities for lying have so much increased. And therefore lying is more prevalent today than ever before. And this element of mendacity can become all-pervasive and extend into all departments of life, permeating everything from the officially fabricated ideologies to the cigarette advertisements, which must at all costs give an 'open air activities' impression, so that no-one shall really know what the true effect of cigarettes is.

To this extent education in truthfulness has to begin in the *private* sphere of human relations: in a simple and natural honesty, in a conscious process of personal self-immunisation against the persuasions of the advertisers to the effect that various things are actual necessities, against their lies (an education in the art of not succumbing to the convenient lie which we find agreeable, and which we accept even though we know that it is a lie, for one can recognise a lie for what it is and still believe it – this too certainly belongs to the education in truthfulness of which we are speaking). We must also learn to be critical of our own opinions, which tend to be cliché-ridden and unduly influenced by public opinion, of our cheap over-simplifications, and 'closed minds'. We must learn to revise our earlier opinions, which we thought we had acquired once and for all. We must strive not to confuse the preconditioning of our minds through habit with evidence in the real sense in arriving at an opinion. We must practise ourselves in facing up to disagreeable situations without evading them, in the courage which enables us to submit to the criticism of others, in bravely suppressing our antipathy towards our critics. We must exercise ourselves also in acknowledging our own mistakes (how rare this is even among those in authority, even though there would be no question of their authority being undermined by such admissions). We must make efforts really to take seriously the opinion of others first, even when we are ourselves of a 'different opinion' on the grounds that one must recognise that it is just as possible for one's fellow to have hit upon the truth as for one's self.

In this connection there is admittedly one deficiency, which must be mentioned here. It is one that has a bearing upon the ethic of truthfulness of which we have been speaking, and which is, in itself, all too sorely needed today. This is the fault of tactlessness, over-bluntness and self-assured presumptuousness, which is often present in the so-called 'candid criticism' of others as practised today. There is no principle which lays down that one ought to say everything that one thinks or that one supposes one has seen. On the contrary there is a principle of charity according to which the truth, even when it really is such (and not every opinion arrived at instinctively, not every expression of sympathy or antipathy, not every kind of prejudice is *ipso facto* a truth) must be either stated or withheld only as the circumstances demand. Moreover if such truth is expressed it must be done in a form which does not offend the dictates of true charity. It must always be in conformity with the particular situation. Perhaps the simplest and most practical criterion for ascertaining whether one is prompted by motives of genuine truthfulness and honesty towards another or by those of a loveless arrogance and over-bluntness is to ask one's self whether one would be ready and willing, not only in abstract theory but in concrete practice too, to recommend another to criticise one's self in the same way as one criticises others. At any rate genuine truthfulness and honesty are not to be confused with sheer lack of manners in the way in which one offers criticism. For when criticism is proffered that is officious, over-strong, over-blunt and wanting in the respect due to the individual, then what such criticism reveals is not the attitude of truthfulness in the sense of a selfless love of the true and the objective, but an emotional and obstinate clinging to one's own opinions and one's own subjective attitudes. This is not objective at all, but rather due to impulse and lack of control (and therefore imprudent and presumptuous). Admittedly an over-sensitive attitude towards criticism can reveal the same lack of interior truthfulness with one's self. For if one so hypersensitive to criticism were to be wholly truthful with himself, then he would indeed recognise that he too was restricted, limited, and therefore liable to error and misapprehension. Not only would he recognise this, but he would also accept these limitations of his, and yet realise that at the same time he was, both in his person and in his official work, hidden in God. Then, feeling less insecure, he would have no need to reject criticism so strenuously, or to be so eager to spring to his own defence.

IV

We come now to a fourth form of truthfulness. For the truthfulness of which we have been speaking, which is practised in private life and in personal relationships between individuals, is reproduced on a larger scale and elevated onto a different plane when it becomes truthfulness in the public life, properly so-called, of society, the nation, the Church and the world at large.

Christianity has a quite specific and peculiar bearing on this virtue of truthfulness in public and social life. Christianity is, in fact, that in which the personal truth of God, the self-disclosure of God to humanity as a whole, becomes revealed. In respect of its content, of those to whom it is addressed, and of the actual Revealer himself, this revelation demands intrinsically and of its very nature, to be complemented by an act of *attestation*, and that too in a form in which it can reach 'everyman' as well as the accredited upholders of this message, for it is 'for each and for all'. Now since the divine revelation consists, in the last analysis, not in the imparting of factual information but rather in the personal self-disclosure of God, and since the response which is 'connatural' can be achieved only in a wholly human, personal, free act of faith, in which this personal truth is received in a spirit of humility and love, this revelation requires to be imparted in a form which is itself connatural both to the actual revelation itself and to the mode, corresponding to this, in which it is accepted. In other words it requires what we call 'witness'. And in this it is different from the mere transmission of a piece of factual knowledge in which the transmitter is not personally engaged in his own message.

Revelation needs witness as an act of personal engagement. Witness is the imparting of a message in which the imparter himself first lives out what he imparts in his own personal life, in which he becomes in his own person involved in the message he imparts. It must further be recognised that this divine revelation is directed to all and not to any kind of esoteric circle, and further that God, as the God of interior grace, can and does entrust every man with the ultimate capacity to understand this threefold self-disclosure of his. Moreover he is ready to awaken this understanding and bring it to the surface by the promptings of his own interior grace. Finally we should notice that this message is intended to touch not only the hidden interior of the individual man with its saving grace, but is also intended to produce in *all* the spheres of human living the effects of redemption and divine grace. For all these reasons the Church, as the imparter of this truth which she has to express in her own witness, must address herself to *all*. And this means to the groups and communities into which mankind is organised as well, to the corporate bodies of men, to the public at large, and in all this it must be realised that in addressing her message to mankind at these different levels the Church has to vary and adapt the manner in which she presents that message according to the particular level for which it is intended. And because *every* Christian is a member of the Church, because everyone is admitted through baptism and confirmation to an active share in the Church's mission, that namely of ensuring that the message of God takes permanent effect by bearing witness to it, therefore every Christian must be a witness to divine revelation in this sense before his fellow men, and that too in their public and corporate lives.

The layman, in virtue of the fact that he is not a member of the Church's clergy, does not have a 'canonical mission' properly so-called. His area of ecclesiastical activity, the area in which he is called, empowered and bound in duty to bear witness in this way, will be confined to *that* sphere of life in the world to which he already naturally belongs. It is here that he assumes his natural place in the world, in the natural social unit, among the neighbours, in the family, in his profession, in the environment in which his public life is passed, and which is in practice accessible to him. And it is here that he too must be a witness. But the witness that he must bear does not consist only, or even primarily in doctrine and doctrinal instruction. Rather it is witness in the sense which we have already defined, and for this reason the layman will not normally have to give any kind of catechetical instruction. Nor does he need to stand at street corners disseminating the popular writings of the Church after the manner of the sectarian sellers of the 'Watchtower'. At the same time it must be appreciated that man's existence is made actual in a specific context and with the special characteristics proper to a particular epoch. And included in this actual and specific context of his life as one of its intrinsic constitutive elements is the human word which is, of its very nature, directed to his fellow men. It must be emphasised that the human word is not something merely superimposed upon or added to human existence *ab externo*, something which can be absent without altering its essential nature. On the contrary this existence would cease to be human in the true sense at all if it were not given expression (admittedly in the most diverse forms that can be conceived of) in words, and that too at all its levels including the religious one. And it is for this reason that the word of explicit witness too has its place in a specific context and environment, that it is uttered in a world situation which is already given and defined. It is for this reason again that every Christian – the layman too therefore – has the duty of bearing witness openly in that particular public setting and environment in which *he* as an individual finds himself placed. Every Christian is a witness to the specifically Christian truth; every Christian has to bear witness in the manner appropriate to his own particular circumstances and the particular place he occupies in the community at large. The determination not to suppress this witness at the moment of decision is one of the fundamental requirements which characterise Christian living. Whereas in other contexts truthfulness consists in loyalty to the truth which it has been given to one to perceive, the truthfulness that is specifically Christian entails as one of its absolutely essential elements the courage to bear witness in this way.

In this connection we of today must realise two things: first that this public confession of Christian belief has been modified in many respects and for the most divers reasons in its actual mode of presentation, or, to put it another way, that the variations in the actual manner in which it has been received and understood are far from insignificant. But the second point, which it is no less important for us to realise, is that the essence of this specifically Christian truthfulness which we practise by bearing witness to the truth has not been altered and cannot be altered. To appreciate the first of these points we have only to ask ourselves whether modern man has actually become cowardly in the manner in which he bears witness and avows his 'convictions'. For the way in which this duty of bearing witness to the faith is discharged has undoubtedly changed, and we of today are tempted to attribute this change to cowardice. If it is not cowardice, then we must ask ourselves what the true explanation of this phenomenon of modern times really is. We who are spiritual and anti-materialist in outlook often feel that this makes us out of place in modern society – at least in any of the situations which being a member of this society involves. It is not immediately obvious to us that we should bear witness to our Christian faith always and in all circumstances by our outward appearance, by the very clothes we wear. The procession through the streets can, in certain circumstances, give the impression of being inappropriate and embarrasssing even to ourselves. Is it so immediately obvious to us that when we are having a meal in a public restaurant we should demonstrate the fact that we are Christians by saying our grace? Or to take the case of one who always and in all circumstances, and in every possible situation, tries to bring the conversation round to matters of faith – is *he ipso facto* the most effective and the most apostolic Christian? And if in the society in which we live, with all its complex ideological currents, there are many of our acquaintances – even close acquaintances – with whom we have never yet talked about matters of religion, is this necessarily and in all cases due to the fact that we suppress our Christian belief and fail in our duty to bear witness to it simply from motives of cowardice? Not for one moment, of course, must it be denied that behind these and similar manifestations of modern Christianity many human faults may truly lie concealed: faults of cowardice, anxiety (*Angst*), untruthfulness, weakness of faith, a falling-off in religious self-commitment, a succumbing to religious relativism etc. It would be naïve and foolish to attempt to dispute this. And it is precisely the Catholics of the so-called civilised sphere of central Europe who would do well to have the truthfulness and honesty to admit this.

1

These, then, are a few small examples which are intended to serve as indications of the manifestations of modern times which we have in mind. But is everything in these modern manifestations to be ascribed to a cowardly reluctance to confess the faith and bear witness to it? I believe not. What is making itself felt here (even though this is not the only factor) is that modern man draws a *sharper distinction* in his attitude to religious, as distinct from profane reality, than was usually the case with men of former ages. Modern man feels the reality of God and of religion in general in a quite radical sense as mystery, as 'inexpressibly' exalted above his world. He is inclined to feel that to speak about it is irreverent and almost indecent. He is acutely aware of how radically different in kind religious reality is from the reality of this profane world in which he lives. That this latter has come to be regarded as in a very radical sense remote from God and 'profane' is to a large extent due to Christianity itself, with its belief in the mere creatureliness of all this is not God. And indeed this must be so because for Christians the realities of this world neither can be nor are so numinous as they are for the devout pagan (who has still continued for a long period to live on in the Christian, and ought so to live on in him, but does not necessarily do so). And because the Christian of today experiences the radical difference between the predicamental and the transcendant, between the world and God, between the profane and the numinous, he can no longer speak in the same unrestricted and unembarrassed way of God and of his own attitude towards religion as he does of the other phenomena which belong to this world. He cannot find it very easy to speak of the 'good God' (Even when he does manage to realise God's absolute personhood in its true sense) as did the men of former ages. He cannot think of God as though he were the sole and supreme head of all beings in the universe, whose plans and ideas were fairly well-known to man, and upon whom man could count to make sure that the world would follow that course which man himself had mapped out as it ought to be. Now he no longer relies upon mere distant hearsay for his knowledge of the immense differences between men's opinions in religious matters, but has experienced them for himself, and in the light of this he is no longer bold enough to find it easy to imagine that he himself is sure of being able to say what he really means in such a way that the difference between his tenets and what other people are aiming at in their ideas is unambiguously clear and certainly the only version that is correct. He recognises difficulties but is still, perhaps, very far from feeling that these need necessarily undermine his ultimate and basic self-commitment to belief, or his readiness to believe, which he bashfully keeps to himself (In this respect modern man is presumably more modest than the representatives of the 'enlightenment' characteristic of the last two centuries of central European civilisation). But these difficulties are such as he cannot really solve, and they inhibit him at any rate from giving free and unrestrained expression to his religious convictions in the presence of others. He feels that today the whole area of religious matters has grown almost unmanageably complex, with its shifts and variations of nomenclature, and the multiplicity of facets, points of view and personal experiences which it has come to include. And this complexity is based on such an accumulation of knowledge and such a proliferation of experiences that it seems impossible within the limited span of one human life ever to catch up with or wholly to comprehend the knowledge and experience of one's fellow. Conversely that fellow himself receives the impression, based on similar grounds, that he is neither understood nor able to make himself understood. Against such a background as this, therefore, it seems useless to embark on any religious discussion.

Modern man has not, by the very nature of his calling, lived over a long period in a milieu which is ideologically homogeneous and therefore favourable to discussions of this sort, so as to have an opportunity gradually to grow accustomed to them; such a milieu as we know, rightly or wrongly, how to create for ourselves. He has not thereby habituated himself to such discussions (and even given these favourable conditions what heart-searchings it often requires to do so!). In fact if modern man is to enter fruitfully into such discussions at all then he must adopt a different approach from that which was taken in former times (and which we still often take today). He must be quiet and reserved in what he says. He must speak sparingly and wait until the *climate of discussion* is really suitable for such an exchange of ideas as is envisaged. With regard to particular questions of theology he will make it a principle to speak of these only when they are relevant, and when, in the situation of those participating in the discussion, they manifestly do contribute to that view of the whole which must be achieved for such questions to be discussed as they should be at all. The situation of those taking part in the discussion must be one in which they are reduced to astonishment and perplexity by the ultimate mystery of existence which encompasses us. They must have an attitude of basic reverence, for only so can the ultimate forces of life be present. And when such matters are not so much discussed as 'torn to shreds' in contests of words modern man will be silent. In the light of this it is not simply cowardice and timidity in the face of the rational and the conceptually unambiguous that makes men less ready to discuss the rational justifications for belief put forward by apologetics in the *'preambula fidei'*. One is justified in receiving the impression that even these can be discussed only when there is hope that one's observations will meet with due understanding and respect, and when the discussion takes place certainly in an atmosphere which is realistic and unemotional, but at the same time with an attitude of interior wonder, in which the whole man is deeply aware of being confronted by his own ultimate responsibility and by the mystery of existence.

This evident *change of style* in the manner in which we bear witness to the faith is not unjustified, but it must be thought out, explained and distinguished from cowardice and from that state of mind in which the convictions of faith are denied either wholly or in part. It must be purified and freed from false forms of this kind in order that it may remain clear that today as always the Christian is equipped, called, empowered and commanded in duty to confess his faith. Otherwise there is always the danger that the demand itself will be refused because, for want of reflection and due consideration, it will be required of the Christian not only that he shall bear witness to his faith, but that he shall do so in the manner appropriate to former ages, a manner which is today impracticable and unrealistic at least for many, in view of the intellectual and cultural differences between themselves and their predecessors. The result of this may be that from motives of their own interior truthfulness they believe that they can and must refuse the demand of the specifically Christian truthfulness, in other words the decision to uphold the truth of Christianity as the word of salvation for all even in their public lives. We still have much to re-appraise, much to put to the test and to try out in practice along these lines with regard to the way in which Christians should bear witness in the present climate of central Europe by confessing their faith before we can once more move on from the level of mere abstract principles to that in which we can have concrete and effective examples.

But while much might still be said about this witness which is demanded of us with regard to the form which it should take in order to meet the special needs of our own times, there must be no doubt about the actual fact that such witness is demanded of us. All Christians must be witnesses.

ON TRUTHFULNESS

All Christians must be truthful not merely in general but also in the sense that they really do confess the truth which has been bestowed upon them as the grace of faith.

But in order that this bolder (and more joyfully unrestrained) spirit to confess the faith may grow and develop, care must also be taken to encourage truthfulness and courage in avowing the faith in the communal life within the Church herself, in other words among Catholic Christians. Let us allow opinions to be expressed even when we ourselves find them disquieting. Let us really allow 'public opinion' to have a place in the Church herself, where we are in a position to expand or to restrict the opportunities for expressing such opinions. Certainly there are non-conformists who are such in principle, people whose one principle, which dominates their whole being, is the conviction that they discover the truth when they hold a different opinion from those about them, or from the convictions held by the generality of Catholics in their country, the ecclesiastical authorities etc. But such non-conformism (which is, incidentally, an extremely conformist kind of non-conformism, because it can always claim solidarity with the chronic grousers) must not prevent us from giving genuine and honestly held opinions their due hearing even when they are uncomfortable, from taking honest criticism in good part even when it is directed against the prevailing opinions. Such tolerance towards manifestations of integrity, truthfulness and independence of thought within the Church is never comfortable, and rarely appreciated. It is much easier and more rewarding to be prejudiced in one's ideas, whether one seeks support and confirmation from the faction in power or the opposition, but genuinely decent behaviour – and truthfulness is included in this – has never been the *most* profitable course, and this applies to communal life in the Church as well. And surely this must be so in the nature of the case even in the Church. For even here worldly values cannot altogether be avoided.

This truthfulness in the communal life of the Church, which is a necessary prior condition for truthfulness in the witness which Christians have to bear outside the Church requires, amongst other things, that our official utterances too shall be genuine and truthful. Now this is not the case if we act as though everything in our teaching and our tenets were always clear, as though we had patent ready-made solutions in stock for any and every problem, as though the only pity was that people did not apply to us for solutions from the first. It is not consistent with such genuine truthfulness when we who belong to the clergy act as though we found it easy to make our weak and cowardly flesh obedient to the commandment of God, as though everything among us was perfectly in order, as though we did not find it necessary to listen to those 'outside' the Church. If in our apologetic for Christianity, whether of the offensive or the defensive kind, we measure ourselves and our opponents by two different standards then this is irreconcilable with the sort of truthfulness of which we are here speaking (and often it is not only pagans who do this, but Christians too). Similarly, if we use unfair methods in controversy, or when we cannot listen to what others say we offend against truthfulness. Even in cases in which the position which we were defending at the beginning of the discussion was true and right, still, when the discussion itself is conducted in a serious spirit, we are still offending against truthfulness if our own opinions in all their breadth and fulness, with all their manifold perspectives and variations of emphasis do not undergo some modification as a result of the discussion. All these and similar matters have something to do with truthfulness, because truthfulness is not only the will to achieve formal accuracy in the propositions one puts forward, but also extends to the actual manner in which the correct proposition is put forward, for this too must be true. And truthfulness extends still further, and requires that man shall adopt a critical attitude towards himself in view of the fact that he is a sinner and knows that he has to appear before the judgment of God without first having been able to judge himself in any really adequate manner. For the rest it must be emphasised once more that truthfulness and criticism must not dispense with prudence in their operation within the Church's interior life. Otherwise we may find ourselves handing over all initiative in areas of controversy (both within and without the Church) to those who seek to gain advantages by being untruthful.

V

In the contemporary scene we should, perhaps, speak also of a fifth form of truthfulness considered as the determination to achieve the truth. This is a strange form, and one that is probably seldom adverted to and still more seldom – if indeed ever – thought of as falling under the general concept of truthfulness. I mean the attitude of love towards, and faith in the hidden truth and the unity inherent in that truth which is in one's fellow man and which underlies all his contradictory opinions, opinions which we cannot ourselves accept. This, therefore, is truthfulness considered as openness and sensitivity to the truth which is in another, which has not yet emerged into his explicit awareness but is still concealed under what may in certain circumstances seem to be the contradiction of it.

What is meant by this may briefly be explained. In the concrete environment of thought in which we live we feel ourselves to be men who are cut off one from another, disunited; men who, in the ultimate interpretations they place upon existence, in the ultimate attitudes on which everything counts, are divided. In earlier ages those who were divided in this way in their ultimate interpretations of life were also divided 'geographically' by the empty spaces which intervened, by political boundaries, social strata, distinctions of milieu etc., to such an extent that these differences of faith did not really constitute a significant factor radically affecting the particular kind of human existence of their times, and thus the individual lived in a milieu which was, from the 'ideological' point of view, homogeneous. Today, however, the position is fundamentally different. From his position among his fellows in the field of his calling and in public life it is brought home to modern man every day that he is the one who 'thinks differently' (from his immediate neighbour). The inevitable result of this is that modern man is exposed to a cruel and frightening burden. In the manner in which he lives his life both interiorly and exteriorly he naturally strives to develop that basic image of how life should be lived which is given to him as a constitutive element of the particular philosophy of life in which he is brought up and of his faith. And he constantly feels himself restricted in this, disowned by his fellows, his position radically called in question by the fact that those about him have a radically different outlook. The consequence of this is that all too many degenerate into a sceptical relativism with regard to all philosophies of life, all metaphysical interpretations, or again merely take as their guide for living the fragmentary remnants of standards still held in common (those of humanitarianism, of decency, of good citizenship etc.). For in the general collapse of any unified picture of the world which was once held in a particular society these have still survived. But let us consider the case of one who is unwilling to adopt either of these attitudes, who recognises that in fact this relativising scepticism of which we have been speaking is itself in its turn a point of view which is open to question, and for this and many other reasons is incapable of providing any effective guide to life; one who experiences that a life based on the fragmentary survivals of the spiritual achievements of earlier ages is not enough, and who implicitly acknowledges to himself that one cannot make any progress along these lines, because otherwise the desiccation of the spiritual element in life will extend still further; one who, on the other hand, has resolved to live uncompromisingly by Christian standards in all their fulness, bravely holding out in a situation which has become spiritually hostile and will certainly remain so for an incalculable period; one who takes this attitude even when it means that from the point of view of an outsider he will be living in a tiny minority, for this is that 'little flock' to which, according to age-old prophecy, it has always been the fate of real and genuine Christianity to be confined. It comes to constitute a strange and exceptional group within society at large. Must this be *all* that he says to himself – simply that such a situation as this must precisely be endured because it does not actually contradict the real nature of Christianity as the act of living one's faith, or the call which the individual experiences interiorly which is a pure act of grace? Or must he develop *another* attitude *over and above* this first one, this second attitude helping him by lightening the burden of responsibility which he bears in isolation before God and his conscience alone, cut off as he is from his fellows and not sharing their convictions? For this second attitude too has its origins precisely in this same faith. I believe that here such a supplementary attitude really is possible and in the long run necessary also, even though it has not yet been sufficiently thought out and developed among Christians.

To understand this we should remind ourselves first that our faith lays down that God wills the salvation of *all*, and wills it truly and effectively. In other words he also wills the salvation of those who live all round me in a community that is manifold and varied in its ideological tenets and to a large extent not even Christian at all. The Christian hope, which is orientated towards the Lord, his Cross and his Easter victory, gives the Christian himself the right to accept, and the assurance to hope that this salvific will of God, viewed in its application to the *whole* of mankind and its history, finds expression not merely in a straightforward *offering* of salvation on God's part, which is then refused, but does effectively and actually succeed and is victorious. Now if we are not to contradict the norms of Christian faith which lay down that Christianity irrevocably and inalienably imports salvation, this victory cannot be achieved as a *concomitant* of Christian grace and as a concomitant to the true and genuine faith. It must be a victory *of* that faith which the Christian confesses and *of* that grace by which he lives. Now if this victory of the salvific will of God is so far-reaching in its effects, and extends far beyond the spheres in which the Christian faith has, as a matter of history, visibly implanted itself and officially been embraced, and if this victory must still endure precisely as a victory of Christianity itself, then it follows that there must be an anonymous Christianity (It is difficult to find any other description for it that is so succinct and clear), a real Christianity which has so far simply failed to be recognised for what it really is, a Christianity which is already latently present even when it has not yet realised its own nature. What this must mean is something with which we are all familiar under different names. We say that when somebody declares that he does not believe in God it may well be that in spite of this he does believe, and does so in truth, but at a level which is so deep within him that he has not explored it, the level at which he takes a genuine moral decision determining the shape of his whole life. We speak of the baptismal desire which is implicitly elicited (even the Holy Office does this). We maintain that it is possible that the light of interior grace which God offers to every man achieves, without any deliberation on the part of the individual, but nevertheless in a real and effective sense, quite simply and without any outward sign, the ultimate orientation of that individual's whole spiritual existence towards the absolute fulness of the life which is interior to God. We also maintain that in cases in which this life is accepted it is possible to speak in a fully theological sense of a supernatural faith in revealed truth such that if it is fulfilled in love for this mystery of existence which silently draws the individual concerned towards itself, it justifies him and in this sense makes him a Christian. This does not mean, however, that the individual himself becomes conscious, in a manner which he could articulate or express, of what Christians explicitly and 'officially' believe, or realises that he is in agreement with this.

What has been said above is only an indication. It is neither intended to be, nor capable of being, anything more than this. But this was necessary by way of paving the way for our understanding of the point which we have now to discuss. In order to alleviate the existential situation of the Christian of our own times, and of the complexities of the society in which he lives with its varied and manifold ideological tenets, it seems that it would be of considerable value to take seriously the possibility of which we have been speaking. The Christian can find it far easier, less restricting and less oppressive to be a Christian if he knows that according to his own Christian faith and his own Christian hope the fact that so many men are not officially Christians is to a large extent to be attributed to outward appearances, to what can be apprehended at the external level, to nomenclature (For in many cases the real existential situation which lies behind this, and which has been accomplished by grace, is quite different). But the recognition of this fact will not make the Christian regard his own personal and explicit avowal of Christianity, precisely as explicitly avowed, any the less important or any the less salvific in its effects. For this in fact constitutes that realisation of himself which is bestowed upon him by grace. It is a realisation of how he himself is related to his own salvation, and how he intends to be related to it, and this state of self-comprehension is, in fact, once more the moment of maturity and fulness in that which does thus achieve its own self-explication. But the Christian can take a less restricted view of the world which is in fact his own. In the light of this he sees men who already honour and adore the God whom they do not know, the God whom he himself consciously venerates. In the light of this he is, at one level, constantly the one who is isolated and cut off from his fellows. This is the level of the historically apprehensible, the level of common parlance, of public avowal, of the 'proclamation' of salvation throughout the social order (which is intended to be such). But at the same time the Christian is no longer the one who is hopelessly isolated at *all* levels of life. He can see himself to be the one who has already advanced further than his fellows (this advance being due to *grace*), the one who already knows what he is and what he hopes that others too are. He does not have the impression of saying something that is wholly strange and alien to them when he bears witness to his Christianity in their presence. Rather he feels that he is telling them what they themselves already interiorly are without knowing it.

The actual ability to recognise this anonymous Christianity in one's fellow men not merely as a deduction worked out in the abstract and hypothetically but in the concrete experience of life is something which is developed by practice and cultivated. It is the ability to make the hidden truth that is in one's fellow apparent, in the first instance at least, to one's self; in other words, as I believe, this too is a kind of 'truthfulness', the truthfulness, namely, which consists in being able enough and bold enough to let truth emerge for what it is in itself (and that is still truthfulness). This truthfulness is one which is of inestimable significance for Christians, and above all for the young Christians of today, especially in view of the fact that these young Christians are no longer in the least willing to adopt a certain attitude which has characterised Christian pedagogy and the Christian approach to learning hitherto. This is the attitude of standing aloof, as far as possible, from the world of complex and conflicting ideologies and (even if only in ever more restricted circles) to confine themselves to the homogeneous world of those professing the same faith.

Of course this is only to define the *task* for the modern Christian. What we have said does nothing to solve either the theoretical or the practical problem of how to give the Christians of today the vision to practise this mysterious kind of truthfulness. If we understood this kind of truthfulness, the truth of Christianity, its intrinsic reality would reveal itself to us far more clearly and unmistakably from the world about us; the world would be far less liable to give the impression of total profanity and de-Christianisation, the impression which we so often receive and which we find painful and testing to our faith.

In the Old Testament truth and truthfulness (faithfulness) are expressed by one and the same word, *emet* (*emuna*). This is not merely a sign that the language is still at a relatively primitive stage of development, in which such distinctions have not yet been drawn. It is a manifestation of a quite specific interpretation of being and life which is essential to the revealed religion of the Old and New Testaments. Reality is essentially not the objective status of things which cognitive being is 'set over against' as something independent, alien and separate. Reality in the ultimate sense is present where being *is itself* totally, and without any break in its continuity. It is of itself something illumined from within. It possesses itself in knowledge and love. Reality is ultimately spirit and person, and in the measure that a given reality is not this, is incapable of realising itself, is not objectified to itself, is not apparent to itself, in the same measure the being of this reality is itself as such weak and lacking in ultimate validity. And in this sense truth, as the givenness of a thing to itself, is an intrinsic element in reality itself, so that a given entity has being and exists to the extent that it realises itself, stands out to itself, discloses to itself the truth that is its own nature. From this point of view, therefore, truthfulness is not, in the first instance, a virtue, a moral prescription which regulates human intercourse, but the connatural projection outwards to *others* of the truth that is inherent in reality considered as the 'being present' of a thing to itself. Truthfulness is the self-confrontation of a reality in so far as this self-confrontation is faithful and really reproduces this 'being to itself' clearly and luminously, undistorted and really achieved, expressed and accepted.

It is here, then, that truthfulness towards others as well has its source. It imparts to the other person only what the individual himself is. It makes his own unique personality emerge from its hidden background and appear before that other pure and undistorted. This truthfulness is in the first instance the free self-disclosure of one's personal being as rendered present to one's self, made available to others, the conveying of one's own personal truth to others. And for this reason it is true that truth and truthfulness are at basis the same: the act of uttering one's own truth faithfully to others. Truth is in origin not the emergence of any kind of thing, but the self-bestowal of being upon itself. As such it is essentially personal, and truthfulness is the disclosure precisely of this personal being to others in freedom and love.

It should be noticed that such an act of self-disclosure, in which one gives one's personal being to others, is, in the very nature of the one who does disclose himself in this way, always a free act. Furthermore being is not simply and in all circumstances that which is open in itself, but rather that which has to be disclosed, to be bestowed. Thus the nature of truth, and of the inner structure of the act of self-disclosure itself as free, means that truthfulness is always a 'grace' too, a favour, a gift. Now Christianity is nothing else than the one joyful message that the absolute mystery which is personal being in the absolute, spirit and freedom, has willed to be absolute truth and truthfulness, in other words the absolute grace of a triumphant self-disclosure to us too. Hence too all that truthfulness which is required of us is not, in the first instance, a law and a prohibition of lying, but rather the power, bestowed upon us as a free act of grace, to disclose ourselves and (since we are finite beings) thereby precisely to come to ourselves, to confront ourselves in our own truth. For we only experience ourselves as that which we are, that which we can be and that which we will be precisely *in that* we open ourselves to the All of being, God himself in the act of opening ourselves to others. For man too, therefore, truthfulness is not simply a connatural extension of truth in which he possesses himself, but also an indispensable mode for this discovery of his own truth. In the last analysis every liar denies the truth of his own self most of all. He withholds his own truth from himself because in being untruthful to others and to the outside world he also prevents his own truth from appearing.

Now one who loses his own truth is lost indeed, because one who has lost himself cannot possess God either. But he who finds this truth, he who accepts it in an attitude of truthfulness, lives it and makes it manifest, has God, who is *the* Truth, and this truth is freedom and eternal life.

23

PARRESIA (BOLDNESS)

The Virtue that the Christian Needs for the Apostolate

IN the last analysis all 'striving for Christian perfection' can consist in nothing else than in love of God and one's neighbour, in the fulfilment of that one greatest commandment. It should be noticed that what is required of us in order to fulfil this commandment is that we shall seek God and our neighbour and not ourselves and our own perfection. This fact alone means that it is not a commandment in the true sense at all. Love of neighbour as expressed in selfless service of him belongs integrally to this task, ancient yet ever new, which is laid upon the Christian. And because of this every Christian has a mission, an apostolate. He may have a very developed and explicit awareness of this or, on the other hand, it may remain at the implicit and hidden level as a quality inherent in the tasks imposed upon him by the necessities of his everyday life. Thus everyone has a specifically Christian task to perform in regard to his neighbour, an 'apostolate', a 'mission'. Now if this applies to every Christian it applies with twofold force to the priest, the ambassador of the faith, and to all others who have a defined and official position and function in furthering the Church's mission. Nowadays one's own native land has become 'mission territory' (although great care has to be taken in how this term is applied). It follows from this that in the contemporary scene the specifically 'missionary' virtues have become the virtues of every Christian who does not forget that he has a mission to his neighbour. Something must be said here concerning one such virtue, because it is one that is often forgotten or overlooked. It is so inconspicuous that it does not really have any distinctive and proper name of its own at all. But precisely for this reason we too often fail to take it sufficiently into account in our Christian living, when we reflect upon the tasks our mission imposes upon us, the difficulties they entail and the holiness which should shine out from them.

1. In order even gradually to be able to clarify, what is meant we must begin by calling attention to certain specific words in scripture. Thus for instance Paul admonishes us that we must be heralds of the word and preach it even *akairos*, 'out of season' (2 Tim 4:2). There is a word, then, such that to all appearances – that is viewed from the human standpoint and not from that of God – it must be spoken on an occasion, *kairos*, which is not right, not the appropriate moment, not the right situation. Paul says that he is not ashamed of the gospel (Rom 1:16), and the very fact that this has to be particularly emphasised implies that this attitude of boldly refusing to be ashamed must be intended as some kind of *counter* to an interior shrinking, a reluctance to speak out, a feeling that preaching the word or any other kind of 'coming out into the open' with the hidden reality and truth of Christianity into the 'world', which is uninterested and irritated by it, is out of place and inappropriate. Jesus declares that it is not enough merely to believe in him. One must also 'confess' him, and that too 'before men'. Evidently, therefore, he holds not only that belief in him is difficult and is the ultimate act for the spirit and heart of man, but that man has the further and supplementary task of confessing him before men. And this too is something that man can refuse to do. This is not so immediately obvious. For if a man already believes why should he feel that confessing this faith of his before men is a further and supplementary task and a still more difficult one? And if we simply reply to this: It is because the other men who do not believe persecute this faith of his, then the question is not solved but only deferred. For what does this really amount to? Simply that when the Christian makes public profession of his faith before others in this way they react to it not as to some strange opinion which is to be tolerated in another since that is what he seems to want, and so to relegate it to the sphere of everyday experience (as with so many other views and opinions), but as to something so provocative, so inappropriate and so dangerous that it is calculated to arouse contradiction, hatred and mortal enmity. Once more, therefore, the ambassador of the faith must have the courage to do something which is anything but obvious. He must have the courage to proclaim the unpreachable, the gospel which provokes contradiction, to act in a manner which is untimely, *akairos*.

Thus as presented in the New Testament the act of 'confessing' the faith has the character not merely of an unrestrained declaration of one's own opinion, something which is, in fact, understandable in itself in human society (in other contexts men are, in fact, quite eager when 'they have something to say' or can listen to something), but the character of daring too, to speak the Word of God into a world which is absolutely closed to it, has no comprehension for it, offers it no foothold, to bring light, and threatens to quench it. And therefore the ambassador or messenger of faith has need of a quality which scripture calls 'parresia'. In German we have not, properly speaking, any precise term for what this means in the religious and specifically the Christian context. For here it designates a virtue, but a virtue which is a gift of God, which at once sets us a task and bestows upon us the means to fulfil it. It is all very well to take the dictionary translation 'candour', but this does justice neither to the political nor to the moral overtones which are essentially inherent from the very outset in the Greek term. Nor does this rendering 'candour' express an idea which, in the history of our language and thought, has come to be charged with religious meaning, as the term 'parresia' has as used in the Old Testament (LXX) and the New. For instance we cannot speak of the candour of God. And it is only by straining the term that we can think of it as a quality of prayer or something which makes prayer possible. The term as used among us cannot express the act of standing in God's presence in free and joyful openness, nor can it stand for something which is an essential characteristic of the self-manifestation of Jesus in the world. Hence it is that it is only with difficulty that we can translate this word in contexts in which it stands for an apostolic virtue. For when we use the term 'candour' or some similar term, then we are referring to a virtue which is common to mankind as a whole, if, indeed, it is not simply a quite neutral specification of the attitude of unconstrainedness, unembarrassment and ease in self-expression – attitudes, therefore, which do not in the least measure up to the distinctive and specific element in this apostolic virtue. For this virtue is exercised only in preaching, considered as the actualisation of the event in which God himself is revealed to a world enclosed in sin.

2. Thus we propose to put forward certain ideas concerning this virtue as it is in itself. These are only few in number. For the most important factor of all must here remain unexpressed. It is that which provides the proper and true basis for this virtue of the apostle and of his mission, namely the parresia of God and of Christ himself.[1]

[1] For a treatment of this idea which brings out its full depths and significance cf. H. Schlier, *T.W.N.T.* V, pp. 869–884.

PARRESIA (BOLDNESS)

The Christian messenger is in a situation to which he does not of himself, i.e. in virtue of his own nature and qualities, belong. He is, in fact, on a 'mission'. He has been 'sent'. Necessarily, therefore, he is intruding upon areas which are not, naturally speaking, his own. He comes to men who are in a very true sense foreign to him. His presence is troublesome to them, and he is troubled in turn. He must in some sense seem like an intruder. With his word, the word that is God's word, he intrudes upon a world which is unwilling to hear it, which is mysteriously hostile to this word, because it is a word which brings to light the hidden contents of the heart, because it goes too far, because it makes too many demands upon man, because it summons him out of the sphere of the comprehensible, because it objectifies and makes explicit things which naturally belong to the horizons of human experience, which are present only in a muted and indirect manner: conscience, guilt, death, judgment and finally the living God with the actual summons which he addresses to men. He who conveys this word to others is one who, by his own faults and by his failures to live up to the word he conveys, continually disowns it. He casts his own shadow over the light which he brings. Even while he brings salvation to others he himself must tremble lest he become a castaway. His own word can sound in his ears like sounding brass or a tinkling cymbal. What he utters is in truth the love of God at its deepest and most intimate offered to man at the most interior and immutable level of his being. It is a miracle of love, a grace which is inexpressibly tender and loving, and yet the Christian speaks of it (how could he do otherwise?) as though it were the most humdrum of matters. He handles it as one handles the everyday affairs of one's life as an ordinary member of society. He teaches the children, he gives instructions, he is constantly in danger of confusing the means, namely the well-being of the Church, with the end, namely that God shall be freely loved. That which is nameless he calls by a thousand names, and he is for ever speaking of him of whom he himself says that he 'is ineffable and exalted above all that is and that can be conceived of apart from himself' (First Vatican Council).

Besides this there is a further factor to be considered: that elemental embarrassment which is involved in being a man extends to the soul as well as the body. The priest and every other 'apostle', provided he is a true man (this may easily be something that is inherent in human nature as such) is, of his nature, one who would rather be silent, one who prefers to leave the unutterable unuttered, one whom it troubles to have to speak out and to lay the incomprehensible mystery of his heart open to the public gaze. And further it seems that modern man finds it particularly difficult to make the mystery which cannot be named a subject for discussion. He has come to realise how vast and complex his own world has become, to gain a more and more detailed knowledge of its inner workings and the mystery and complexity of its laws. Hence it becomes increasingly impossible to confuse these with God himself. And because of all this he realises how far the God who really can be called God is from our own earthly experience, how far he is above all the possibilities of human expression. He almost has the impression that it is impious to practise any kind of formal religious exercises, any kind of organised religion. He almost has the feeling that from motives of sheer reverence he cannot give his adherence to those who believe that they have already obtained an insight into the designs of God. Still less can he belong to the official representatives of God who have to help him (God) in order that he can survive in the world at all. Does not all this make it difficult to be an official minister of religion, or to 'come out into the open' with one's Christianity in any other way either? Is it not difficult to make it one's calling to speak of God, the ineffable, difficult even before one encounters the malice of enemies who refuse to hear, before the contradictions have commenced? Does not the very nature of religion itself make it difficult when one has any understanding at all of what this is?

Now the virtue which provides us with strength to bear and overcome these difficulties is the Pauline virtue of parresia. Religion, if it is authentic and true, carries with it in its initial stages, a dumbness which is deathlike in its intensity. Parresia is the strength which enables us to overcome this and to speak out in spite of it. It is that indefinable attitude of courage which enables one to say in one's heart: *Credidi propter quod locutus sum.* In the silence and solitude of his divinity the Father utters the Word. This becomes flesh and forces its way into the empty void of the world in order to make itself heard in a dimension in which, naturally speaking, the only thing that can be heard of him is silence and nameless mystery. And when the Word took flesh in this way it occasioned immense pain and called for immense endurance. Parresia is simply the virtue which enables us to continue this endurance and bring it to its due consummation. It is because God himself has spoken 'in spite of' hostile dispositions in the world that the Church too has found a voice and utterance in the word of avowal, in the word of praise, in the cry of joy, in the prayer for grace whispered by the weeping suppliant. And now we must go right back to the start, and read once more those passages in scripture which treat of the word that is preached *akairos*, out of season, of the 'shameless' refusal to be ashamed of the gospel, of confessing God before men, of that special kind of boldness which is called parresia, and which is proper to Christianity alone.

But in order to obtain a deeper, and perhaps a still clearer spiritual insight into the significance of this virtue, which every Christian needs in order to accomplish his mission, we must point out certain consequences which follow from what has already been said.

Anyone who has not had the experience of being forced to speak out when he would really have preferred to keep silence is a mere petty propaganda-monger, one who has no true comprehension of the significance of what he is speaking of – not in any sense a priest or a 'confessing Christian' speaking in the power of the divine virtue of parresia. There are those, on the other hand, who do feel the pain involved in the exercise of this virtue, who sometimes have the feeling, so powerful that it seems to threaten their very lives, that they had better impose silence upon themselves, or at least make mention of God only indirectly and, so to say, by means of an embarrassed silence. But this does not mean that they are any the less called to the priesthood or to the mission in which all Christians are *ipso facto* summoned to take an active part. It does not mean that they have a weaker missionary vocation than one who finds that the name of God comes easily off his lips. If the difficulties which this virtue entails are experienced less and less, then one must ask one's self whether this really is a sign that one is already speaking by the charisms of the Holy Spirit, with the tongues of angels, and in harmony with the exultations of the heavenly choirs, or whether in reality one only appears to be speaking of God, and his living presence is no longer in one's words at all. But one who deliberately evades the pain which this virtue entails, and who really is silent, one who occupies himself with something else in order not to have to speak of God, such a one as this is no apostle of the incarnate Word of God. He betrays his status as a Christian at its most basic level, the level which is referred to in the passage which runs: 'Do not say, "I am only a youth", for to all to whom I send you you shall go, and whatever I command you you shall speak' (Jer 1:7).

The opinion has been put forward (notably in France) that the 'witness' which the Christian layman has a mission to bear consists simply in (silently) being a Christian. In other words he does not, on this view, need in any sense to be the sort of apostle who speaks out unless he voluntarily accepts a supplementary 'commission' from the Church's authorities. But this is not true. Certainly the layman does not extend his activities beyond the confines of his own natural sphere of life (his family, his natural milieu, the community in which he lives and works, his neighbourhood). This is the sphere to which he naturally belongs, and as a layman he is not called to leave it (at least not in any permanent or definitive sense) in order to fulfil his duty as a Christian. But in this sphere he must also bear witness to his Christian mode of existence by speaking out and making it known in words. And for this he too needs this virtue of parresia, which is so difficult. And it would be true of him too that he would be betraying his status as a Christian if he were to evade the pain which this God-given virtue entails. If he tried to evade the duty of exercising parresia in this sense by keeping silent, by making no attempt whatever to speak of God (maintaining that the parish priests do quite enough in this direction, and are actually paid to do it), then he would be offending against his own mission because it is a duty laid upon every man from his natural position in society to bear witness in words too (with restraint and discretion perhaps, but still precisely with parresia too) to what God has wrought upon him and to the source from which his reserves of strength derive.

It has to be something that people notice in us that we find it difficult to utter the Word of God which God himself has placed upon our lips. For only in this way can this word become credible to others. Only in this way does the content of what we speak retain, even as we speak it, the ring of holiness, the quality of silence which it must carry with it if it is not to be confused with the mere noise of this world. We have to ensure that the true power to speak in this sense does not degenerate into the false, over-facile and Godless loquacity of the mere babbler or the manager of an enterprise, something which no longer conveys God but rather one's self. And for this purpose our speaking of God must always proceed afresh from our sense of mission, from a background of prayerful silence. Anyone who would not rather be silent and who cannot endure the silence of God himself does not speak in the true sense at all. His word is not a word proceeding from that parresia which is a grace and a miracle of God. It belongs, rather, to the busy-ness of men, which makes a noise because it is afraid of the silence of God.

There remains our Christian lot as presented in Mt 10:27 (and, in a form which has been completely altered, in Lk 12:3): 'What I tell you in the dark utter in the light, and what you hear whispered proclaim upon the housetops'. The message we have to utter is one that can only be heard where the light of this world is swallowed up by the divine darkness, and the voice of God comes in a quiet whisper which is not to be found in the noise of many human words. And yet this message must be uttered by us from the roof-tops and the pulpits, in the classrooms and in the factory workshops, in canteens, during factory breaks and on Sunday afternoons after the cinema, finally in the humming of the world's presses (in the manner appropriate to each particular context). The message must be spoken in these contexts in order that God may be present even in them, and in order that men may be made to notice and hear where God quietly utters the Word that is himself. Indeed it is for this purpose that the string of our tongue has already been loosened in baptism (Mk 7:31–37), and not only our ears but our mouths too have been opened in order that we may no longer be dumb servers of dumb idols, but that we may be able to 'confess' by praising God and avowing our faith in him (1 Cor 12:2), strengthened for both of these acts by the virtue of parresia.

We are all the poor servants who must, of their very natures, be silent in God's presence once we realise who we are and who *he* is. And it is in the light of this that we must understand what it means when we say on our own behalf the prayer of Acts 4:29: 'Grant to thy servants to speak thy word with all boldness (parresia)'. What we are praying for here is that the closing words of Acts, which were spoken of Paul, may be true of all God's servants too, ourselves included: 'He preached the kingdom of God and taught about the Lord Jesus Christ quite openly and unhindered' (Acts 28:31).

24

THE WORKS OF MERCY AND THEIR REWARD

When one sets out to treat theologically of the rewards of the works of mercy one very quickly finds one's self overtaken by the deepest embarrassment. And it may be that the best reward of all is to be placed in this position of embarrassment.

The problem arises from the fact that when someone exercises compassion towards those who are his equals he very often becomes condescending and enjoys this attitude of condescension. At least this very often seems to be the case. One of the etymological roots of the Old Testament concept of compassion concerns this. Compassion is conceived of as a 'stooping down'. And the other root (envisaging parental or mother love) seems not wholly to disagree with the first. But this is terrible. Who wants to be treated condescendingly? Does not the recipient of such charity not seem to be deprived of his basic dignity – the dignity of the poor and the suffering, the greatness of whom appears precisely in their lowly state? Of course it might immediately be objected in response to these apprehensions that all this makes no difference. The hungry man who is filled, the sick man who is healed by the charity of another – these will not spend much time in asking whether the charity which brought them succour was the outcome of pride, self-assurance or condescension. But even if we allow this to be the case – and even so does not the recipient of alms often feel himself mortally wounded in his personal dignity even as he eagerly grasps for these alms? – it would nevertheless still be possible to maintain that this alien kind of charity should be done away with in favour of an approach based on justice, with all the necessary and reasonable means of applying this, in which all are placed on an equal footing, an approach in which everyone is accorded his due rights and so everyone is helped. This would, in effect, circumvent the situation in which one man has to 'condescend' to the need of another, feeling compassion for him from his own position of material security and the abundance of his resources whether interior or exterior. Has not wounded human dignity often enough explained furiously, 'I want not alms but my rights!' Thus it could be said that true compassion must find a way of doing away with itself in order that that poison which is inherent in its own nature, namely pride, may disappear. And let us not be too ready or too quick to reply that compassion is the practical sympathy of the *poor* and the *suffering* for the poor and suffering, and therefore far from all self-assured pride or condescension. For we have to recognise, however regretfully, the obvious fact that the poor cannot make the poor rich. He who is really in a state of despair himself cannot truly console another. Such as these can do nothing effective to answer the other's need. Was not the doctrine of the Stoa and the Diatribe right in assigning pity and charity to the list of vices? Is there any other way of helping than turning one's face away as one comes to the help of another, and doing so in such a way that one is manifestly only giving him his due? Is there any other way of helping than by setting out in a reasonable and practical way to give what is needful as something to which the recipient himself, and not the giver, has a legitimate claim? Is the genuinely charitable man not one who feels guilty in the presence of the other, and feels that the 'resources' (and this means more than merely money) on which he draws in order to help that other are so much ill-gotten gains? When we follow the words of scripture in saying that God is compassionate, and we, as creatures and children, live by his mysterious compassion, then this simply raises the same tormenting question in a still sharper form. Is it not easy to be compassionate from the pure fulness of glory and blessing which belongs to God alone? To bestow when one loses nothing thereby? To forgive when what is forgiven could not have done any injury to God? To be patient towards those imprisoned in time from the position of eternity, which no time affects? Is not God precisely the prototype of a kind of compassion which cannot be ours because it humiliates him whom it pretends to raise?

And yet the message of the gospel does preach that love which stoops down to poverty, a love which, unlike Eros, does not catch fire from the beauty of the beloved, but loves him out of compassion although, or because he is poor, lowly and nothing. The condescension involved in such love may be terrible, but so too is the attitude of mind which refuses to 'receive anything in charity', the claim to be able to help one's self – this is a still more terrible pride. Are not both kinds of pride together at one in their spirit of mortal enmity, by which giver and recipient are divided, and do not both together represent the one single state of need of sinful creaturehood? Who can give without showing himself proud in the very act of giving? Who can receive without losing his dignity in the very act of receiving, without having his resentment kindled?

It is quite evident that there is only one who can give in such a way that in doing so he does not seem to be 'graciously' condescending. It is he who is conscious that he himself and his gift are continually being given and loaned to him by another in order that they may be handed on; one, therefore, who never for one moment loses sight of the fact that he himself is the subject of charity in the most basic, absolute and all-encompassing sense, so that it is not that which is his own which he gives to others but that which he has received. And he gives it as something which he has received, and which he must project further beyond himself because it was not given to him in the first place in order that he could retain it for his own use. A man can only be charitable, therefore, without at the same time becoming frightful, when and to the extent that he is conscious of being himself the object of compassionate love, and to the extent that he accepts himself as such, when he gives in virtue of the fact that he himself is receiving love. Only he who is loved with the love of Agape can be charitable in a spirit of Agape. Only he who has attained to this attitude of humility which consists, once more, in receiving his own self as a gift of love from God, only he who makes this humility the basic fact of his whole existence will avoid becoming proud in the exercise of his charity. Only in this way can he practise charity, and in the very act of doing so reveal not his self-assurance and his riches, but his own poverty, from which the other can allow himself to be given what he needs. And when he who is doing a work of charity looks upon him whom he is helping he sees in him the reflection of his own poverty and need. He is one with him in a spirit of brotherhood, in which all the poor and all the needy have their wants supplied from one and the same fulness, and so he receives from his brother more than he gives: a new insight into his own emptiness. For it is only in this insight that he can avoid losing his own riches, which he has received from the hand of another. *Simul dives at pauper.*

But in that case are we not all the subjects of that condescending charity which we call the love of God? Do we not, in that case, simply hand on the humiliating gift which has itself put us in a position to be charitable? And is not the result of this that this attitude of charitableness, which has produced and continues to produce its own acts of charity, does not heal but simply carries the process of destruction further? And if the source and origin of all reality and all goodness, that which is present in our innermost being, yet at the same time immeasurably exalted above us (setting an infinite distance between itself and us) is called God, can we then speak in this way? Does he too humiliate even as he gives? Does he bring about the unfathomable pain of nothingness when it is brought face to face with itself and realises itself for what it is? Does he do this by the very act of supplying the immediate need? Or is it rather that when he bestows his grace on man, provided it is really accepted, it is always accompanied by that miraculous love for himself in which one can accept the gift and still not be humiliated precisely because the blessing one receives exceeds the riches and glory of him who gives? Is it not rather that one can receive gifts from this giver because in the gift he gives *himself* as well? Truly, if in bestowing the gift of compassion one can and does give one's self too, handing one's self over, then no offence is done to him on whom the gift is bestowed. But can *we* do this in contexts in which it is a question of charity, which can only be expressed in the giving of gifts, rather than of love, which gives itself and by that very fact sets itself and the loving subject free? And further, may it not be that in relation to God it is the absolute sin of sins not to allow gifts to be bestowed upon one? Do we not inevitably here pass from the realm of mere knowledge which is still uncommitted to any particular course of action to that precisely of act, the act namely of love in its receptive aspect, which has its own light in itself and nothing apart from itself?

But there is another answer too to the question of God's act of bestowing, in which he does not destroy by the very fact of willing to give. It is something that can only be expressed with stammering and hesitation. But are we to be silent about it merely because what it expresses seems the most improbable answer of all? God himself has assumed a creaturely status, and made it his own, and has thereby himself endured our state of need. He gave himself to our nothingness, assuming it as his own fate, and therefore he is in a position not to look down upon us or to be condescending when he bestows his favours upon us. In fact he has identified himself with the poor in their tears, their hunger and their death. This may sound like a myth which is no longer applicable to the contemporary scene. But must we not regard the situation in this light: On the one hand we have the absolute fulness, and on the other ourselves, our emptiness and nothingness. Now the fulness creates the empty and, moreover, creates them in a *meaningful* way (How could it be otherwise when it really is the fulness of light and meaning and goodness?). And if this is the case, then the fulness makes itself responsible for the nothingness. The fulness that is God has committed itself in such a way that it is no longer 'able' to repel the nothingness, to set it at an infinite distance from itself and so to demonstrate the triumph of its own untouchability. It is no longer in a position to thrust the nothingness away from itself and thereby to condemn it to the absolute pain of a wound that is constantly open and never healed. Now that it has committed itself as a free act of love it is under a certain 'compulsion' in virtue of that love to take upon itself the burden of the nothingness. Moreover by accepting creaturehood in this act of absolute self-bestowal God has not only penetrated to the innermost depths of man's being (in the act which we call grace), but actually 'appears' in the concrete dimension of history, the dimension in which alone we find ourselves. And this is what we mean by saying that God has achieved his epiphany in the flesh of that man who is the Son of the Father. Furthermore if modern man finds nothing illogical in pantheism or panentheism, then he has no right to relegate to the realm of myth that *free* act by which God bestows himself upon the creature in grace and in the incarnation of his Son, which gives the world a share in God's own life. But we have almost lost the thread of our argument. All that we mean to say here is that on the Christian understanding of existence even God in his act of compassion humbles himself, empties himself and bestows himself upon the one to whom he gives gifts from his fulness; that even God encounters himself in the creaturehood he mercifully accepts, sees himself there as a compassionate man who sees his own need in the beggar whom he succours. For the Word has become flesh, has become the Man of Sorrows and the crucified one.

But the most sublime miracle of human compassion is this: He who is really compassionate loses himself, identifies himself with his brother in his need, dares to commit himself to the unknown. His freedom achieves its ultimate act of daring, that of abandoning himself. And then it can be said of such a one (even when it is only the Christian that says this): Many a man has already encountered Christ without knowing that the one with whom he was in contact was the one whose life and death had achieved for him a destiny of blessing and redemption; that by the boldness of his compassion for others he had, so to say, won a place for himself in this life and death of Christ; that he was encountering the one whom the Christians rightly call Jesus of Nazareth. Freedom as exercised in the creature always entails a certain boldness in committing ourselves to those unknown and incalculable factors which, whether we recognise it or not, lie concealed within that course which is visible to us and upon which we decide. Factors which are *totally* unperceived or *absolutely* other cannot be taken into our calculations when we make our free decisions, for the object of these must necessarily be that which is defined and limited. But because something is unexpressed and unformulated it does not necessarily follow that it belongs to this category of the totally unperceived and unintended. Now the grace of God and Christ are present in everything as the mysterious essence of every reality which can be the object of our choice. And for this reason it is not so easy either to reach out to receive something from another or to bestow something upon another without thereby having, in some way or other, to do with God and Christ. Let us therefore take the case of one who, even when there is no question whatever of any explicit verbal revelation, accepts the poverty of his own existence as something bestowed upon him (that in itself is not so easy!); one who receives and gives charity in patient silence, or better in faith, hope and love (whatever names he may give to these basic attitudes and motivations). In doing this he accepts his own human nature precisely as that mystery which lies buried in, and at the same time leads on to the further mystery of eternal love, the mystery that carries life with it even in the womb of death. Such a one as this gives his assent to something in such a way that it is equivalent to entrusting himself to the immeasurable and the incalculable. For in fact God has filled this situation with the immeasurable and the incalculable, that is with his own self. The Word has become flesh. Such a man as this is, in fact, without realising it, giving his assent to Christ himself, for he who lets himself go and takes the plunge falls into depths which are there in objective fact, and not merely because he himself has imagined them. He who accepts without reserve the humanity which belongs to himself and his brother (something which is, indeed inexpressibly difficult so that the point at which we really do achieve it in fact remains obscure) has thereby accepted the Son of Man, because God has accepted man in him. When scripture states that he who loves his neighbour fulfils the law then this is the ultimate truth, that which is true in virtue of the fact that God himself has become this neighbour.

Thus every time we accept and love our neighbour we *ipso facto* accept and love in him him who is at once nearest to, and most remote from us. In other words in surrendering ourselves to, and bestowing ourselves upon our brother we ourselves receive a still greater gift: the fulness upon fulness of our compassionate God, and in this himself for his own glory.

25
PROVING ONESELF IN TIME OF SICKNESS

The Question Which Sickness Raises for Man as a Whole

WE shall be attempting here to develop only one single line of thought, that namely concerning the unity, the wholeness of man and the bearing which sickness has upon this.

Christian theology and philosophy recognise the unity and the wholeness of man. Naturally when we Christians assert that man consists of body and soul we are quite right. Indeed a sick man could say with justice that he experiences this duality in his own being only too clearly. But for all this man, that is to say that objective entity with which each of us is directly confronted as a matter of his own personal experience, is originally one, one with a unity which is not the mere outcome or result of a chance combination of two prior entities. It follows from this that what we *experience* as soul is in reality our own being which is objectively speaking a single and whole entity as viewed from within. And what we call our body is ultimately this same entity in its oneness and wholeness as experienced from without. This is not to deny that this being of ours in its oneness and wholeness, which we are faced with in our concrete living experience, has not behind and beyond this experience two meta-empirical or metaphysical elements in it such that the distinction between them cannot be obliterated and they cannot be identified one with the other. But the objective reality which we encounter directly when we apprehend ourselves as a matter of authentic experience is always the whole and single entity, always man in his oneness. In apprehending this single objective reality that is ourselves we do not always penetrate to the same level of reality in it. But it is no less true that in apprehending it we never apprehend merely one constituent element in this whole in such a way that it does not necessarily bring the other constituent element to our awareness as well.

It is not possible at this point to describe the various approaches which Christian theologians and philosophers have devised in order to give intelligible expression to this basic unity of man, or the various attempts which have been made to express this, without falling into the errors of materialism on the one hand, which seeks to deny and existence of the soul as a distinct principle, or into those of an abstract and over-spiritualised approach on the other, which tends to deny the reality of the body. But whatever the differences in approach may be, for Christian theologians and philosophers the body is neither the prison of the soul nor a mere container for it, but rather an integral element in man as a unity. Similarly the soul is not a thing which controls the body rather as an operator controls a machine, but this too is rather an integral element in man as an unity which, as one might express it, only achieves its true identity in virtue of the fact that it is itself embodied, and has a body belonging to it, complementing the body so as to constitute the true spiritual reality. Body is not something added on to the soul. Rather it is a concretisation of it, the projection of soul as basic life-force into an already existing sphere of space and time. Thus in a certain sense it is that in the soul which causes it to exist in that concrete dimension of space and time in which it comes (figuratively speaking) to its due fulness and flowering.

For this reason when the Christian intends to confess that in which he believes the final perfection of the whole man to consist he speaks of the resurrection of the flesh, and for the same reason we recognise that we are redeemed through the physical death of the Lord, through his Blood, precisely because the act of obedience and love performed by the Lord in its inconceivable sublimity could only really be achieved in and through what became of the physical side of his nature, his flesh. And for the same reason in its further projections too, in its application to our own soul, salvation history becomes intelligible, acquires a body, in a human word, in the community of the Church as a visible historical entity, in the gestures of the sacraments which touch the body.

What is the significance of all this for sickness and for those who suffer it? We have seen that the man whom we experience in ourselves and whom we name according to our experience is not a compositum made up from body and soul as from two separate pre-existing entities, but is rather a being who is completely one and whole right from the origins and prior to any such distinction, so that any account we can give of body and soul in man presupposes this prior unity of his as something that is already given. Now it is in accordance with this that on the Christian interpretation when an event such as sickness befalls man it always affects him as a whole, as a single entity, one in which body and soul can indeed be conceptually distinguished, yet the unity of which is objectively speaking indissoluble.

Again the experience of so-called physical sickness contains (even though one can often only understand this with difficulty) a statement concerning the sick man as a person who is spiritual and free, a statement about the tasks which his own sickness imposes upon him whether he has already managed to fulfil these or has failed to measure up to them: tasks of courage, of honesty with himself, of patience, the task of turning the experience to good account in the religious sense, finally the task of integrating this intervention from without which we call sickness into the single overall meaning which a man has to find in his own existence, a task at which he may already either have succeeded or failed. By the time one becomes aware of sickness in one's self as an objective fact one has already taken up a definite attitude towards it, and this taking up of an attitude is an integral element in the sickness itself.

Admittedly – and in considering the indissoluble unity to be found both in man himself and in his sickness this is the obverse side of the coin – there is no stage in sickness or aspect of it in which man's awareness of himself is confined solely to the spiritual side of his being, or to the level of personality. Something which seems to belong purely to the realm of the spirit and the mind when we are ill can in fact be something extremely physical, something which does not belong to the level of personality at all, but has impinged upon us from without. When a sick man is suffering from the extremes of depression and even despair this may be not so much the expression of his basic attitude as a person but rather a symptom of the external affliction as this impinges upon his personhood, the reflection of something external and alien to his real personality. And it may be that in the same man who seems to be in such a distressed state spiritually speaking what seems to be merely physical and material in his power of resistance, the hold he keeps on life, is in fact to a large extent only the embodiment of a spirit that is fundamentally sound, at one with itself and also with that which has been imposed upon it because it is at peace with God.

It can also be the case that the body has more to tell us about the spirit and the spirit more about the body than either can tell us about itself. Our concrete experience of sickness is never such that we are in a position unequivocally to distinguish between the spirit and the body as two completely separate compartments. We can never say with certainty 'This factor has come upon me from without and is my lot which I must accept and bear. *That* factor, on the other hand, in the sickness I am suffering from is something intrinsic to myself, something which is the outcome of my own free action, for which I myself bear the responsibility. It is, of course, true that a diagnosis which distinguishes between the physical and the spiritual factors in an illness is, provided it is prudently conducted, quite legitimate, and, indeed, necessary from a therapeutic point of view. But however true this may be, when it comes to the ultimate judgment, we can never have any absolute certainty as to which of the various symptoms from which the sick man suffers are to be ascribed to the affliction visited upon him *ab externo*, and which are the outcome of his own free acts as a person.

Now all this means that what is true of man in general applies in a special and heightened sense to the sick man: he is made aware of experiencing himself, yet at the same time the ultimate significance of this experience remains obscure to him. Man experiences himself as mystery, as a question to which he has no answer. He experiences his own existence as obscure and almost inexplicable not because it is lacking in objective reality, or because there is nothing real behind the experience, but because the full depths of being in this self which he experiences exceeds his powers of penetration.

But if man experiences himself as mystery, if he accepts this mystery in silence and is submissive enough to accord its full value precisely to that in his experience of himself which is too much for him to question, if he accepts this question to which he can find no answer not as something which is devoid of meaning and dark, but rather as a light which is too blinding for his eyes, a light which only the eyes of another, of him whom we call God, are strong enough to look upon, then the sick man is at one with God. For he has submitted himself to God, to him to whose charge the indivisible unity of action and passion, the lot that is sent us and the acts which proceed from ourselves as free beings, must remain committed in order that we can come to terms with our sickness even when it remains a mystery.

In sickness man is brought face to face with himself in a particularly uncompromising way. He achieves a state of isolation with himself. And yet he does not know exactly what this state is into which he has fallen, whether he is to regard himself as the controller or the controlled. But he does become aware of this: that that which is under his own control and which he decides upon for himself has, in its final outcome, to be decided for him by another, and that which he recognises as his own act of control and decision is something which in his sickness he experiences as subject, once more, to the silent and more remote control of another, which presides over his own controlling act.

Sickness sharpens a man's awareness of both factors in his life, both that he is in control and that at the same time he is subject to control from without. But he must accept that these are two distinct aspects of what is ultimately one and the same situation, namely the state of being ill, just as body and soul are two distinct elements in the single entity that is man himself, and just as an openness to outside influence and the power to direct himself are intrinsic to his own nature. And if he does this, if he accepts his sickness as a single reality involving both action and passion but ultimately a mystery beyond our own personal control, then both the sick man himself and his sickness are in God's hands. Then the sickness acquires a redemptive value.

Patience

In offering these few brief considerations on the time of sickness I should like to say something about patience. The relevance and appropriateness of this to the situation of the sick will surely be apparent to all. At the same time, however, we should not be too ready to discourse about the sick and the patience they should exercise, for this is not a subject on which the healthy should have much to say.

As soon as the subject of 'patience' is introduced one is immediately reminded of the opening words with which Cyprian of Carthage introduced his treatise on patience seventeen hundred years ago, to the effect that the listeners must already have what the speaker is trying to recommend to them, namely patience, for without this he would not have any listeners at all. And in fact, if one were totally devoid of patience in any sense, then one would never be able to acquire it either, because the very act of acquiring it in itself entails the exercise of patience over a long period. Some degree of patience, therefore, must be numbered among the basic attitudes of man, one that is deeply rooted in his nature. The reason for this is that it must, to a certain extent, support itself. It must already be there in order that it may be summoned up. It must be ready to hand in order that the higher degrees of it may be sought after.

Patience derives from something which is fundamental to the nature of man as such, namely that he is both a person endowed with spirit and simultaneously a being subject to the limitations of time. Beings that are of their nature eternal have no need of patience. They have no further perfection to achieve beyond their present state. They do not look for anything further because the sheer eternity with which they are endowed means that their natures are already in the state of their due fulness and perfection. Again beings which are non-spiritual do not need patience because their consciousness is always limited to the present moment, and precisely in virtue of this fact they know nothing of continuous change as such, of the past and future as these affect them, even though they themselves are constantly undergoing a process of development and change.

But we are beings who are both endowed with knowledge and subject to time. We carry our past with us, and in our cognitive faculties we already reach out for that which has still to come in the future. We actually and consciously live through the process of change to which we ourselves are subject. The interplay of past and future acquires reality as our experience. Not only are we unable to hold back the process of transition and change, we cannot even conceal from ourselves our own inability to do this. Our existence is governed by a single and uninterrupted process of change. We are empowered to see this existence of ours as a whole and to recognise as a law of its very nature that it must constantly press on to further developments. To recognise and accept this fact is what we might call 'existential' patience, patience at the existential level. We patiently accept the fact that our existence is subject to change in this way, and yet that it retains its unity throughout the process of change. But the very fact that we are this kind of being and cannot avoid being so, that we have this kind of nature and cannot escape from it – this in itself, once more, presents us with a task to accomplish, one in which it is possible for us to fail; something which we must do for ourselves, exercising courage and faithfulness, being consciously and deliberately true to our own nature in order to achieve it. For a person endowed with freedom and with spiritual faculties has in his make-up factors which are given, inevitable and inescapable, *and* at the same time other factors which are mysterious and unpredictable. It is this that sets him the task of exercising his freedom responsibly.

Man, therefore, must freely and consciously come to terms with this special quality in his own nature. He must recognise and accept himself as a being subject to constant and purposive change, and at the same time endowed with cognition. He must not suppose that he is able to interrupt this change, must neither attempt to hold himself back at the stage which he has already achieved, nor attempt prematurely to achieve a stage which still awaits him in the future. In other words he must patiently accept the change to which his existence is subject for what it is, and recognise that it has a meaning and is directed towards a goal. Only then can he be said to be patient with this existential patience of which we have been speaking.

The point to be realised is this: What man has to recognise and accept with this elemental kind of patience is not simply those factors arising here and there in his life which are disagreeable, and which seem to him to be part of a meaningless lot imposed upon him from without. What he has to tolerate and endure with patience at its deepest and most elemental level is rather *himself* – himself considered as one who is on the way to some future goal, one who may neither stop and remain where he is, nor suppose that he is journeying into an empty and indeterminate void without any ultimate point of arrival. Our impatience with everyday vexations is simply a sign of the fact that at a deeper level of our life we have not succeeded in freely attaining to the virtue of this existential patience and making it our own.

There are those who seek to cling on to the circumstances of the present moment with its pleasures, its successes, its seeming self-sufficiency even though all these are, of their nature, precisely transient and fleeting; those who cannot let go of what belongs to yesterday until what belongs to tomorrow has already been proved to be harmless and reassuring; those who cannot freely enter into new situations which seem to be more arduous or to hold out less promise, who cannot entrust themselves to the darkness or to that which is under the control of another; those who take fright at the silent power which presides over and controls our lives, and which is God, even though he alone knows and decides where this transitory existence of ours began and where it will end. Such as these are incapable of attaining for themselves this virtue of existential patience. They betray the fact that they do not possess this virtue by the impatience which they exhibit in their daily circumstances, and when they meet with the shortcomings, the pains and toils which belong to human life even at its most commonplace and everyday.

On the basis of this too we can understand why sickness above all and pre-eminently should be the situation in which the genuineness of patience is put to the test and proved. For in sickness a still higher degree is demanded of us of that patience which we have to exercise in any case in our everyday lives. And hence it is a situation which really reveals whether we possess this virtue of existential patience or not, or, to put it more modestly and more accurately, whether we have the *will* to possess it.

It might be supposed that sickness is a pause, an interlude that temporarily suspends the process of change in our human lives, one in which nothing happens, in which one is condemned to a sort of suspended animation, in which one becomes feeble and poor, and so that sickness is a kind of suffering which should not exist, so that the most that can be said is that we must painfully reconcile ourselves to it in order to prevent it from being even worse. But the process of change and progress in human existence is carried further precisely in sickness itself. Sickness takes us out of that state which we had regarded as stable and constant, out of a life which had seemed so full and fulfilling, so unvaryingly right for us, and therefore fixed and unchanging, out of our work, which had acted as an opiate masking our secret existential *Angst*, out of the business of everyday, out of the state of health which we had taken for granted. In sickness we are carried beyond all this into a state which is unmistakably transitory and not enduring, a state of pain and enfeeblement in which we are manifestly no longer in control, but rather at the mercy of unknown and alien forces. In this sense the real process of change and transition in human existence is accelerated in sickness. And once we have been forced out in this way from a state which only seemed to be fixed and stable, the question presents itself insistently and in a manner which cannot be denied of whether this is a sign that our existence is meaningless and destined soon to collapse into a void of nothingness, or rather a sign that it is being controlled and directed towards an ultimate goal of blessedness. Thus in sickness we are still more inescapably faced with the question of whether or not we do possess the virtue of existential patience.

Patience, therefore, is a quality that is inherent in the very nature of human existence. Now when man finds himself summoned by this to exercise patience freely and consciously as a virtue he can, of course respond by taking refuge in doubt, and this doubt can in its turn be disguised as an optimism that is over-facile and out of place. Another way in which he can evade the question is simply to employ the resources of chemistry and drugs to suppress it and silence it in his heart. But to the question of how to exercise and acquire this virtue of patience as the outcome of a consoling and strengthening faith both of these answers would be false. Impatience in sickness is tantamount to admitting and disclosing the fact that one is deficient in that deeper existential kind of patience in which one keeps one's eyes fixed trustfully upon the underlying unity which persists throughout all the process of change in one's life; in which one recognises that this underlying unity points one on to the still deeper and more mysterious fact that that life is being directed and controlled by a power beyond one's comprehension, a power that one accepts precisely in its incomprehensibility as loving and benevolent, and that one calls God.

Of course impatience in the sick may simply be due to a nervous condition without being in the least a manifestation of the basic attitude of the sick person's innermost heart. And no-one can say exactly which of these two conditions is making itself felt in the painful restlessness of the sick at any given point, or how far such restlessness is due to either condition. Not even the sick person himself can say unequivocally whether his impatience is to be taken as a sign of the former condition or of the latter. Our patience or impatience too is something which, in the last analysis, only God can judge. But for all this there is one thing that we can and must do: we must examine our consciences with regard to the impatience which manifests itself on the surface of our everyday lives during sickness, and see from this what sort of patience in the truest and deepest sense we have managed to achieve. We must recognise that we are called in a special sense to this elemental kind of patience, and must be responsive to this call. It is a patience that takes the form of a certain gentleness and quietness of attitude (and so of holiness too: for it is the outcome of grace) in recognising and reconciling ourselves to the constant change and transition to which we are subject, and which runs as a single uninterrupted process beneath the surface of our lives. We must submit trustfully and without any clinging to the past to this process of transition, in which our lives are carried gently yet relentlessly onwards to that final goal in which their ultimate consummation can be attained. For provided this existential patience has been transformed into the virtue of patience, i.e. into a conscious and deliberate acceptance of, and submission to this process of change and transition in a spirit of faith and love this can bring us the fulness of blessing in which our ultimate perfection consists.

Man has to learn freely to accept himself as a creature of God in his eternity, a creature which is at once subject to time and endowed with self-knowledge, and which therefore has to direct itself towards its own due consummation through a process of transition in time. To achieve this without either clinging on to the present or succumbing to anxiety (*Angst*) about the future – that is what it means to turn existential patience into a consciously exercised virtue of patience. Patience in our everyday affairs and patience in time of sickness have to be practised and so to bear witness to the fact that we have patience at this deeper and more elemental level within us too. The former kind of patience has to be nourished and strengthened by the latter, and so to prove that it is authentic and true.

26

ON CHRISTIAN DYING

THE death of Christ is not simply an event of the past. On the contrary it is, as all Christendom believes, an event which, even though in the external and superficial sense it belongs to the past, still has an eternal validity in God's sight. For it is that unique occurrence in the history of mankind for the sake of which God in his eternity has once and for all determined to keep mankind for ever enfolded in his compassion and love. But the Christian has to think of this death of Christ in such a way that he reverently and solemnly accepts its enduring validity, and by faith makes its redemptive power effective in our lives also. And in order to do this, and in order really to understand what the message of this death is meant to convey to him he must strive to gain an understanding of the nature of death in general. Of course he can learn something of the meaning of death in general precisely *from* this message of the death of Christ. But however true this may be, still, in order to have any real understanding of what it means to say 'At that point one died for all' he has to bring to bear on the question an idea of death which is as vivid and as fully developed as possible.

In what we shall be saying about death here we shall be taking it not in the strictly biological or physiological sense of the term, but rather in that sense which it bears in the context of the Christian understanding of human existence. This is not because the latter is in contradiction to the former, but rather because precisely as person endowed with freedom and with spiritual powers man is more than a biological 'case'. The purely biological aspects of death, those, roughly speaking, which fall within the field of medicine, constitute only one element in a broader and more comprehensive whole, and it is with this broader field that theology is concerned because it has to view man as a person endowed with spirit and therefore responsible, a being which has an eternal validity; for under this aspect too death comes as the supremely decisive event in man's history.

The primary factor to which the Christian understanding of death directs our attention is the universality of death. This first point seems platitudinous, and simply to reiterate a fact recognised by all as a matter of natural and common experience. However there is more to it than this. The message of faith on this point is actually addressed, in the first instance to each one of us as *individuals* as a truth which expresses the ultimate significance of the existence of each one of us taken as a whole, a truth which we must accept and opt for as an act of our own personal freedom. Viewed in this light this initial point is not so self-evident. Certainly we are aware that 'one' has to die. But this is far from implying that 'I' personally have really understood that *I* have to die, that I myself am already on the way to this death, that all my life through I am advancing inexorably and undeviatingly towards this moment of my death. It is far from implying that I constantly take the recognition of this fact as my starting-point in directing the course of my life, that I never suppress it and never act as though I myself were not already a dying man. But it is this that the message of faith concerning the universality of death is intended to convey to me first and foremost as the most basic truth of my personal life. And further, if this assertion of the universality of death were based, even from the Christian point of view, merely upon the fact that at the biological and physiological level all previous experience bears it out, then indeed it might be possible to regard it as a principle which has only been valid up to the present, but which can now be abrogated. On this view it would have the same degree of validity as the statement that 'Many die of the pestilence', a statement which was indeed true formerly, but which is not so now. It might even be possible to imagine that one day medicine will actually find a way of doing away with the 'unpleasantness' (as it has been called) of having to die on the grounds that strictly speaking biologists are unable to explain why a cell or a group of cells should not continue to survive indefinitely.

But in contrast to this the Christian assertion of the necessity of death has an absolute validity. This is because it is based not merely upon biological considerations, but on human nature as a whole. There is a factor in man, in his very nature and in the way in which he was originally fashioned, which makes it impossible for him ever to escape from or do away with the necessity of dying, that makes it absolutely certain that he will always die. Death is not merely something that is 'appropriate' to man in the sense that it is appropriate to a precious artefact not to be broken because to break it would be an outrage to its very nature and the purpose for which it was designed. On the contrary man is subject to death as a necessity of his innermost nature. It is on deeper grounds than merely biological ones that human nature inherently and inexorably tends towards death as its inevitable goal.

The deepest and most ultimate reason for the connection with and orientation to death which is most intimately inherent in man, which makes him mortal and in virtue of this fact renders all men now and for ever subject to death in the truest sense, is the freedom of the spirit. It is this, ultimately speaking, that makes man mortal, and mortality in the biological sense is only the manifestation and the realisation in the concrete of this mortality, which has its origin and basis in the freedom with which man is endowed as spiritual. How then can this be the case? Freedom is not the power constantly to change one's course of action, but rather the power to decide that which is to be final and definitive in one's life, that which cannot be superseded or replaced, the power to bring into being from one's own resources that which must be, and must not pass away, the summons to a decision that is irrevocable. If freedom were capable of achieving only that which could subsequently be abolished by a further free decision, then freedom would be nothing more than power over that which is purely neutral and indecisive, that which is always open to subsequent revision, a miserable sort of freedom, condemned, as it were, to proceed in futile circles without any final resting place, ultimately meaningless. If, therefore, man *is* personal freedom, then it follows that he is one who uses the resources of his own innermost nature to form himself by his own free act, for by the exercise of this freedom of his he can definitively determine the shape of his life as a whole, and decide what his ultimate end is to be, the ultimate realisation of his own nature, beyond all possibility of revision.

Now the physical side of man's nature, in which he actively works out the shape of his life as person and brings it to its consummation, is so constituted that it sets him in the dimension of that which is constantly open to further development. It follows from this that while it can be the dimension in which freedom is exercised *in fieri*, it cannot be that in which the fulness of freedom is achieved, the dimension of that consummation to which freedom finally and definitively attains. Freedom enters into the dimension of becoming and of openness to further development only in order to achieve its own consummation. To this extent it is exercised at this physical level of man's being only in order to pass beyond it and transcend it, and so to attain to its definitive goal. The free man is willing to accept the limitations of mortality only in order that the exercise of his freedom on this plane may enable him to attain to that true immortality which lies beyond, and which consists not in an unending evolution in time but in the achieved finality of eternity itself – in that, therefore, which is beyond time.

At its deepest level the exercise of free decision bears upon death itself. It must do so because, in order to arrive at its own final perfection it must will death as that which puts an end to the mere prolongation of temporal existence. It is only on the surface of our awareness that we shrink from death. At its deepest level this awareness of ours craves for that which is imperfect and incomplete in us to be brought to an end in order that it may be finally perfected. Indeed if anyone told us that our present state would last for ever we would regard this in itself as tantamount to being damned, for it would mean that every fleeting and transitory moment of our existence was *ipso facto* deprived of its true value, a value which consists in the fact that each of these moments provides us with the possibility of making a decision of final and permanent validity. For the outcome of the free act is always something which endures.

Of course Christianity recognises a special kind of perfection to be attained through the exercise of freedom, one that goes beyond that which death brings, namely that state of perfection in grace which the first man was offered the possibility of attaining to in Paradise. In this situation of primæval blessedness too man would not simply have enjoyed an indefinite prolongation of his earthly life; here too his freedom would have defined some state of final perfection which would have been achieved by some radical transformation of the physical side of his human nature as realised in the concrete. But in Paradise the physical side of the man who had attained to the state of Paradisal perfection would have undergone an extremely radical change. It would have been raised to a state of glorification in which it was no longer subject to constant change and flux, unfolding itself in an unending series of transformations. At the same time, however, primordial man would not have relinquished the physical side of his nature as we have to relinquish it now in order to achieve our own perfection. To that extent this necessity of death to which we are subject is a sign of the guilt in Adam of the whole race, a manifestation of the sinfulness of all. But even this does not derogate from the fact that death precisely *as* that which perfects us and raises us above the continuous flow of time, as the incursion of that finality which is posited once and for all in freedom, is on a higher level than the mere process of becoming which we now call life. The one death which comes to all is natural and in harmony with our natures inasmuch as it is the birth of that finality aimed at in freedom which is the ultimate object of man's will at its most basic and fundamental. Death is 'unnatural' in its immediate effect upon the physical side, which is an essential part of man's nature, inasmuch as in death this cannot at once be transformed and raised in glory to that state of final perfection for which man's life, taken as a single and continuous whole, is designed. Instead at first this physical side of our nature simply falls away from us as something which we have to transcend and get beyond, and is relinquished as though it were of no permanent significance.

Thus from our consideration of the universality of death, inasmuch as this is an article of faith, we have been brought spontaneously and inevitably face to face with quite different and far deeper factors which are essentially inherent in death. Death is the breaking in of finality upon mere transience – that finality which is the concretisation of freedom come to its maturity. But when we make this assertion we intend it as the Christian answer both to the materialist teaching that at death man ceases totally to exist, and to the teaching of the transmigration of souls, which implicitly denies the unique and final value of this earthly life and its importance as providing the opportunity for absolute decision (in reality this latter doctrine recognises only the miserable fate of being condemned to the eternal cycle of birth and death). But while all this is true as far as it goes, a further point must straight away be added to it: this act of freedom which ultimately determines what man's final state is to be comes to its fulness, as we have seen, in death. For that very reason it constitutes the absolute climax of the process of enfeeblement and deprivation of power in man.

The freedom which is exercised on the physical plane is, in fact, that freedom by which man lays himself open to intervention from without, submits to control by another power or powers. The physical side of man's nature constitutes the sphere in which the interplay takes place of action from within himself and passion as imposed from without. As a physical being endowed with freedom man has to take cognisance of the fact that he occupies an intermediary position. He is neither wholly self-directing nor wholly subject to control by another, but half-way between these two. The mysterious interplay between action and passion in the exercise of human freedom appears above all in the fact that it is precisely at the very point at which man freely achieves his own perfection that he is, at the same time, most wholly subject to control by another. The ultimate act of freedom, in which he decides his own fate totally and irrevocably, is the act in which he either *willingly accepts or definitively rebels against* his own utter impotence, in which he is utterly subject to the control of a mystery which cannot be expressed – that mystery which we call God. In death man is totally withdrawn from himself. Every power, down to the last vestige of a possibility, of autonomously controlling his own destiny is taken away from him. Thus the exercise of his freedom taken as a whole is summed up at this point in one single decision: whether he yields everything up or whether everything is taken from him by force, whether he responds to this radical deprivation of all power by uttering his assent in faith and hope to the nameless mystery which we call God, or whether even at this point he seeks to cling on to his own autonomy, protests against this fall into helplessness, and, because of his disbelief, supposes that he is falling into the abyss of nothingness when in reality he is falling into the unfathomable depths of God.

On the basis of this it is possible for us to realise that death can be either an act of faith or a mortal sin. In order rightly to understand this we must consider (and perhaps it would have been clearer to make this point right from the first) that the actual act of dying does not necessarily occur at that point in time in the physical order at which doctors suppose it to take place, and at which it is considered to take place in the popular estimation when men speak of the final departure and of death as coming at the end of life. In reality we *are* dying all our lives through right up to this, the final point in the process of dying. Every moment of life is a stage on the way to this final goal, a stage which already carries this end within itself and derives its significance from it, just as when one sees a shot fired one can already estimate, even as it is travelling, where the impact will fall. Life, therefore, is in a true sense a process of dying, and what we are accustomed to call death is the final point in this life-long process. Dying takes place throughout life itself, and death when it comes is only the ultimate and definitive completion of the process. Now this death in life or living death, as it may be called, can become one of two things: it can be made into an enduring act of faith in the fact that our lives and destinies are being directed and controlled by another and that this direction is right; the willing acceptance of our destiny, the ultimate act of self-commitment to that destiny, a renunciation which we make in anticipation of our final end because in the end we must renounce all things; also because we believe that it is only by this poverty entailed in freely accepting our own destiny that we can free ourselves for the hand of God in his unfathomable power and grace to dispose of us as he wills. *Alternatively* this death in the midst of life can become an act of desperately clinging on by main force to that which is destined to fall away from us, a protest, whether silent or expressed, against this death in life, the despair of one who is avid for life and who imagines that he has to sin and so to obtain his happiness by force. The death that is accomplished in life, therefore, must be really the act of that loving and therefore trustful faith which gives man courage to allow himself to be taken up by another. Otherwise it will become the mortal sin which consists in the pride of seeking one's own absolute autonomy, anxiety (*Angst*) and despair all in one.

Now in both modes of dying there are, whether we realise it or not, others who have gone before us. We are not the first to die, but are rather the successors of these, caught up in a struggle between life and death which takes place on a more comprehensive scale. Certainly each individual dies his 'own death'. Certainly each individual is unique in the inexorable solitude of his own death because each individual life, despite the opposite impression of a meaningless existence *en masse*, in which many – all too many – are involved, is unique and unrepeatable in its free moral decision. But even though this death is personal and unique to the individual in this sense, still it is the death which has been ushered into this world of the embodied spirit (a death, therefore, which only the superficial will equate with the death of animals) by the rebellion of the first man. And at the same time it is the death which the Son of Man freely takes upon himself. Our death is modelled upon the death of both of these. For it was precisely the death of Adam that the Son of Man willed to die in order to redeem this death. And because it is never possible for us to say of ourselves with complete certainty which exercise of life we commit ourselves to with the ultimate decision of our free will, we cannot ultimately know either whether it is possible for us to say which of the two deaths we are dying, the death of perdition or the death of Adam which has been redeemed; in other words whether the death of Christ imports life for us or judgment, whether it is the death of despair that we are dying or the death of faith. Both modes of dying are *concealed beneath the surface* in the everyday process of dying.

Death affects every aspect of our personal lives and being. It constitutes the transition between the sort of being that is becoming and the sort of being that is final completion, from the freedom which has been given up to the achieved finality which is at the same time the moment of radical enfeeblement. To the extent that we regard ourselves from the point of view of this world, to the extent that we are those who are quitting it and not those who are coming into it, to this extent we are, so to say, losing possession of ourselves. And for all these reasons we have no clear vision of what this definitive and final state of death will mean for us. In dying we strive to attain to the inconceivable. It is not immediately clear in the here and now what the fruit of life which we are bringing to maturity will one day be worth. But it is precisely because death is concealed from us in this sense that it is (to reiterate) the situation *par excellence* in which we can make the most radical and absolute option possible between faith and despair, between the death of Christ and the death of Adam. The dying man passes into a state of silence and solitude which engulfs everything in its own stillness. It is a state to which he has been drawing ever closer throughout his life, the situation in which he is faced with a question, an option to be taken, in which a decision is demanded of him, the situation either of the faith that redeems or of the despair that kills. The fact that death is concealed from us in this way makes it possible for us to choose either of these alternatives.

We have spoken much about death and yet said little. For who can say much about the mysteries of human existence, especially if they are followed through to the mysteries of God himself, whose eternal Word has taken our death upon him and thereby imparted to death a divine value, a divine mystery and an eternal grace? And yet we must think about death, not merely because our life is that mode of existence which of its very nature leads to death, but still more because it is the mystery of Christ the Lord in his Good Friday. Since Christ has died for the salvation of the world, since the life of God and his glory has definitively entered into the world there has been no more decisive factor in the world than precisely this death. By comparison with this every other event in the world is transitory and ultimately unimportant, or important only in virtue of the fact that it precisely does have some part to play in this history of the death of Christ.

If we have been given the vocation and the grace to die with Christ in this death of his, then the everyday and banal occurrence which we call human death, and which awaits each one of us also, has been elevated to a place among God's mysteries. In order to understand these mysteries and to be able to put them into practice in the liturgy of our life we need only to look to the death of the crucified Lord, and hear the words which he spoke, and which express what is most terrible and at the same time what is most sublime in his death. These are words which we too can hear and repeat in life and death: My God, my God, why have you forsaken me? Father into your hands I commend my spirit. For if we understand death as supremely *the* state of abandonment by God in which we fall into the hands of the eternal God, then we have already understood and endured death itself.

But together with this one crucified Lord – and the implications of this symbolism are frightening – there are two other dying figures, two men who cursed their fate of death because they did not understand it. Who indeed can understand it? But one of the two looked to the death of Christ. And what he saw there was enough to enable him to understand his own death also. For when one says to the dying Christ 'Think of me when you come into your kingdom' then one has indeed understood death, understood it rightly and received it as one's own salvation. And the Son of Man, he who shared in our fate of death, redeemed it and made it a gateway to life, said to this dying man: 'Today you will be with me in Paradise.'

But he says this to us also. If we have ears for it we have already solved the baffling riddle of death. But in order that the message of the blessing which our death will bring shall not remove from us that holy fear which is so needful for us precisely to obtain this blessing in our death he says to the other thief... precisely nothing. The darkness and silence which hung over this death serve to warn us that death can also be the onset of a deeper death still, a death that is eternal. But even as we fear and tremble we can also listen to the joyful message, the Christian gospel of the death that is life; of the coming of the Lord who is that life which knows no death even though it comes to us in death. This reality is still veiled beneath the solemn and humbling experiences which we have to undergo in death. But the death of Good Friday, the death which issues in life and eternal goodness in God's presence – that is the truth about death which faith enables us to know.

INDEX OF PERSONS

Albercuis of Hierapolis 174
Aquinas, St Thomas 176
Archimedes 238

Balthasar, H. V. von 12 n.7
Bäumer, R. 18 n.19
Benn 7
Bonaventure, St 39
Becht 7

Calvin, J. 25 n.3, 28
Cyprian of Carthage 279

Descartes, R. 39
Dirks, W. 22 n.30
Dolch, H. 18 n.19
Duval 22 n.33

Favre-Dorsatz, A. 25 n.3
Feiner, J. 113 n.1
Francis of Assisi, St 40 sq.
Francis of Sales, St 33
Funke, G. 22 n.29

Gagarin, Y. 18
Guardini, R. 32

Herrler, P. F. x

Ignatius of Loyola, St 25 sqq.

Kant, I. 39
Kriegbaum, B. x

Lahitton, J. 42
Lehmann, K. x, 113 n.1

Löhrer, M. 113n.1
Luther, M. 34

Metz, J. B. 19 n.21, 22 n.30, 32, 39 n.6

Paul, St 72 sqq., 153
Pius XII 75
Philothea 18
Przywara, E. 46 n.9

Reiners, H. 26 n.5

Schleir, H. 262 n.1
Schultz, H. J. 22, n.30
Splett, J. x, 22 n.30
Stolte, B. 22 n.30

Weger, P. K. H. x
Wisser, R. 22 n.30

SUBJECT INDEX

Abandonment:
  of Christ and Christians 139, 141
Apostolate (cf. Witness):
  paressia as virtue needed 260 *sqq.*
Ascension:
  relevance to Christ's living-on and his return 177 *sqq.*
  festival of the future of world 181 *sqq.*
  festival of nearness of God 184
  festival of preparation for Pentecost 185
Asceticism:
  new form in consumer society as imposing one's own limits 19 *sqq.*
Assumption:
  dogma has little impact now 30
Atheism:
  observation on problem of Christian living in situation of militant A. 13 *sqq.*
  salvation of atheist 17 *sq.*

Baptism:
  implicit desire 254 *sq.*
Being:
  as such is basis of knowledge and Truth 233
  death as transition between B. that is becoming and B. that is final completion 292
Boldness:
  as virtue Christian needs for apostolate 260 *sqq.*

Charisms:
  in the Church 75 *sqq.*
Christ '(of God)'
  God's self-bestowal in history 63 *sqq.*, 188

credibility of dogma of Incarnation 67 *sqq.*
belief in Resurrection as reasonable 70 *sq.*
incarnate Word of Father 107 *sqq.*, 133 *sqq.*, 157 *sqq.*, 211 *sqq.*
festival of Christmas 121 *sqq.*, 127, 132 *sqq.*
death of Christ as answer God has given to question of what we are 138 *sq.*, 140 *sq.*, 285 *sqq.*, 293
was truly dead 147 *sqq.*, 151 *sqq.*
our life hidden with C. in God 153 *sqq.*
joy of resurrection 155 *sqq.*
at heart and centre of earth 157 *sq.*
elements of Easter experience 164 *sqq.*
encounters with Risen Christ 169 *sqq.*
as shepherd 173 *sqq.*
as God's act of bestowing 271 *sqq.*
Christianity:
  Christian living formerly and today 3 *sqq.*
  'new age' not an age of un-Christianity 39 *sq.*
  intellectual honesty 47 *sqq.*
  'ultimate essence' 59 *sq.*
  grace and task 98 *sq.*
  and truthfulness in public and social life 244 *sqq.*
  anonymous C. 254 *sqq.*
Christmas:
  the festival of eternal youth 121 *sqq.*
  as holy night 127 *sqq.*
  and peace on earth 132 *sqq.*
Church: (cf. Christianity):
  difficulty of analysing present unrest 1, 3 *sqq.*
  Christian living Heritage and Commitment I, 5 *sqq.*

297

Church—*continued*:
   perspectives of Christian living in the future II *sqq.*
   life in the world and service to world 16 *sqq.*, 88 *sqq.*
   'discernment of spirits' and future of more forms of Christian living 23 *sq.*
   Christian and Catholic faith as a whole 58 *sqq.*
   eschatalogical presence of God's truth and love by word and sacrament 64
   obligation not to stifle Spirit 72 *sqq.*
   Spirit indispensable 74 *sq.*
   in diaspora situation becoming C. of believers 92 *sqq.*
   community must not become ghetto 95
   faith in 100 *sqq.*
   as subject of sending of the Spirit 186 *sqq.*
   projection of historicity and visibility of Jesus through space and time 188 *sqq.*
   necessity of witness 245 *sqq.*
   public opinion within 251

Communication:
   question of knowledge as communication with reality 230 *sqq.*
   mass media and relation to truthfulness today 242

Compassion:
   works of mercy and their reward 268 *sqq.*

Confession:
   necessity of constructive approach to frequent C. 7 *sq.*

Conscience:
   and intellectual honesty 48 *sqq.*
   and its masking 235 *sqq.*

Cross:
   modern 'way of C.' 159, 168
   and Eucharist 217 *sq.*

Death:
   picture of a dying man 136 *sqq.*
   scandal of D. 140 *sqq.*
   meaning from state of having died and being dead 147 *sq.*, 152 *sq.*
   interpenetration with life 149 *sq.*, 153 *sq.*, 286 *sq.*

Descent into Hell:
   meaning as descent into realm of dead 145 *sqq.*

Despair:
   Risen Christ as hope of despairing 169 *sqq.*

Detachment:
   as consequence of Obedience to God 34 *sq.*

Devotions:
   luxury of elaborate systems ruled out today 13 *sq.*

Dogma:
   scandal of D's 100 *sqq.*
   human history 115 *sq.*

Doubt:
   inescapable but can be consoling 143 *sq.*

Easter:
   joy of different types stemming from resurrection of Christ 155 *sqq.*
   experiencing E. 159 *sqq.*
   whole of E. experience greater than sum of parts and is 'sui generis' 164 *sqq.*
   linked with Pentecost 186 *sqq.*

Ecumenism:
   dialogue must not appear to be between two ghetto-like ideologies 96 *sq.*

Education:
   truthfulness today and implications 241 *sqq.*

Eschatology:
   return of Christ 177 *sqq.*
   Ascension as feast of future of World 813 *sq.*
   eschatalogical triumph of grace of grace of Spirit manifests itself in responsibility 198 *sq.*

INDEX

Eternity:
  Present in time and emerges from it 162 *sq.*, 179
Ethics:
  new asceticism must become morals in the concrete 22
  significance of maxim 'A.M. D. G.' for existential ethic of today 42 *sq.*
Eucharist:
  dangers of rejecting Eucharistic devotions 8
Eucharist (cf Sacrifice):
  and our daily lives 211 *sqq.*
  sacrament of the everyday 216 *sqq.*
  sacrament of the everyday put into practice 221 *sqq*
Examination of Conscience:
  dangers of self-centred form 43 *sq.*
Exegesis:
  related to Spirit's work in Church 117 *sq.*

Faith:
  role of 'fides implicita' today 14
  intellectual honesty and exercise of F. 50 *sqq.*, 66 *sqq.*
  Christian F. considered as a whole 58 *sqq.*
  in Church 100 *sqq.*
  only possible within Church 109 *sq.*
  and its festival, the Ascension 181 *sqq.*
  eye of F. must see into significance of the everyday 226
  truthfulness to self as experience of F. 239
  salvation only through F. 255
  death as act of F. 290 *sq.*
Freedom:
  in any creature is subject to pre-existing conditions 35 *sqq.*, 137
  structure of choice in St Ignatius 41 *sqq.*
  and authority 91 *sq.*
  truth setting man free 237 *sqq.*
  as basis of mortality of man 287 *sqq.*

God:
  present experience as incomprehensible II *sqq.*, 125, 135, 164, 240 *sq.*, 248
  being open to G. as ever greater 25 *sqq.*
  in His divinity as the Mystery of Human existence 60 *sqq.*
  self-bestowing model of Christian's compassion 271 *sqq.*
Grace:
  truthfulness towards self as G. of God. 238 *sq.*
  interior G. given to all men 254 *sqq.*
  penetration of God to depths of man's being 272
  perfection offered to first man in Paradise 288
  to die with Christ 293

Hierarchy:
  and the Spirit 84 *sqq.*
  and Word of God in history 108, 114 *sqq.*
History, Church :
  Ignatius standing at turning point of ancient and medieval from Church of New Age 32 *sqq.*
  man as historically conditioned even in recognition of truth 58
  human H. of divine Truth 115 *sq.*
Honesty:
  intellectual H. and the Christian faith 47 *sqq.*

Ideology:
  and criteria of Truth and Pragmatism 231 *sqq.*
Incarnation:
  cf. Christ

Knowledge:
  idea as most radical mode of communication with reality threatened 230 *sqq.*

Layman:
  role as witness 246

Legalism:
  danger in religion 45 *sq.*
Lie:
  nature and subject 240 *sq.*
Life:
  belief in eternal L. related to Christmas 124 *sqq.*
  true L. begins with death 143 *sqq.*
  interpenetration with death 149 *sq.*, 153 *sq.*, 223

Magisterium:
  of Pope and Bishops within Church 113 *sqq.*
Man:
  necessity today to accept plurality of human nature 16 *sqq.*
  as being 'in fieri' 27, 136 *sqq.*, 287 *sq.*
  essentially the one who must plan and live from day to day 37 *sq.*
  portrait of the intellectually honest 47 *sq.*
  intellectual honesty and human decision 48 *sqq.*
  perceptible existential difference in intellectual life between what is implied in very act of living and what is outcome of scientific speculation 53 *sqq.*
  lord of nature not servant 206 *sqq.*
  appeal to inner experience of modern M. to attain truthfulness 236 *sqq.*
  question which sickness raises for M. as whole 275 *sqq.*
Mercy:
  works of M. and their reward 268 *sqq.*
Metanoia:
  for stifling of Spirit 80 *sq.*
Mission:
  difficulty today of reconciling 'family of faith' and open missionary community' 97 *sq.*
  essential to Christian 263 *sqq.*
Mysticism:
  necessity today of working out a theology 14 *sqq.*

Neurosis:
  stemming from over-reflection on self 41

Obedience:
  as given to God and consequent detachment 34 *sqq.*, 63
  necessity of true and bold interpretation in Church 81 *sqq.*

Parresia:
  as virtue Christian needs for apostolate 260 *sqq.*
Patience:
  necessity in times of transition 23, 83 *sq.*, 154 *sq.*, 280
  in itself and related to sickness 279 *sqq.*
Peace:
  scriptural meaning 132 *sq.*
Pentecost:
  meaning of festival 186 *sqq.*
  linked with Easter 186
Politics:
  cannot be dismissed by Christian as 'dirty business' 19, 90 *sqq.*
Poverty:
  and love of God 269
Prgamatism:
  sceptical P. related to values of Truth 231 *sqq.*
Prayer:
  value of silent meditation 8 *sq.*
  question of whether man of tomorrow will be man of P. 9 *sq.*
  questionable procedure of intercessary P. 12, 16
  necessity regarding work of Spirit 86
  for boldness 267
Pride:
  and the works of mercy 269 *sqq.*
Priest:
  and virtue of 'paressia' 260, 263 *sqq.*

Rationalism:
  value and dangers in religion 44 *sq.*

INDEX

Redemption:
  Christmas and Easter as festivals of beginning of R. 127 sq.
Relativism:
  modern prevalence and effects on disregard of Truth 230 sq., 253 sq.
Religious Life:
  value of monasteries of contemplative life 8
  distinctive aims and spirit always far from exclusive to members of an order 30 sq.
Responsibility:
  as deriving from Holy Spirit 198 sq.
Resurrection:
  as transformation and consummation 156 sqq., 168
  implied in Ascension of Christ 184
Resurrection of Christ cf. Christ
Revelation:
  needing witness as act of personal engagement 245

Sacrifice:
  in Mass say 'yes' of faith to that S. as ours 205
Salvation:
  wanted for all by God 254 sq.
Sanctity:
  obligation of every Christian 26 sqq.
Scepticism:
  weary S. not demanded by intellectual honesty 56
  modern prevalence and its effects 230 sqq., 253 sq.
Scriptures:
  meditation as practised today 1, 7
  not self authenticating but authentic because integral to Church 108, 112 sq.
Sickness:
  Christian significance 275 sqq.
Silence:
  the S. in which heart is reborn 171 sq., 192
  and obligation to speak 264 sqq., 267

experience of self in S. during sickness 278
of death 293
Spirit, Holy:
  obligation not to stifle Spirit's work in Church 72 sqq.
  gifts of H. S. 73 sqq.
  metavoia for stifling Spirit 80 sq.
  courage to take risks and endure antagonism 81 sqq.
  works through and in spite of human history of Church 117 sq.
  necessary for Easter commitment 166 sq.
  Ascension festival a watching and praying for H. S. 185
  Pentecost feast of descent of H. S. and permanent dwelling 187 sqq.
  life always included in fold of Church 189 sqq., 194 sqq.
  that is over all life 193 sqq.
  source of responsibility and trust 198 sqq.
Spirituality:
  problem of Christian living today 4 sq.
  Christian living in the Church today as Heritage and Commitment 5 sqq.
  Christian living in the future 11 sqq.
  experience of God as incomprehensible 11 sqq.
  life in the World and service of the world 16 sqq.
  new form of asceticism 19 sqq.
  significance of A.M.D.G. 25 sqq.
Sunday:
  the day of the Lord 205 sqq.
Symbolism:
  ambiguity of religious symbols 128
  S. of night 128 sqq.

Tact:
  and its absence in candid criticism 243 sq.
Technology:
  use in controlling environment 231 sq.
  characteristic honesty affecting modern man 235 sq.

Time:
  would become illusion if unfulfilled 161 *sq.*
Theology:
  difficulties for intellectual honesty in usual approaches to fundamental T. by Catholics 51 *sq.*
Trust:
  deriving from Spirit of Pentecost 199 *sqq.*
Truth:
  Christianity not a fortress of truth with innumerable windows but one single aperture 61 *sq.*
  Church as foundation and support 115 *sqq.*
  deeper levels of meaning of truthfulness 229 *sqq.*, 258
  as analagous entity 234
Truthfulness:
  as will to Truth 229 *sqq.*, 257 *sqq.*
  regarding one's self 235 *sqq.*
  in human intercourse 239 *sqq.*
  in public and social life 244 *sqq.*
  determination to achieve the Truth 252 *sqq.*

Witness:
  as act of personal engagement 245 *sqq.*
  change of style today 249 *sqq.*
Word:
  of God in the mouth of Church 102 *sqq*
World:
  Christian in his world 16 *sqq.*, 88 *sqq.*
  neither authorities in Church nor members immune from spirit of the world 85
  diaspora situation has positive meaning 89 *sqq.*
  Ascension as festival of future of W. 181 *sqq.*

Youth:
  Christmas, the feast of Eternal Youth 121 *sqq.*
  the honesty of modern Y. 235 *sqq.*